Christianity in Asia

Series Editor: Michael Nai-Chiu Poon

Asia today consists of many young nations that emerged from centuries of colonial and missionary experience. How do Christian communities in the region respond to the new socio-political challenges of today? The *Christianity in Asia* series, commissioned and edited by the Centre for the Study of Christianity in Asia, Trinity Theological College, Singapore, explores how young churches in Asia understand their identity, reflect on their own mission practices, engage the state and society, and contribute to fresh understanding of Christianity in the contemporary world.

First published 2006

Published by
ATF Press
An imprint of the Australasian Theological Forum Ltd
P O Box 504
Hindmarsh
SA 5007
ABN 90 116 359 963
www.atfpress.com

Series on Christianity in Asia: I

Pilgrims and Citizens:
Christian Social Engagement in East Asia Today

Edited by Michael Nai-Chiu Poon

Foreword by Bishop Robert Solomon
Introduction by Archbishop John Chew

ATF Press
Adelaide

This collection of essays is the first volume in the series on Christianity in Asia. This, its first fruit, is dedicated to the China Christian Council, as a token of the long-standing partnership between Trinity Theological College, Singapore, and the Church in China.

Contents

Contemporary Engagements

Concluding Reflections: Ways Forward in Seeking the Welfare of the City

Foreword

Robert Solomon

For four days in mid August 2005, about one hundred local church and civic leaders engaged academics and church leaders in the region and beyond in an international conference in Singapore, to reflect and explore how faith communities can contribute to the well-being of our societies, cities, and nations. *Seek the Welfare of the City*—the theme of the conference, underlines an important and timely concern in today's world. This importance is punctuated by the rare joint participation of top leaders from the State Administration of Religious Affairs (SARA) in the People's Republic of China, China Christian Council (CCC), and the Institute of World Religions of the Chinese Academy of Social Sciences in the conference.

1. Positive engagement with the world

Christians have a rich heritage of praying and working for the peace, prosperity, and well-being of the cities that we live in, the nations to which we belong, and indeed, of the earth which is our common home.

This arises from a worldview that accepts God as the creator of all, who loves and cares for all, that God is a God of order and has established institutions and governance for the larger good of human societies. Hence Scripture urges Christians to submit to governing authorities that have been instituted to maintain order, justice, and peace. As Paul wrote in the epistle to the Romans, 'Give everyone what you owe him: If you owe taxes, pay taxes; if revenue, then revenue; if respect, then respect; if honour, then honour (Romans 13:7).'

The Christian faith is therefore not a world-denying faith or a faith that calls for withdrawal from the world and the society that we live in. Rather, it calls for positive and redemptive engagement with the world that will contribute to the betterment and transformation of human societies. Such a perspective is rooted in a spirituality that has to do with the peace and reconciliation that we believe is offered to us through Jesus Christ our Lord. As Scripture points out, we are ministers and ambassadors of reconciliation. We long to see our societies flourishing in peace, prosperity, righteousness, and justice.

Robert Solomon

This is exercised in our day to day living as we rub shoulders with our fellow human beings in the hustle and bustle of life. In the midst of many human and social problems caused by human sinfulness and frailties, we are challenged to live in a redemptive way, made possible by the grace of God. Hence Scripture tells us:

> Do not repay anyone evil for evil. Be careful to do what is right in the eyes of everybody. If it is possible, as far as it depends on you, live at peace with everyone . . . If your enemy is hungry, feed him; if he is thirsty, give him something to drink (Romans 12:17–18, 20).

Our challenge is not just to co-operate with the authorities, and to live harmoniously with our neighbours, and uprightly in our society. Beyond that, we are called to reach out to the needy in our communities, with whatever compassionate help we can give.

In the agricultural societies of the Old Testament, farmers were required not to harvest their entire crop, but to leave some for the poor of the land so that they and their families could have some food to eat. In the more urban environment of the New Testament, there are many wonderful illustrations of how the Christian community cared for widows and orphans, who otherwise, in that society, would have no means of survival and sustenance. In fact, James defines pure religion this way:

> Religion that God our Father accepts as pure and faultless is this: to look after orphans and widows in their distress and to keep oneself from being polluted by the world (James 1:27).

This religious instinct and habit is rooted in the command Jesus gave to his disciples, as a summary of the entire religious and moral law: 'Love the Lord your God with all your heart and with all your soul and with all your mind', and, 'Love your neighbour as yourself' (Matthew 22:37–9).

Vertical devotion and piety must be accompanied by horizontal compassion and kindness. Our love must be directed towards heaven and earth. This has been expressed throughout church history. There are many cameos that one can paint to demonstrate this.

One could think of the terrible plague that struck the world in CE 250. It is named after a bishop and called Cyprian's plague, not because he caused it but because he mobilised the church to respond in such a way that the world noticed. It was probably a smallpox epidemic, a highly contagious and deadly disease. It killed more than 5,000 people daily and lasted for sixteen years. There was much panic and some even blamed Christians for the epidemic. Those who did not know the hope that is in Christ were extremely afraid. They did not go near the sick. They discarded the dead bodies of loved ones on the streets. Cyprian got the Christians to go out to care for the sick and dying and to bury the dead.

Or one could think of the social plague of an international slave trade that marred the well-being of human society about two centuries ago. In that context, we remember people like William Wilberforce, a British parliamentarian and deeply committed Christian who fought very hard to abolish the abominable slave trade. Or countless others, whether in the medical professions, other sciences and the arts, who devoted entire lifetimes to bringing innovations and ideas that improved the lot of the human race.

2. Christian contributions in Singapore

We have seen the same in our own nation of Singapore. This year, as a nation, we celebrate our fortieth National Day. Our history, of course, goes back earlier. When Christianity came to our shores in significant ways in the nineteenth century, the faith community was quick to set up institutions and ministries to help alleviate human suffering and to improve human society. The National Council of Churches of Singapore (NCCS) publication, *One Faith, Many Faces*, tells this story well, of how the church had contributed to the development of the nation.[1]

One of the ways this has been done is through the provision of education for the young. From the outset churches had established schools, and over the years these have become well known for quality education, having produced generations of men and women who would provide leadership and service to the nation.

While the government-established schools have grown significantly in number since our independence and significant growth in population, the schools established by and still associated with the founding churches form about fourteen percent of all the state schools in Singapore. The government and society as a whole continue to appreciate the educational legacy we have

1. The National Council of Churches of Singapore, *Many Faces, One Faith* (Singapore: Armour, 2004). See also Bobby Sng, *In His Good Time: The Story of the Church in Singapore 1819–2002*, third edition (Singapore: Graduates' Christian Fellowship, 2003).

created and the holistic education provided by our schools, including the instilling of moral values and social responsibility. In addition to schools, churches have also been active in running good kindergartens.

In addition to the schools, the churches have also established youth organisations such as the Boys' Brigade and Girls' Brigade that have an on-going presence in Singapore schools. Such organisations help train the young to be spiritually, morally, and socially responsible and to be good citizens.

The churches have also sought to establish medical and nursing facilities, including those for the elderly. There are a number of hospitals and nursing homes that seek to minister to the needs of the elderly and the sick.

The needs of families have been met through the establishment of family service centres and counselling facilities. Twenty-eight percent of family service centres in Singapore are connected with churches.

The churches have also made strong and significant contributions in the treatment, rehabilitation, and aftercare of drug addicts—a very intensive and difficult ministry. In fact, two-thirds of the aftercare institutions in Singapore are run by churches. Collectively we have accumulated a lot of expertise and experience in this area.

Other areas have also not been left behind. Churches have been active in ministering to those with special needs such as those with mental and physical disabilities. Many Christians are also providing leadership and service in the emerging hospice ministries.

Contributions to the well-being of our nation have also been made by Christians in other ways. In the professional and commercial world, Christians have played a key role in spending time and careers in improving the lot of our society and making the nation a peaceful and prosperous place to live in. Even in politics and public service, Christians continue to play key roles.

Two-thirds of doctors are Christians. About a half of our teachers are Christians. In many of these public service arenas, Christians continue to make significant personal contributions to the well-being of our nation.

Together in the NCCS, the churches here have worked together very well in contributing to all these needs and meeting these challenges. In recent years the NCCS has also addressed matters related to social and moral values, and issues in the life sciences and the arts.[2] Besides our relevant publications, we

---

2.   Note here the National Council of Churches of Singapore's publications on contemporary issues: *The Christian Church in 21st Century Singapore*, edited by Isaac Lim (Singapore: National Council of Churches, 2000); *A Christian Response to the Life Sciences* (Singapore: Genesis Books, 2002); and *A Christian*

have often been invited to give our views in various matters. Our aim is to see our nation, strong in its foundational values and habits, and prospering with harmony and peace.

3. Co-operation with other faith communities

We are not, of course, saying that Christians are the only ones concerned about the well-being of our nation or making significant contributions. There are others in our multi-religious and multi-ethnic society who share our interests and concerns. It is therefore imperative that we discover ways in which we can continue to make our contributions in partnership with others, as our own particular context demands. The NCCS has been in dialogue with other faith communities, such as the Muslims, on issues of common interest and concern. We trust that this will only strengthen the national harmony and well-being of our country. In the increasingly globalised setting of our modern lives, our concern has to also reach beyond our own shores to assist others elsewhere in other cities and nations, who also have similar aspirations, needs, and challenges. In this respect, I am glad that our churches have reached beyond to other countries. We have sent many to these needy nations to help establish educational, medical, and social welfare institutions. We are gaining new vision, energy and expertise in these areas. Many of the people involved in these ventures are those who have been trained at Trinity Theological College. This college is a testimony to the close ecumenical working relationships between the churches. This college continues to serve the people of this country and beyond. Many of our students come from several Asian nations. We believe that the friendships forged here would help to improve international relations and co-operation and result in global partnerships.

I mentioned earlier the presence of friends from China in the conference. I remember that in March 2002, we welcomed to Singapore a group of twelve distinguished visitors from SARA and CCC. We shared with them how the churches work with the government in helping to develop the nation. We had very fruitful discussions. Subsequently, a team from the NCCS visited China on the invitation of SARA. In a way, *Seek the Welfare of the City* conference was a continuation of that mutual sharing.

Response to Homosexuality (Singapore: Genesis Books, 2004). *A Christian Response to the Arts and Popular Culture* will soon be published.

I am very pleased that the Centre for the Study of Christianity in Asia, Trinity Theological College, is making the conference papers available to a wider readership. I hope that this publication will stimulate further discussion, and lead to deeper friendships and partnerships, so that wherever we are, we can all contribute to the well-being and welfare of our cities, nations, societies, and our world.

Introduction

John Chew

It is with special joy that I pen this introduction to the collection of papers of the *Seek the Welfare of the City* conference in August 2005. The conference was first proposed in Beijing more than two years ago, during an official visit of the National Council of Churches of Singapore to the State Administration for Religious Affairs (SARA) of the People's Republic of China in late 2003. In the course of our conversation we suggested that, similar to other parts of the world, Asia was entering a critical new phase of development at the turn of the millennium. We need to re-examine how the 'old' and the 'new' in our societies can contribute together towards formulating new visions for the young nations in Asia today. This suggestion when mooted was immediately welcomed by the host. This led to the planning of the conference. Looking back, not only has the conference successfully taken place, it has gone beyond our initial expectations.

The conference is both historic and strategic. It is historic because this is probably the first occasion in Asia that has brought together church leaders, academics and civil servants in both Singapore and China to engage in open dialogue and self-analysis. It is strategic because the subject matter of the conference relates to an urgent and common concern whose solution demands the mutual trust and co-operation between the three parties mentioned above. The issues have to be frankly and yet humbly articulated and discussed, to the end that the conference would lead to practical ways that all parties would be able to encourage one another and work together to promote the common good.

The presentations from the biblical, historical and contemporary contextual perspectives discussed how Christians have contributed to the welfare of communities in which they found themselves. We were reminded how Christians worked for the common good in their daily lives, even under very challenging and diverse circumstances. Indeed, the Christian community from its very early inception stood in line with the ancient people of God in discharging their social responsibilities (see Deuteronomy 4:1–8; 10:12–22; 26:1–15; Amos 5:14f, 21–24; Micah 6:8).

It is of no little significance that this core concern of the biblical faith and ethics in seeking 'the welfare of the city' and its people surfaced in very poignant and heart-breaking ways. The people of God were called to be a blessing while they were in exile under very difficult and challenging circumstances (Jeremiah 29:7). This central vocation of the people of God was brought to focus in Jesus, our representative. Jesus continued to bless through his preaching, teaching and healing ministry (Matthew 5–7, especially 5:1–11; 9:35-38), while setting his face to go to Jerusalem (Luke 9:51). He chose not to do otherwise; though he knew full well that he would be ironically rejected by the very 'city' he came to bless (Luke 13:31–35). When he drew near and saw the 'city' for the last time, knowing how he would be treated 'he wept over it (Luke 19:41)'. Nonetheless he still sought its *peace*—its true welfare— to the very end. Poignantly, he accomplished this on the cross, outside the 'city' (Hebrews 13:12–14).

The experience of coming together for the conference augurs well for further interactions of this kind in Asia. Through these encounters, we hope that important contributions could be made as we all try to seek the welfare of the cities that we are all in, and to discover our lives, concerns and welfare are indeed interrelated and inseparable. I hope and trust in these very challenging times, this publication would promote further discussion on Christian social responsibilities in our societies, and lead to practical efforts to make our cities a better place to be for the future generations.

Many have contributed tremendously to the design and preparation of the conference. In particular, we thank the leadership in the China Christian Council, the State Administration for Religious Affairs of the State Council of China, and the Institute of World Religions of the China Academy of Social Sciences, for their friendship and confidence in the churches and Christians in Singapore. More especially, we are very grateful to Mr Ye Xiaowen, the Director-General of SARA, for making the conference a success not only by his valued presence but also delivering one of the opening addresses. Their support and participation is a key factor to the success of the conference.

Editor's Introduction

Michael Nai-Chiu Poon

This volume of essays, from the conference *Seek the Welfare of the City* held in Trinity Theological College, Singapore in August 2005, marks a fresh approach to articulate the character of Christian social engagement in East Asia today.

The conference presented a welcomed opportunity where key institutional interpreters of Christianity in China and Singapore, together with colleagues in the West, came together to reflect on a topic that is important and relevant not only to the church, but is also of considerable interest to the secular authorities and those of other faiths. The conference was important in the following respects.

The conference took place at a time when East Asia—for the first time since the end of the Pacific War—has by and large emerged from its colonial and missionary past, and have become a relatively socially stable, politically secure, and materially increasingly affluent region. At the same time, there is a concern that this remarkable achievement can be undermined by religious and ethnic divides. East Asian nations find it necessary to engage religious leaders for the sake of continuing social progress. China affirmed recently that religion can play an important role in 'building up a harmonious society'.[1] Zhuo Xinping's 'The Christian Contribution to China in History', the keynote address at the conference, marks a fresh departure on the interpretation of Christianity in contemporary China. The opening addresses by Lim Siong Guan (former head of the Singapore Civil Service, Government of Singapore) and Ye Xiaowen (Director-General of the State Administration of Religious Affairs, People's Republic of China) underline the political context of the discussion on church and society in East Asia today.

---

1. Chinese President Jiang Zemin affirmed, in the National Meeting on Religious Activities held in Beijing, 10–12 December 2001 that religion plays an important role in the development of China's national life. Premier Wen Jiabao officially announced the policy on building up a harmonious society in the National People's Congress and the Chinese People's Political Consultative Conference in March 2005. Cao Shengjie's paper explores the ramifications of this new policy for the church.

Those who are concerned with Christianity in the global South will find this volume of essays a welcomed contribution to the lively discussion on the future of Christianity. The experiences of Christian social involvement in Singapore and China may well offer a fresh model for Christian social engagement today. Philip Jenkins in *The Next Christendom* draws attention to the transformation in Christianity worldwide.[2] In particular, he traces the adaptation of liberation theologies in Latin America, Africa and Asia, and observes how churches came increasingly to be identified with political reform and revolution. He contrasts this paradigm with the segregation of religion from public life in the West. It is remarkable that he referred only to the Philippines and Korea in his assessment on Asia.[3] Are there fresh approaches to Christian engagement with the political and social order, other than that of the late-modern liberal practices in the West and liberation theologies in the South? Will the future of Christianity inevitably follow the social dynamics that Jenkins and other interpreters of global Christianity in the West identify? It is striking that churches in the global South often remain as objects under investigation in these prophecies of the future. Seldom do they draw on the self-assessment from churches in the global South itself. Can we conceive of fresh ways of relating to the wider world other than that of a recluse or political activist, the two prevalent models we find in contemporary Christianity in the West? Daniel KS Koh explores some of these issues in his essay 'Resident Aliens and Alienated Residents'.[4]

Singapore and China—in spite of their obvious dissimilarities—share similar desire to make religion a positive factor in promoting the common good. The hard-earned social stability, after all, can be undermined by ethnic and religious conflicts. The on-going political and social engagement by Chinese and Singaporean Christians hence should be of immense interest to both academics and practitioners. Cao Shengjie, Robert Solomon and Richard Magnus offer insightful reflections on what Christians can contribute to harmony in their nations and societies. Christians in this region often engage the West in dialogue, but seldom among themselves. The conversation among

---

2.   Philip Jenkins, *The Next Christendom: The Rise of Global Christianity* (New York: Oxford University Press, 2002).

3.   *Ibid*, 150–2.

4.   I am grateful to Daniel Koh for his permission to include his essay in this collection. Another version of this essay appeared in *Trinity Theological Journal* 13 (2005): 103–124. Koh chaired the session on Historical and Theological Reflections in the conference, and made several important contributions in the Question and Answer sessions.

East Asians in this volume, which is sometimes punctuated by honest difference in opinion, makes for fascinating reading.

This tension is sometimes expressed in terms of that between 'pilgrims' and 'citizens'; the one refers to the Christian community's spiritual identity, and the other that of its secular role. Christians hence engage critically with the wider world. How should Christians in East Asia situate this critical engagement? Must it necessarily be negative? Our particular deeds of love must lead us to a more coherent understanding of human community, which in its turn helps us to interpret our practical tasks. Oliver O'Donovan's analysis of authority in his essay 'All Authority is from God' offers a theological framework for Christians in East Asia today to interpret their practical tasks in social and political responsibility. He points out in his follow-up essay 'Fellow Citizens with the Saints' that 'wherever the church makes its home, the local community and its political relations can only be purified and strengthened by having the church in their midst'. Kenson Koh and Michael Nai-Chiu Poon draw insight from the early church and Roman Catholic traditions, and offer examples of how the community of believers, itself as the renewed society, can be the critical edge of transformation for the wider society. The citizenship in the heavenly city informs the character of citizenship on earth. Hwa Yung reminds us in his essay of the unique Christian contribution in the emergence of civil society in history.

The papers presented in the conference did not of course pronounce the final word. Our journeying, discerning, and contributing are continuing tasks of love. Oliver O'Donovan, Zhuo Xinping, and Daniel Koh have kindly offered their further reflections on the conference, and suggested helpful ways forward for Christian communities in East Asia, with the hope that they would find renewed vision and confidence to make their distinct contribution to the welfare of our fellows in East Asia and the wider world.

I am very grateful to Bruce Winter, whose seminal work *Seek the Welfare of the City* inspired the title of the conference. Both he and Paul Barnett have been faithful mentors of God's Word for many of us in Singapore. Together with Tan Kim Huat, my colleague in Trinity Theological College, they underpinned the conference with elucidation from the Holy Scripture and the biblical world. I am grateful to Bishop Robert Solomon and Archbishop John Chew for writing the foreword and introduction.

Lee Soo Ann, Kua Wee Seng, and James Wong kindly assisted in the conference. Ngoei Foong Nghian, Principal of Trinity Theological College, offered the Centre for the Study of Christianity in Asia his staunch support. I thank Michael Mukunthan, Librarian of Trinity Theological College, Mrs

Judy Lim, and Mrs Michelle Chan for their assistance in the preparation of this volume.

The National Council of Churches of Singapore and Tyndale House, Cambridge, co-sponsored the conference with the Centre for the Study of Christianity in Asia. I am grateful for their partnership.

This collection of essays is the first volume in the series on Christianity in Asia published jointly with ATF Press of the Australasian Theological Forum. I thank them for their participation in this project. I dedicate this first fruit of the series to the China Christian Council, as a token of the long-standing partnership between Trinity Theological College, Singapore, and the Church in China.

Michael Nai-Chiu Poon
The Centre for the Study of Christianity in Asia
Trinity Theological College, Singapore

Contributors

Paul Barnett is a retired Anglican Bishop of North Sydney, Australia, research fellow in ancient history at Macquarie University, Sydney, Australia and research professor at Regent College, Vancouver, British Columbia.

Cao Shengjie is the President of the China Christian Council, People's Republic of China.

John Chew is the Archbishop and Primate of the Anglican Province of South East Asia. He served as Principal of Trinity Theological College.

Hwa Yung is the Bishop of the Methodist Church in Malaysia, and was the former Director of the Centre for the Study of Christianity in Asia, Trinity Theological College.

Daniel KS Koh is the Director of the Centre for the Development of Christian Ministry and Lecturer in Christian social ethics and pastoral theology, Trinity Theological College.

Kenson Koh is the Procurator, St Francis Xavier Major Seminary, Singapore.

Lim Siong Guan is the Permanent Secretary, Ministry of Finance, former head of the Singapore Civil Service, Government of Singapore.

Richard Magnus is Senior District Judge, Singapore.

Oliver O'Donovan is Regius Professor of Moral and Pastoral Theology, University of Oxford.

Michael Nai-Chiu Poon is the Director of the Centre for the Study of Christianity in Asia, Trinity Theological College.

Robert Solomon is the Bishop of the Methodist Church in Singapore, and served as Principal of Trinity Theological College.

Tan Kim Huat is the Dean of Studies and Chen Su Lan Professor of New Testament, Trinity Theological College.

Bruce Winter is the Director of the Institute for Early Christianity, Tyndale House, and Fellow of St Edmund's College, as well as a member of the Faculty of Divinity, University of Cambridge.

Ye Xiaowen is the Director-General, State Administration of Religious Affairs, People's Republic of China.

Zhuo Xinping is the Director of the Institute of World Religions, Chinese Academy of Social Sciences, People's Republic of China.

Preliminaries

1

Religion in Governing a Country: A Positive or Negative Factor?

Lim Siong Guan

I wish simply to make a few remarks on the question: 'Religion in governing a country: a positive or negative factor?' All I can do is offer you my perspective simply as an observer, as an interested citizen of a country whose life and hopes are built upon a society which is safe, stable and secure.

What I am about to say are purely my personal views and do not necessarily reflect the views of the government. They are based on many years of watching and learning the principles of governance in Singapore, and how they are translated into policy and practice. I have to say also that my observations are purely about Singapore. I make no claims on whether they are relevant to anyone else or to any other country.

1. Religious harmony

Many of you would have watched Singapore's National Day Parade yesterday. You were present personally at the *padang*, where you would have soaked in the energy and excitement of Singaporeans, and seen first hand the unity amidst all the diversity of race, language and religion. Or you watched the parade broadcast live on television.

I hope you can recall the segment in the programme where everyone stood up, placed his or her right hand over the heart, and together said the National Pledge:

> We the citizens of Singapore,
> pledge ourselves as one united people,
> regardless of race, language or religion,
> to build a democratic society
> based on justice and equality
> so as to achieve happiness, prosperity and
> progress for our nation.

3

Every Singaporean student says this pledge and sings the National Anthem regularly in our schools.

Social stability is an absolute must in Singapore. Economic and social progress depend completely on it. So a huge amount of effort is put in by the government to promote racial and religious harmony. Singaporeans grow up living in this reality. The principles of governance for the survival, security and success of Singapore are enshrined in the six National Education messages, which are taught and reinforced continually in our schools and during National Service which every able-bodied eighteen year-old Singaporean must serve fulltime for two years. The National Education messages are:

> Singapore is our homeland; this is where we belong.
> We must preserve racial and religious harmony.
> We must uphold meritocracy and incorruptibility.
> No one owes Singapore a living.
> We must ourselves defend Singapore.
> We have confidence in our future.

You will notice how critical the idea of preserving racial and religious harmony is, so critical that it is a centrepiece of the education and the daily living of Singaporeans. Why is this so essential? The answer lies in two areas: the make-up of Singapore society and, if I may say so, the nature of human beings.

2. Make-up of Singapore society

The Singapore Census of Population in 2000 shows the racial breakdown of Singapore residents as:

- Chinese 76.8%
- Malay 13.9%
- Indian 7.9%
- Others 1.4%

The Census also gives the religious breakdown for those fifteen years of age and over as:

- Buddhism/Taoism 51%
- Islam 14.6%
- Christianity 14.9%
- Hinduism 4.0%

- Other Religions 0.6%
- No Religion 14.8%

The critical thing to note about these figures is the extent to which religious affiliation goes with ethnic group. Note the following:

- 99.6% of Malays are Muslim
- 55.4% of Indians are Hindu, 25.6% are Muslim and 12.1% Christian
- 64.4% of Chinese are Buddhist/Taoist, 16.5% are Christian and 18.6% have no Religion

What we find is that practically all Malays are Muslim, practically all Muslims are Malay or Indian, and practically all Hindus are Indian, while Christianity is spread between the Chinese and the Indians. The level of religious affiliation is much higher for the Malays and Indians than the Chinese. The census also found that the higher the education level among the Chinese, the greater the chances that they will either have no religion or are Christian.

I hope these statistics show clearly enough why racial and religious harmony is so critical that the government has to continually work at getting the message across to all citizens to respect each other's beliefs. This is done in school and in public speeches. The nature of race and religion is such that it only needs a spark of misunderstanding to create a major incident.

3. Make-up of the human being

Let me now deal with the point of why, despite the fact that racial and religious relations are such a sensitive aspect of Singapore life, the government cannot dictate the process. Why is it not possible for the government to simply say that all citizens should forget about religion, and in that way avoid the tensions and differences that religion brings about?

The Straits Times (Singapore's largest circulation English language newspaper) of 16 July 2005 published the salient findings of a survey it conducted on Singaporeans and their religious inclinations. Not only do eighty-six per cent have a religion but among those with no religion, seventy per cent believe in God.

All in all, we have a picture of a nation of believers, with over ninety-five per cent saying they subscribe to a religion and/or believe in God, and at least fifty-nine saying religion has a real place in their daily lives. The question is: Is such a situation unique to Singapore, or does it apply more universally to human beings wherever they may be? If it is unique to Singapore, then the government could, if it wished to, seek to modify it or redirect the trends. But if it is a statement about human beings and their need to have a reference beyond themselves which they call god—because there is a spiritual aspect of man beyond his physical body and the intelligence of his mind and the emotions of the heart—then a government that seeks the support of the people cannot expect to change it, but must accept it and accommodate it and provide for it.

Since in religion we are dealing with forces, or a force, beyond just the intelligence and emotions of man, it is necessary to figure out how to manage it in the governance of a country. For Singapore, to ignore it is out of the question, to accommodate it is necessary. But can we go further and harness it as a positive factor, rather than view it as a negative influence which government must guard continually against?

4. Preventive policies

Race and religion need to be actively managed. I name two 'preventive' measures the Singaporean Government has taken to help sustain racial and religious harmony, just as examples. One is the move to group a number of constituencies together—four, five or six constituencies—under what is called the Group Representation Constituencies (GRC). Rather than one Member of Parliament (MP) being elected for each constituency, a group of MPs from the same political party is elected for each GRC at the General Elections. The rule is that each group of candidates cannot all come from one racial group. Given the predominance of Chinese in Singapore, the minority races could easily fail to get a single candidate into parliament, as a Chinese candidate appealing just to Chinese voters can get elected without caring about the interests of the other races. The GRC system ensures that there will be continuous representation of minority races—the Malays and Indians especially—in parliament.

A second example of such a 'preventive' policy is the racial distribution policy for the public housing estates which you see all over Singapore. We have a rule on the maximum percentage in each block and each zone that may be owned by any one racial group. Thus no block of flats may have more than twenty-five per cent of Malay households or thirteen per cent of Indian households or eighty-seven per cent of Chinese households, and no neighbourhood may have more than twenty-two per cent of Malay households or ten per cent of Indian households or eighty-four per cent of Chinese households. This compares with the population as a whole having fourteen per cent of Malays, eight per cent of Indians and seventy-seven per cent of Chinese. The policy ensures that we will never have a block of flats or neighbourhood where practically all the owners come from just one race. It is a policy to ensure that Singaporeans in general will always grow up, and have to learn to live, in a diverse racial and religious environment. The idea is to foster mutual understanding and relationships at the grassroots level that bridge racial and religious divides.

There is in Singapore a Maintenance of Religious Harmony Act which provides for the maintenance of harmonious relationship among all the religions, and ensures the separation of religion and politics. The Act was enacted in 1990 because some religious groups, including the Buddhist, Christian and Muslim, were becoming rather fervent in their beliefs and evangelistic activities, and overly zealous in their proselytisation. Also a number of Catholic priests and activists had used social action to take on the government with liberation theology.

The security services are always on the alert for elements which seek to create disharmony and foster discontent between people of different races and religions. *The Straits Times* article that I referred earlier quoted the pastor of a large church congregation in Singapore to have said, 'In a small country like Singapore where people highly value religious harmony, it is very hard for "aggressive evangelism" or "fanatical faith" to thrive. And it is foolhardy for anyone to even dare to try.' Another pastor said that his congregation is 'very sensitive to the Muslims because their faith is a communal one—it is associated with the entire Malay community'. On the other hand, the adviser to the Hindu Advisory Board has said, 'The Hindu community is concerned over Hindus being converted out of the religion. Hindus never ever attempt to convert others into the Hindu religion.' Obviously religion is an extremely sensitive matter, and the government has to find a way to allow for the freedom of citizens to choose their own religion, as provided for in the country's constitution.

Unless carefully managed, race and religion can easily be exploited to generate social discord, undermine public confidence, foster suspicion and distrust, and incite hatred between the communities. Indeed, Singapore experienced riots in 1964 when race and religion were exploited for political ends: Malays killed Chinese and Chinese killed Malays in about equal numbers. The riots were symptomatic of tensions between Singapore and Kuala Lumpur and resulted in Singapore separating from Malaysia in 1965 and becoming the independent state it now is. Singapore celebrated forty years of independence yesterday. But the need to wisely and sensitively handle matters of race and religion never goes away.

5. Religious extremism

In December 2001, authorities in Singapore uncovered a plot by a terrorist network known as Jemaah Islamiya (JI) to attack American, Israeli, British and Australian nationals, buildings and interests in Singapore. JI is based in Southeast Asia with links to Al-Qaeda. It recruited and trained extremists in the late 1990s, with the stated goal of creating an Islamic state comprising Brunei, Indonesia, Malaysia, Singapore, the southern Philippines, and southern Thailand. JI was responsible for the bombing of the Marriott Hotel in Jakarta in August 2003 as well as the Bali bombings in October 2002.

Following the December 2001 plot against Singapore, Singapore Malays and Muslims found themselves on the defensive. The government had to act very fast to get religious and community leaders to take the initiative to ask the people to come together and re-create trust and confidence in each other. Multi-racial and multi-religious Inter-Racial Confidence Circles (IRCCs) were formed at the grassroots level—all still active today—comprising community leaders and leaders of churches, mosques and temples in the area. The kinds of repercussions in attacks on mosques and churches in Holland after the murder of film-maker Theo van Gogh in the Netherlands, and the attacks on mosques which Britain saw after the London bomb attacks last month, were avoided in Singapore.

The government also introduced a Declaration on Religious Harmony in June 2003 which reads:

> We, the people in Singapore, declare that religious harmony is vital for peace, progress and prosperity in our multi-racial and multi-religious Nation.
>
> We resolve to strengthen religious harmony through mutual tolerance, confidence, respect and understanding.
>
> We shall always
> Recognise the secular nature of our State,
> Promote cohesion within our society,
> Respect each other's freedom of religion,
> Grow our common space while respecting our diversity,
> Foster inter-religious communications,

and thereby ensure that religion will not be abused to create conflict and disharmony in Singapore.

The declaration affirms the values that have helped to maintain religious harmony in Singapore, and serves as a reminder on the need for continued efforts to develop stronger bonds between religions in Singapore.

So these are what you might call the 'negatives' of religion. It requires governments to be alert, to take preventive steps to minimise causes of tension and distrust between races and religions, and to take proactive steps to build up mutual understanding and confidence. Government must accommodate these differences in religion, because banishing religion is not a choice: it is an integral part of culture, of society, and, most critically of all, of the nature of man himself. Nevertheless, there is a point at which tough action may be necessary against particular groups, should they threaten national unity or undermine deep national interest. As an example in Singapore, the government banned the Jehovah's Witnesses, because they had opposed National Service, which is military service all young males in Singapore must perform.

6. Moral education

Religion is obviously not all negative. Otherwise they would have long disappeared from the world. When it comes to ethics and moral education and social education, all religions and cultures teach much the same thing. It is wrong to steal and to kill. It is right to honour your parents, to provide for widows and orphans, to look after the needy, the sick and the handicapped, to help our fellowman where you can.

But in Singapore, the government has taken the strict stand that religion is a personal decision, and that while there is freedom of worship there shall be no aggressive, insensitive proselytisation. As a result, the schools try to teach moral education without religion. This is, of course, very difficult. Imagine a teacher teaching his students to be kind and caring and understanding and honest and sincere, and the next thing that happens is the students seeing him shouting away at an old lady or disclaiming responsibility for a mistake he had committed. Teaching moral education within the context of religion would allow the teacher to say:'This is the ideal, and this is what is right and what is wrong. I don't care what religion you believe in but this is what your religion teaches about behaviour in society and the way to treat other people. Sometimes, even I fail, but we all must keep trying to do what is right and stop doing what is wrong.' By teaching moral education without religion, the need for personal example by the teacher is very great, and his teaching fails when the students do not see the teaching to be true for his life.

7. Schools teach religious knowledge

I should say, however, that it has not always been the case that moral education is taught in our schools without religion. Dr Goh Keng Swee, who was then the First Deputy Prime Minister and Minister of Education, made Religious Knowledge a compulsory subject for all upper secondary school students from 1984. They could choose any one of six Religious Knowledge subjects to study—Bible Knowledge, Buddhist Studies, Confucian Ethics, Hindu Studies, Islamic Religious Knowledge and Sikh Studies. Dr Goh's idea was that studying religion for its ethics was the way to produce morally upright citizens. When he introduced the idea to the public in January 1982, he said that when he was in charge of the army, he noticed that one common occurrence in battalion camps was that if you left your wallet or watch unattended for more than ten seconds, it disappeared. 'So,' he continued, 'one day I told the Prime Minister that the schools are turning out a nation of thieves and that something must be done about this in our educational system.' Summing up his views on religious education, Dr Goh said:

> The aims of this exercise are modest. We don't believe we're going to make all Singaporeans upright. Every society has its black sheep. But at least when they've gone through a course on religious knowledge, most of them will leave school believing it's wrong to lie, cheat and steal. Many now do not.

The then Minister of State for Education, Dr Tay Eng Soon, said in a speech in February 1982:

> The societies and civilisations from which we have descended have all been shaped and moulded by great religions and ethical teachings. Hinduism for example has permeated through Indian culture and thought for several thousand years. The Chinese civilisation has been profoundly influenced by Confucian ethics. These civilisations have undergone great upheavals, wars and change. It would be true to say that it was their moral and religious beliefs which have provided the continuity and given their peoples

the strength to survive these changes. We would be foolish not to learn from what the great religions and ethical disciplines can teach us, especially in our present scientific and materialistic age. We can readily observe what is happening to those societies which have abandoned or lost the time-tested moral and religious beliefs of their forebears. They have become amoral; they are permissive and self-indulgent, they are also turning to all kinds of fads and cults. And the thoughtful members of their societies are worried about these trends. We do not want this to happen to us. The teaching of religious knowledge and ethics can certainly reinforce the moral values of our children and provide them with a moral compass for life even though we know that there are many other factors such as the home, the example of elders and so on which greatly influence the moral character of children. The teaching of religious knowledge and moral education in our schools will not solve all our problems. But if well taught it could provide an anchor in the midst of the cross currents of change which are going on around us.

8. Schools stop teaching religious knowledge

The policy of compulsory religious education in upper secondary school, however, did not last. Dr Goh Keng Swee's successor, Dr Tony Tan, reversed it after six years. He explained to Parliament in a Ministerial Statement in October 1989 that:

> There is today a heightened consciousness of religious differences and a new fervour in the propagation of religious beliefs. This trend is world-wide and it embraces all faiths. It can be seen in the growth of Islamic fundamentalism, enhanced Christian evangelisation and resurgence of activity and interest among traditional religions such as Buddhism. If carried to extremes, this trend towards greater fervour in the propagation of religious beliefs can disrupt our traditional religious harmony and religious tolerance which are pre-requisites for life in Singapore. It is not possible for government to

ignore this new development. We must take cognisance of it and we must implement measures to ensure that it does not upset the present climate of religious tolerance in Singapore. I think we have to face this fact squarely. But to avoid any suspicion of partiality in formulating and implementing the measures, it is essential for government to be seen to be scrupulously neutral and even-handed in the handling of religious matters in Singapore. Now, to avoid any misunderstanding, I want to clarify what is meant by the phrase 'to be neutral and even-handed in the handling of religious matters'. What the phrase means simply is that government cannot and should not be perceived to lean towards or to favour any particular religion. The phrase does not mean that government is against religion.

Dr Tan continued:

All Singaporeans, including the government, are well aware of the enormous contribution which religious groups have made to the life and progress of our country, particularly in the field of education. The schools which have been established by the major religious groups in Singapore have made a great contribution to the cause of education in Singapore. We hope that they will continue their good work and we can assure them of the government's support for their educational efforts. But to be neutral and even-handed in the matter of religion must mean, at the very least, that government should not give the appearance even unintentionally of giving preferred status to any particular religion or of using government institutions or government-supported institutions such as schools to help propagate any particular faith. It follows then that schools as government-supported institutions should, in my view, not be used as a means to impart religious beliefs to children. The teaching of religious beliefs, of what guides a person through life, what impels a person to be what he is, this is the province of the home. It is not the province of the schools. And parents cannot abdicate this responsibility to the schools or to government. It is the responsibility of parents to be moral exemplars, to set examples for their children, to teach them their religious beliefs and to bring them up in the religion in which they would like their children to follow. Schools can at most play a minor supporting role but the prime responsibility must remain that of the parents.

Dr Tan concluded:

If we accept the principle that the proper province for the teaching of religious beliefs is not in the schools but in the home, then it must follow that Religious Knowledge should not be made a compulsory subject to be taught within curriculum time in schools.

In place of the Religious Knowledge programmes, the Ministry of Education extended the Civics/Moral Education Programme, already being taught in the lower secondary school levels, to secondary three and four, also incorporating aspects of nation building, an awareness of the national shared values, and an appreciation of the beliefs and practices of the various religions and races in Singapore.

9. A moral society

If we simply become a society where what is legal is right and what is illegal is wrong, then we would have reduced morality to the law and thereby the whole moral fibre of society would be damaged. Law should be the expression of what is right and wrong, and set the boundary beyond which the individual will be trespassing onto the rights of others or posing a danger to them. But when a society becomes one where the law defines what is right and what is good, rather than the law being the expression of what the conscience of society and the intuition of the individual indicate to be right and good, then the law must become tighter and tighter to tell the individual in greater and greater detail what he must do and what he must not do. And government will then become more and more autocratic, and behave more and more like a god. Society will then weaken, as the conscience that resides in each one of us becomes silenced.

Where the conscience in the individual is strong and where people have the fear of God—which very often is a fear of divine retribution and of what may happen to them in this life or after they die—people will behave responsibly even when there is no one to catch them and punish them. The weak society is where people need to be forced to do things, and lose their sense of concern and responsibility for their fellowman. This is where religion plays the role only it can play, of bringing to people a consciousness of god, even a fear of god, that will cause them to do what is right and good even when there is no law to force them to do so, or no policeman around.

Allow me to quote some verses from the Bible to make the point about religion expecting people to do what is good and right because it is good and right, and demands accountability from the greatest superpower of all—God himself:

> Do not commit adultery, do not murder, do not steal, do not give false testimony, honour your father and mother (Luke 18:20).
> Love the Lord your God with all your heart and with all your soul and with all your mind and with all your strength . . . Love your neighbour as yourself. There is no commandment greater than these (Mark 12:30–31).
> Obey your leaders and submit to their authority. They keep watch over you as men who must give an account (Hebrews 13:17).
> Give everyone what you owe him: If you owe taxes, pay taxes; if revenue, then revenue; if respect, then respect; if honour, then honour (Romans 13:7).
> In everything, do to others what you would have them do to you (Matthew 7:12).

The last is the golden rule, stated in positive terms. The same rule, teaching much the same thing but stated in negative terms, can be found in various ancient cultures and religions. For example, Confucius taught: 'Do not impose on others what you do not desire others to impose upon you.' The Hindu sacred literature Mahabharata says: 'Let no man do to another that which would be repugnant to himself.' The Buddhist sacred literature Udana-Varga says: 'Hurt not others in ways you yourself would find hurtful.'

The difference between the golden rule stated in positive terms and in negative terms is that the rule in negative terms means: 'Leave people alone, don't hurt them,' whereas the rule in positive terms means: 'Help people, do good for them if you can.'

Imagine a society where many live according to the precepts I have quoted from the Bible. More than that, imagine a civil service with many officers who live and work by these precepts. What a difference it would make to the quality of government and the social environment of a country! Confucius had said of government:

> If the people are governed by laws and punishment is used to maintain order, they will try to avoid the punishment but have no sense of shame. If they are governed by virtue and rules of propriety are used to maintain order, they will have a sense of shame and will become good as well (*Analects* 2.3).

10. Conclusion

Let me summarise. Singapore is a multi-racial, multi-religious society. We must preserve social harmony and social stability at all costs. But religion cannot be wished away. It is intrinsic to the make-up of every man that he has a spiritual dimension to his being, and not just a physical body, an active brain and a sensitive heart. Government must recognise the powerful emotions, even explosiveness, of religious feelings, and manage the tensions which can easily come to the surface when communities feel they are being discriminated against. Yet only God in religion can do what government cannot do, namely, keep alive the conscience, and motivate people from within as to what is right and good. The law and the policeman are there to prevent people from doing what is irresponsible towards others. Only religion or god in the heart can move people to act beyond self-interest and thereby move society to a higher level of care and concern and a deeper sense of community and social responsibility.

I remember very well a conversation I had with Dr Goh Keng Swee about a rule to prevent people from having loud parties after midnight. He said it was a rule which tries to be fair: people can have a good time and enjoy themselves with loud laughter and singing and music, but only till midnight. The neighbour must be allowed to have the silence for his sleep after midnight. I asked if it would not be better for people to be educated about social responsibility and caring for their neighbours; then they will naturally stop making so much noise, and perhaps even stop before midnight. Dr Goh, in his usual great and incisive wisdom said, 'Setting the rule is government's business; converting the heart is God's business.'

Finally, what is the answer to the question I started with: 'Religion in governing a country: a positive or negative factor?' As I think it over, I believe it is the wrong question to ask. The right question is: 'Religion in governing a country: how can it be harnessed to raise moral standards, social conscience and responsible citizenship?' In other words: 'How can we make religion a positive factor?'

2

A Message of Peace and Harmony from the East to the West

Ye Xiaowen

My first encounter with the book *Seek the Welfare of the City* was three years ago, when I was visiting Tyndale House at Cambridge University at the invitation and arrangement of the United Bible Societies.[1] Since then, I had wished to have the book translated into Chinese very much, so that more Chinese people would have the opportunity to learn about the valuable ethics embodied in the Bible and highlighted in the book, which are beneficial to the public and society.

I believe, all that is true, good and beautiful are connected; be they religious or secular in form and be they measured by the values of the East or of the West.

This conference reminds me of a remark made by a Chinese bishop, Ding Guangxun: 'The central message of the Bible is reconciliation and peace— reconciliation and peace between God and human beings, and reconciliation and peace among human beings.' Now, I would like to talk on the topic of 'Seeking Global Peace'.

1. The threat of terrorism and unilateralism

The main trend in today's world is indeed towards peace and development. However, conflict and confrontation between different nations, peoples and religions are also becoming increasingly violent. This is a challenge to the collective wisdom and civilisation of all mankind. This challenge, to a large degree, derives from the confrontation between terrorism and what we call 'unilateralism', the tendency of some countries to act in their own interests without consulting or considering the interests of others. During the last hundred years, certain aggressive aspects of Western culture have led to a self-

---

1.   Bruce Winter, *Seek the Welfare of the City: Christians as Benefactors and Citizens* (Grand Rapids: Eerdmans, 1994).

centred conviction in the superiority of Western culture. The inevitable reaction to this sort of 'unilateralism' has been the rise of terrorism.

In Chinese we say 'enemies travel along a narrow path—sooner or later they are sure to clash'. This saying describes very well the clash of terrorism and 'unilateralism'. These natural enemies are in a state of dramatic confrontation and conflict. What they have in common, however, is their self-centred nature. Both demand complete submission from the other, both aim to destroy and replace the other. As a result, some call for a Jihad, while others call for a New Crusade. These two enemies struggle and fight, but neither can replace the other. They can fight and struggle, but neither can achieve victory over the other. Such a confrontational stance leads to numerous conflicts and renewed confrontations. Waves of terrorist attacks, like 11 September 2001 in New York, 11 March 2004 in Madrid, the bombings in London on 7 and 21 July 2005, and Sharm-el-Sheikh blasts on 23 July 2005 in Egypt, continue to send shock waves throughout the world.

Terrorism, is not only lurking, but also lurching. Some Western scholars have described this as 'a clash of civilisations'. Civilisation is an accumulation of human wisdom. A 'clash' between civilisations results when human ignorance replaces human wisdom. Is continued conflict the only prospect for modern civilisation? Can nothing be done about the dilemma in which civilisation finds itself?

No civilisation should be despised. No civilisation should be treated with contempt. Civilisations should respect and appreciate each other. No civilisation should take advantage of its strength to oppress the weak. All should treat other civilisations with tolerance, just as the ocean embraces equally all the rivers flowing into it. Civilisations should not be classified into higher or lower classes. They should not compete for survival, but complement each other. Favouring this one over that, trying to replace some or exclude others will only generate hatred. Mutual revenge will only lead to greater tragedies. Violence will only lead to more violence, and hatred will never end while more hatred is being generated.

2. Recovering the true meaning of religion

Harmony and peace are what the world needs now. People turn to religion and pray for peace, since religion always advocates peace. Unfortunately, some religions are distorted and abused. Some people want to use religion to interfere in the internal affairs of other nations, or to create violence and terror under the banner of religion. As a result, estrangements, suspicions and hatred are sown; more tensions, conflicts and confrontations are generated. This is a blasphemy against the holiness of religion. This is an expression of contempt for the purity of religion.

In 2000, the *Commitment to Global Peace of the Millennium World Peace Summit of Religious and Spiritual Leaders* declared that 'our world is plagued by violence, war and destruction, which are sometimes perpetrated in the name of religion'.

Prayers can offer comfort to people, but peace can only be established by great courage and wisdom. Today, we have all come to this conference in Singapore, a country in which diverse cultures and religions coexist in harmony. Beauty lies in diversity; the richer, the better. Actually, the wisdom of harmony lies in diversity. Diversity should be the basis of harmony, and the result of diversity should be harmony, not uniformity.

Confucius said that 'the gentleman seeks harmony but not uniformity; mean people seek uniformity but not harmony'. Attitudes towards 'harmony' and 'uniformity' distinguish the gentleman, or man of superior moral character, from 'mean people', who are concerned only about their own narrow interests.

Our world, after all, is diverse and colourful. Narrow-minded people may consider any diversity as a threat, and any difference as an enemy. But to the broad-minded, diversity is like a beautiful rainbow, where difference makes for unity and harmony.

Some terrorists are constantly proclaiming they will use force to defend Islamic civilisation. However, the original meaning of the word *Islam* is 'peace'. Islam believes that we are all descendants of the same ancestors. We should be forgiving towards our enemies and avoid extremes. We should strive for peace and avoid conflict. Allah said, 'Oh, you who believe, enter into peace, all of you (Koran 2:208).'

Some 'unilateralists' proclaim that they will use force to promote Christian civilisation. However, Christianity by its very nature also advocates peace and reconciliation. The Bible teaches Christians to love their neighbours, indeed to love their neighbours as themselves. Jesus said, 'Do to others as you would have them do to you (Matthew 7:12)'. As Emilio Castro, the former General Secretary of the World Council of Churches, said: 'If a man does not have a normal relationship with his neighbours, he could hardly develop a normal relationship with God.' Bishop Ding Guangxun also pointed out that 'the central message of the Bible is reconciliation and peace— reconciliation and peace between God and human beings, and reconciliation and peace among human beings'.

3. Peace and harmony in Chinese cultures

Now let us turn our attention towards the East. The concept of peace and harmony is expressed in Chinese by the word 'he'. This concept is embodied in Confucianism, Buddhism and Taoism, all of which enjoy a long history in China.

He, peace and harmony, is a major characteristic of traditional Chinese culture. It is the faith of the ancient Chinese sages, and the basis of their philosophies.

Confucianism stresses that 'harmony is precious'. People should 'seek harmony but not uniformity in human relationships'. In Confucianism, diversity and harmony, coexistence and balance, is respected. It is believed that 'the combination of the diverse produces a myriad of things, but the uniformity of the same generates nothing'. Confucianism advocates that a society can only progress through mutual dependency.

The basis of Buddhism is the doctrine of conditional causation. This means that everything is interdependent and coexists in harmony. Buddhism advocates ideas of equality and mercy, such as 'all truths and practices are equal in value'; 'there is no distinction between the self and the other'; 'compassion without causation means looking on all things as being of the same nature as oneself'. These concepts constitute an important basis for the realisation of peace and harmony. Buddhism believes that external peace and harmony come from inner peace and composition. If inner disharmony and external disharmony interact, the mutual agitation will lead to even greater confrontations and disputes. 'If one's heart is pure, it is a spiritual land of Buddha.' This is a quotation from the *Vimalakīrti-nirdeśa sūtra*. It means if your heart is pure, Buddha will be in your heart.

The *Way*, the natural way of the universe, 'Tao' in Chinese, is the highest belief of Taoism. Taoists believe that the fundamental nature of the *Way* is that it produces and accommodates everything. It is natural, mild and unselfish. Taoists let things take their own course and advocate gentleness, avoiding argument or dispute. Taoism holds that 'the *Way* models itself on the Law of Nature' and that 'to know perfect harmony of nature is in accord with the everlasting *Way*'. Taoism stresses an intuitive grasp of the interdependency of the myriad of things and the preservation of harmony. Only in this way can the universe thrive.

- The essence of *he*, peace and harmony, lies in acceptance, respect, gratefulness and flexibility.
- The internal meaning of *he* is human kindness, family concord, social harmony and world peace.

- The basis of *he* is tolerance and the ability to live with differences in a harmonious way, to seek commonality among differences and to thrive together.
- The highest stage of *he* is to appreciate the greatness of others while appreciating one's own virtues and qualities, to let goodness and beauty fill the world with peace and goodness.
- The idea of *he* reflects the general law of the development of things and it may progress and become enriched with the times.

4. One world, one dream

A globalising world needs to be guided by ideals, ideals to turn conflicts into peace, ideals of peace that can cross national borders and are cross-disciplinary. Traditional Chinese culture and religion, which seek 'diversity and harmony' and 'harmony but not uniformity', can contribute the concept of *he*—peace and harmony to the world. China, in the East, has a tradition of peace and harmony. To the West, now facing so much toil and trouble, China would like to bring this message of *he*.

In April 2005, out of concern of the difficulties currently faced by mankind, over two hundred Buddhist masters from all over China held a round-table conference in Sanya, Hainan Province. They made a vow to 'send a message of peace and harmony to the troubled world'.

In Bangkok this May, representatives from forty-one countries and regions took part in *The International Conference on Buddhism*. The Chinese representative proposed the idea of 'sending a message of peace and harmony from the East to the West'. The participants found this idea very attractive. The declaration of the conference approved the proposal to hold a *World Forum on Buddhism* in China to further explore issues of common concern, to deepen the understanding of the idea of peace and harmony in Buddhism and Chinese culture.

China today practises a foreign policy of good neighbourly relationships and peaceful coexistence, and a domestic policy of building a harmonious society and realising peaceful reunification. China's development is a peaceful one and the rise of China is also peaceful. China's development not only contributes towards Asia's stability and prosperity but also towards peace and development of the wider world. China's development does not pose any threat to any other country. It is not simply a political commitment of China to advocate and preserve peace, as it is also a natural extension of the values within Chinese civilisation.

Some people are suspicious of China's peaceful rise and warn of a China threat. They do not understand that 'seeking harmony but not uniformity' is a tradition, indeed one of the national characteristics, of the Chinese people. They have never heard of Confucius' maxim that 'the gentleman seeks harmony but not uniformity, while mean people seek uniformity and not harmony'. They are trying to understand the mind of a gentleman with the mindset of a mean person.

Until now, some people still do not believe that freedom of religious belief is respected in China. Our respect for the freedom of religious belief is sincere and consistent. First, it is our respect for objective existence, for objective processes and for the inherent laws of social development. Second, it is our respect for basic human rights, and it can help rally people around the cause of national rejuvenation and build a better world. Third, it is deeply rooted in our cultural heritage. Throughout China's history, one sees few, if any, massive conflicts between religious believers and non-believers, or between followers of different religions. Fourth, it is protected by the Constitution and the laws. The Regulations on Religious Affairs, that went into effect this March, gave further guarantees to such freedom.

An ancient Chinese sage said: 'When the great principle prevails, the world is a commonwealth. Rulers are selected according to their wisdom and ability, mutual trust is promoted and good neighbourliness is cultivated.'

Martin Luther King had a dream. He dreamt that black boys and black girls would be able to join hands with white boys and girls, walking together as brothers and sisters.

China is preparing to host Olympics in 2008. China also has a dream. It is expressed in the slogan for Olympics 2008: *'One world, one dream'*.

One world: a peaceful world in which different civilisations respect each other and diverse cultures coexist in harmony. One dream: to achieve unity and harmony through dialogue, mutual understanding and tolerance, and eventually to create peace for the whole world. This is the message China wishes to send to the world, a message of *he*—a message of peace and harmony.

Biblical Studies

3

Pilgrims and Citizens: The Paradox for the First Christians According to 1 Peter

Bruce Winter

The first Christians in the Eastern part of the Roman Empire were an enigma to the society in which they lived. They were not Jews—they had no synagogue. They were not a religious cult—they had no temple (Acts 17:24). They were not an association—they had no political agenda. They were not an academy—their teachers used no titles (Matthew 23:8–10). They could not be described by any of the known ethnic or social categories of their day.

Then who were they? What did their compatriots make of them? Some accused the Christians of being Jewish insurrectionists. 'These people who have stirred up trouble throughout the world have come here' in order to free Judea from the yoke of Roman tyranny (Acts 16:6). In an official letter the emperor Claudius had warned the Alexandrians against such 'Syrians'.[1] The Christians had no such political agenda.

Some saw them as atheists, for they had no statues to worship. The god dwelt in the statue. 'Athena is visible in her statue', her devotees said standing before her great image in the temple on the Athenian Parthenon. They said the same of other gods and goddesses.[2] Christians did not worship what Paul declared to be 'so-called' gods, that is, popularly but erroneously called 'gods in the heavens and on earth'. They worshipped one God, the Father and one Lord, Jesus Christ (1 Corinthians 8:6). God did not dwell in temples made with hands (Acts 17:24). They needed no temple.

Others saw that some of what they did was akin to the activities of an association. These were hotbeds of political intrigue against which Augustus took action immediately on coming to power. He forbade them from meeting more than once a month, apart from the Jews who met in the synagogue. To

---

1.   *P Lond*. 1912 (AD 41), *ll*. 96–100.
2.   R Lane Fox, *Pagans and Christians* (London: Penguin, 1987), 115.

hold a meeting would be a felony.[3] Gallio, the noted jurist and governor of
Achaea, declared that Christians in his province were not guilty of any offence
against Roman law (Acts 18:12–15). They had no agenda to overthrow the
Roman order. This was a landmark judgment in the case of the Jews versus
Paul in Corinth.

While Tertullian (*c* 160–*c* 240 CE) actually used some of the activities of
an 'association' by way of an analogy to try to explain to the outsider the
activities of the Christian community and what he called 'the business of the
Christian association (*factio*)', he struggled as he explained Christian meetings:

> I will now show you the proceedings with which the
> Christian association occupies itself. We are a society
> (*corpus*) bound together by our religious profession, by the
> unity of our way of life and the bond of our common hope.
> We meet together as an assembly and as a society . . . We
> pray also for the emperors, for their ministers and those in
> authority, for the security of the world . . . We gather
> together to read the books of God . . . With the holy words
> we nourish our faith.[4]

However, he emphatically denied that the Christian meeting was 'an
association (*factio*)'. 'When decent people, when good men gather, when the
pious and when the chaste assemble, that is not to be called an association.'[5]

Christians and their gatherings could not be readily defined, even when
they used a political, *ekklēsia*, term to describe their meeting.[6] They were not
comfortable fits in the first century social order. In Roman society Roman law
regulated all aspects of life. The focus on social obligations, class structures
and the abhorrence of non-conformity meant that these Christians did not

---

3.   The crime of an association meeting weekly was that of being an illegal
     collegium that carried with it political or seditious implications. See OF
     Robinson, *The Criminal Law of Rome* (London: Duckworth, 1995), 80.
4.   Tertullian, *Apology* 39.1–4.
5.   *Ibid*, 39.21.
6.   See the comment of EA Judge, 'Did the Churches Compete with Cult Groups', in
     *Early Christianity and Classical Culture: Comparative Studies in Honor of
     Abraham J Malherbe,* edited by JT Fitzgerald, Thomas H Olbricht, and L
     Michael White (Leiden: Brill, 2003), 501.

conform to society's norms. There was something of a puzzle about their lifestyle. A later Christian writer was to articulate the enigma that being a Christian created for fellow citizens:

> Christians reside in their own countries, but as if aliens (*all' hōs paroikoi*). They take part in everything as citizens (*politai*) but put up with everything as foreigners *(xenoi)*. Every foreign land is their homeland and every home a foreign land . . . They find themselves in the flesh, but do not live according to the flesh. They pass their time upon the earth, but they have their citizenship in heaven.[7]

The anonymous Christian who wrote this letter to the non-Christian, Diogentus, stated that Christians 'show forth the amazing and admittedly paradoxical nature of their own *politeia* (*thaumasten kai homologoumenōs paradoxon endeiknutai tēs katastasin tēs heautōs politeias*). He admitted quite openly that Christianity was something of a 'paradox' (*paradoxon*).[8] It was not only the amazing consequence of their beliefs. It was also the fact that those who embraced them operated 'contrary to expectation' and continued to do so even when their fellow countrymen did not always understand or appreciate their contribution as citizens.

A first-century person who was not a Christian would also have been amazed on reading 1 Peter because of this 'paradox'. The 'amazing' nature of the Christian faith and its focus is first discussed in detail (1 Peter 1:3–2:9). There then follows another focus that created the paradox. The author of 1 Peter wrote to encourage Christians to continue to live out this paradox, even if others did not understand why they operated as they did. It is the purpose of this chapter to explore the enigma that the first Christians created for other citizens.

1. Focus on the amazing future

1 Peter begins with the blessing of 'the God and Father of our Lord Jesus Christ'. The reason why God should be blessed is because of an amazing act of clemency. The guilty people who deserve execution are forgiven all their crimes against God. This act of pardon was secured, not through skilful

---

7. *Epistle to Diognetus* 5. 5, 8.
8. *Ibid*, 5. 4.

advocates or lawyers pleading special or extenuating circumstances, but was made possible through the death and resurrection of Jesus Christ. His resurrection gave them their resurrection, described as being 'born anew' to a living and sure and absolutely certain hope and confidence about their ultimate future (1:3). 'This was the true grace of God' in which the Christians stood on a rock-like foundation that is the theme of the letter (5:12).

The nature of that future is described as an inheritance for every such person. It is secure, being described as 'incorruptible, undefiled and never deteriorating'. That is the reason why 'every home (is) a foreign land', to cite the letter to Diognetus. It was not because they despised their country or were disloyal to it. The everlasting inheritance is 'reserved in heaven' for them. There will be no inheritance left unclaimed there because of the iron-clad guarantee that the power of God would keep the Christians so that they would finally secure it (1:4–5).

Even the present difficult moments of life have a lasting purpose. They test the Christians' faith just as pure gold is refined in the fire. The complex issues of life have a trajectory into the future because even they 'will be found to result in praise and glory and honor' for God's people in heaven (1:6–7). The best is yet to be. Nothing in the present is a loss. Even their present pain has an ultimate gain.

Overwhelming devotion to Jesus Christ who visited this earth but has now ascended to heaven was a heart-felt one on the part of Christians. They were under a lifelong obligation to their Saviour. They owed him everything. They would one day experience the fullness of the salvation he secured (1:8–9).

God did nothing but first he gave advance notice to his servants the prophets (Amos 3:7). These were like very early press releases of what would come to pass. What the Christians were now enjoying was made known to the prophets well in advance of it happening. These prophets knew the grace that was coming through Jesus Christ. They also knew about the sufferings and subsequent glorification of the Son of God long before his birth (1:10–11). They were well aware that they were not only serving their own generation, but it was revealed to them that they were serving the generation of the first Christians when searching out the time and the events predicted when the Messiah came.

The amazing events of the death and resurrection of Jesus that are the content of the gospel were announced by the Holy Spirit to the first Christians. The angels would gladly have 'traded in' their harps for the opportunity to tell men and women of this totally unexpected grace that would come to them as 'good news' (1:12). All this was the work of the Triune God,

Father, Son and Holy Spirit, who undertook such an amazing rescue operation (1:2–12).

How could this future hope not totally fill the horizons of Christians? They were, in fact, commanded 'to gird up the loins of the minds, be sober, fix your hope completely on grace to be brought to you at the revelation of Jesus Christ' (1:13). With such an everlasting inheritance, the Christians could only be future looking. Did this amazing message mean that Christians were only to focus fully on their ultimate bright future? This is known technically as 'binocular' vision, hence the use of 'binoculars' that focus on a particular distant object, that is, the grace coming to them.

2. The monocular foci of the first century Christians

There are certain animals that have monocular vision. They have eyes on either side of their heads. They can focus on different objects at the same time. Crocodiles and many lizards have this capacity. What is paradoxical about the Christians is that they are to focus fully with 'one' eye on grace that is coming. At the same time they have another very different focus or vision according to 1 Peter. This is the paradox of Christianity.

The second focus is not about living a life of self-fulfilment. It was not about the pursuit of 'fleshly lusts' (2:11). Others wanted to satisfy all their desires immediately. Why should the first century Christians not live like this? If the ultimate future is guaranteed by Christ's resurrection, then why not enjoy 'now' knowing that you will also enjoy 'then', and have the best of both worlds.

There were a number of reasons given why they could not do this. Firstly, the Christians were taught that they were under a deep obligation. The first call on them was to have a different 'lifestyle'. As God's children they must reflect his character. God is holy. 'Like father like son'. His sons and daughters must bear the Father's likeness (1:14–16). They now would be subjected to God's evaluation. The assessment would not be the basis of their acceptance, but they would be held accountable with what they did or did not do. God is not impartial when it comes to assessing how his children have lived (1:17).

God's redemption meant that they must now live pure lives (1:18–22). As the letter to Diognetus stated they 'guard their purity'. It is out of a pure heart that they were to love other Christians earnestly. It was far deeper than being polite. Every aspect of falsehood had to be abandoned and they must continue to be nourished in their spiritual lives (2:1–2).

Secondly, they had to live useful lives. They must never be what they once were. The word 'life-style' (*anastrophē*) was often mentioned in 1 Peter (1:15, 18, 2:12, 3:1, 2, 16) and it was to be a 'good' one (2:12, 3:16). This was not a reference to prosperity or luxurious living, as we would assume when the term is used today. The good lifestyle is one marked by good deeds. These deeds were such that the outsiders would see them. Jesus taught 'let your light so shine before men, that they may see your good *works* and glorify your Father in heaven' (Matthew 5:16). 1 Peter teaches the same truth.

In 1 Peter the Christians were called upon to 'do good' in the two major spheres of life. What existed outside their home in the first century was called *politeia*. It was not restricted to 'politics' but covered the whole of the public sphere, ie everything outside their home.[9] The other sphere was related to the home and the family.

It is interesting that the first domain mentioned in 1 Peter was not home and family. In the first century that was seen as the most important sphere of life. 'Don't sweep the snow off your neighbour's roof. Sweep your own path' may have been what their first century compatriots did but that was not how the Christians operated.

What did it mean to have 'a good lifestyle' in the public sphere? It meant being a good citizen. That meant being subject to all the state and civic institutions, to the ultimate ruler in the first century, the emperor or to his deputies, his provincial governors. They were given the authority (*imperium*) by Rome to govern. In those days the role of government was divided into two spheres. The first related to the courts for the administration of Roman criminal law (2:13–14a).

The other sphere was the official praising of those citizens who undertook civic benefactions that enhanced the governing of the citizens and beautification of the city. In the first century it was expected that those who possessed financial means would use them to undertake honorary public offices for running the city. They would also donate fountains, gardens, buildings and other facilities that would enhance its life. They would provide financial help in giving grain in times of famine, for which there was evidence in Corinth. We know in 50s CE that there were three such famines in the East. They would be 'praised' or officially acknowledged, by the ruling authorities

---

9.   C Meier, *The Greek Discovery of Politics,* translated by David McLintock (Cambridge, Mass: Harvard University Press, 1990), 13ff.

as a 'high-minded and good' person, 'manhood at its best'.[10] Christians were commanded 'to do good' in the public sphere (2:14b–15). The 'praising' meant that the person was publicly announced as a 'civic-minded and good' person (*kalos kai agathos*). This was done if he or she held an honorary public office or had given something to the city to enhance its environs. This was not a sphere of activity to which Christians were forbidden to contribute. According to Tertullian it was said of the Christians that they 'buy provisions (*obsonant*) as if to die tomorrow, and build (*aedificant*) as if they were never to die at all'.[11] This may well be a similar reference to the giving of benefactions to the city.

The effects of 'doing good' in the public domain would be twofold. This would not only benefit others and the city generally but it would also silence the 'ignorance of uninformed people'. They concluded that the Christians were 'evil doers' and not the 'doers of good'. The doing of good in the public domain was declared to be 'the will of God' and it also aimed at correcting misconceptions about Christians (2:15).

1 Peter 2:12ff taught Christians how to relate positively to their city and its inhabitants. This would confirm that 'they take part in everything as citizens', as was said in the letter to Diognetus. It is suggested that it was also the reason why he spoke of 'the paradox' for those with a heavenly focus. Their monocular vision was also fixed on the welfare of those in the city.

3. The paradox with a precedent

Was this teaching in 1 Peter simply a one-off pragmatic decision that aimed to take any pressure off Christians? A paradigm for the role of the Christian in society in 1 Peter can be found in the Old Testament in Jeremiah 29:7. The paradigm appears to have been foremost in the thinking of the writer of this letter, for the description of Christians was expressed in terms of the 'Diaspora' (1 Peter 1:1). In Jeremiah's day, the Jews in Exile were exhorted to settle in Babylon, marry, 'seek the welfare of the city' to which the Lord had carried them, and pray for its peace. The suggested alternative was that the community should perceive its present existence as a temporary one and its

---

10. For evidence see my 'Secular and Christian Responses to Corinthian Famines', *Tyndale Bulletin* 40.1 (1989): 86–106 and 'Acts and Food Shortages', in *The Book of Acts in its First Century Setting*, volume 2, Graeco-Roman Setting, edited by D Gill and C Gempf (Grand Rapids: Eerdmans, 1994), 59–78.
11. Tertullian, *Apology* 39.14.

members as resident aliens in Babylon. Their false prophets saw return from exile as an event that would occur almost immediately (Jeremiah 29:8).

The people of God in that Diaspora, however, were commanded to continue to seek the welfare of their city in which they would dwell for the next seventy years in exile, and then their return to the promised inheritance of their forefathers would occur (Jeremiah 29:4–14). It has been shown that the treatment of the Jews in exile was no different from that experienced by other dispossessed minority groups in Babylon. What was unique was the attitude Israel was called upon to adopt. They were not to plot the destruction of their conquerors, but to seek their blessing. 'The people are to intercede with the Lord on behalf of the well-being of their new home.'[12] Bright notes, 'the command is a remarkable one for the Jews to pray for the hated heathen power, and to seek the peace ie the prosperity of their city'.[13]

The parallel with 1 Peter was not accidental. The Christians were aptly called 'elect sojourners of the Dispersion' (1:1). This was a theological and not a social description of the letter's recipients. It was an appropriate phrase for the elect pilgrim people of God in their present temporal situation. Far removed from their promised inheritance or final homeland, they were assured that they would reach their promised destination preserved by the power of God. They will not be disappointed with the nature of their inheritance (1:4–9). The twin concepts 'to do good' *(poiein agathon)* and 'to seek peace' *(zētein eirēnē)* are picked up later in the letter (3:11) in a citation from Psalm 34:12–16, but the language is also reminiscent of the theme of Jeremiah to 'seek the welfare of the city and to pray for its peace' (29:7). The parallels between Jeremiah 29 and 1 Peter 1 are compelling. In 1 Peter the theological paradigm that demanded that Christians seek the welfare of the city was derived from the Old Testament exile.[14]

How then should the Christians in 1 Peter spend their days on earth? It is clear that as spiritual 'sojourners' and 'alien residents' they must withdraw from the self-indulgent lifestyle of their contemporaries (2:11) and seek the welfare of the society in which they lived. As we have seen, they were instructed to spend their days in this earthly city seeking the blessing of its inhabitants (2:11ff). They were to do good in the city, in the households as bonded servants (2:18), in marriage (3:1, 7), and in every activity (3:11).

---

12.   RP Carroll, *Jeremiah* (London: SCM, 1986), 556.

13.   J Bright, *Jeremiah* (New York: Doubleday, 1965), 211.

14.   For an extended discussion of this see my *Seek the Welfare of the City: Christians as Benefactors and Citizens* (Grand Rapids; Eerdmans, 1994), 15–17.

Why were Christians commanded to 'do good'? It was because they belonged to the God who did good. The God of the Bible is a God of infinitive goodness. That is seen in all he does, in creation, in providence, in general revelation to all humanity, in specific revelation, in redemption, in sanctification and in judgment. All that he did was good. We should not be surprised that his Son went about 'doing good'. He did all things 'well' we are told (Acts 10:38, Mark 7:37). For Christians, it is a case of like Father, like sons and daughters. They must devote themselves to the doing of good deeds in all human activities in the private as well as the public spheres of life.

4. Christians in society—historical and sociological explanations

Seeking the welfare of the city is not how some scholars would describe the activity of the first century Christians. A social historian has suggested that 'Plainly their security [the Christians] as groups was felt to depend to a large extent on their activities escaping public attention'.[15] Social ethics was defined in 1 Peter as 'the doing of good works' in all spheres of life and was every Christian's calling (2:11ff). It has also been said that Christians were required 'to stand aloof from public life'. This attitude came from Epicurean teaching on withdrawing from society. While this comment has not been applied specifically to a discussion of 1 Peter, those conclusions can readily colour our overall perception of the early Christians' participation in, or withdrawal from, public life. In Macedonia they were taught to 'live quietly'. This is seen as a reference to political quietism—the Christian was 'to attend to one's own affairs', and not 'to attend to public affairs' (1 Thessalonians 4:11–12).[16] However the command applied to former clients of patrons withdrawing from disruptive and divisive involvement in *politeia*. It was certainly not a command for withdrawal by all Christians from public life.

Others have felt that the place of Christians in society can be better accounted for by using sociological models rather than social-historical approaches. For instance, it has been argued that 'social marginality' and 'social separation' was actively encouraged in 1 Peter. This conclusion was reached with the use of the sociological model of the 'conversionist sect', which is said to have encouraged 'the maintenance of social distance' in order

---

15. EA Judge, *The Social Pattern of Early Christian Groups in the First Century* (London: Tyndale House, 1960), 73.

16. RF Hock, *The Social Context of Paul's Ministry: Tentmaking and Apostleship* (Philadelphia: Fortress, 1980), 46, and AJ Malherbe, *Social Aspects of Early Christianity* (Baton Rouge: Louisianan State University Press, 1977), 26.

to preserve coherence and distinctiveness as a means of attracting potential converts. In the same way sociologists believe that rigorous religious distinctiveness accounts for the growth of sectarian groups in the twentieth century.[17] This is not to deny that 1 Peter may have been written in part to overcome any temptation to separatist tendencies developing among Christians as a defense mechanism against any hostile pressure towards them. The teaching of 1 Peter did not encourage such a separation from society but rather from sin (see 1:17, 2:11).

There is an alternative sociological model that seeks to show that the opposite activity is occurring in 1 Peter, that is, the integration of this movement into society. This 'acculturation' model was developed from the social patterns of South Pacific peoples and the Indians and Amish people of North America, and has been used to argue that 1 Peter reflects 'the social function of contradictory actions' with an 'enthusiastic reception' of social patterns and at the same time a firm rejection of other behavior.[18] Again this does not explain the motivation for ethical conduct in 1 Peter, nor does the evidence from that letter itself support the view that Christians were aiming for acculturation. The difficulty addressed there is the problem created by society's response to Christians. Recent discussions of social history and sociology seem to offer no explanation consistent with the extant data on the relationship of early Christianity in Asia Minor to the public life of its adherents, which is a major concern in 1 Peter.

5. Conclusions

The teaching about social ethics and civic involvement by the pilgrim people of God in 1 Peter holds together two crucial, but related biblical doctrines, the future hope and doing good in the public and private domains. To stand in 'the true grace of God' demanded a deep commitment to the welfare of the city while focusing on the living eschatological hope. That enabled the Christian to place personal concerns second to the needs of others in the city. The firm, future hope of a secure inheritance meant that nothing in this life

17. JH Elliott, *A Home for the Homeless: A Sociological Exegesis of 1 Peter, its Situation and Strategy*, (Philadelphia: Fortress, 1981), 74–77 citing BR Wilson, 'An Analysis of Sect Development', *American Sociological Review*, 24 (1959): 3–15.

18. DL Balch, 'Hellenistic Acculturation in 1 Peter', in *Perspectives on First Peter*, NABPR Special Studies series 9 (1986): 83. This argues that Elliott has not applied the correct model and that of acculturation is the appropriate one.

was catastrophic for the Christian (4:12). The setting of one's hope on the grace to be revealed at the revelation of Jesus Christ (1:13) provided the perspective for fulfilling the Christian mandate to seek the welfare of the earthly city and not one's personal advantage.

In the 'City of London', Britain's premier financial centre, there is a popular saying that 'the person who dies with the most "toys" wins'. It is certainly not the case for Christians that 'If one does not seek his own welfare, then he will be destroyed by heaven and earth', according to an ancient Chinese saying. Those who seek the welfare of others in the city did not incur 'judgment', but rather secure the blessing of heaven by benefiting other citizens, 'for the eyes of the Lord are upon the righteous and his ears are open to their prayer' according to a more ancient saying (Psalm 34:12–16 cited in 1 Peter 3:10–12). Popular sayings are far from the teaching of 1 Peter on the contribution of Christians in the public sphere.

Public roles today may seem to us to be much more complicated than in the first century. However, they would not be seen as anything but highly complex in the first century. In their day political life operated with interest groups, powerful lobbying by the clients of a patron for the wider support for his vote, conflicting obligations to the Tribes of a city and very robust debates and decision-making processes in the political meeting (*ekklēsia*).[19] But the call to do good remains the same. Christians were commissioned to do good not just in the household, nor only in the household of faith but also in 'the city'. According to 1 Peter, the Christians' 'constitution' 'shows forth the amazing and admittedly paradoxical nature of their [the Christians'] own *politeia*'. It may have been a great enigma to their compatriots and it still can be today but the Christian's mandate from heaven is to seek in the welfare of the city.

---

19.   JE Lendon, *Empire of Honour: The Art of Government in the Roman World* (Oxford: Clarendon Press, 1997).

4

'Seek the Welfare of the City': Contributions of Diaspora Jews (323 BCE–66 CE)

Tan Kim Huat

1. Interpreting diaspora

Attempting to forestall a rebellion by pointing out that the repercussions would be felt beyond the geographical confines of Palestine, King Agrippa II was recorded to have declared that 'there is not a people in the world which does not contain a portion of our race'.[1] The historicity of the statement in Josephus may be disputed but it is undeniable that such a view was shared by many in the first century of our Common Era. Indeed, the experience of diaspora may be regarded as the defining characteristic of Jewish existence not just in the first century but the entire period of the Common Era.[2]

Interestingly, Josephus himself embellishes Balaam's first oracle in Numbers 23:7–10 with themes that both legitimate and extol the diaspora experience of his fellow Jews:

> Happy . . . is the people, to whom God grants possession of blessings untold and has vouchsafed as their perpetual ally and guide His own providence. For there is not a race on earth which ye shall not, through your virtue and your passion for pursuits most noble and pure of crime, be accounted to excel . . . aye and ye shall suffice for the world, to furnish every land with inhabitants sprung from your race . . . Those numbers now are small and shall be contained by the land of Canaan; but the habitable world,

---

1.   *Bellum*, 2.398.
2.   ES Gruen, *Diaspora: Jews amidst Greeks and Romans* (Cambridge MA: Harvard University Press, 2002), 1.

> be sure, lies before you as an eternal habitation, and your
> multitudes shall find abode on islands and continent, more
> numerous than the stars in heaven.[3]

Balaam's first oracle, which emphasises the concept of divine election and
the distinctiveness of the Jews, speaks of them as a people dwelling apart from
the world (Numbers 23:9). This motif is reinterpreted by Josephus to refer to
their moral excellence,[4] together with a slant which capitalises on their
diaspora experience, that is, the Jews' inheritance of the whole world as an
eternal habitation. It is arguable whether in so doing, he is actually turning
what was regarded by the Prophets as a tragedy (exile and dispersion as a form
of judgment) into a triumph (the possession of the entire earth as promised in
the Abrahamic covenant). In other words, diaspora experience can be and has
been reinterpreted as colonising experience.[5] Be that as it may, as the minority
which had a religion that was intimately connected with the possession of the
land, and which was also strongly monotheistic, the reality was such that
exiled Jews had to negotiate the diaspora adroitly, especially when they had
distinctive practices. Their being conspicuously different often elicited many
derogatory and racist remarks from the majority. An anonymous dictum found
in a papyrus was certainly representative: 'As everybody else does, keep clear
of the Jews.'[6]

Needless to say, the response which regarded the Jewish Diaspora as an
evil that must end was also present. The skirmishes and revolts involving Jews
during the Second Temple period, the sentiments found in writings which
yearn for the exile to end, even when a segment of the Jewish people had
already returned to *Eretz Israel* all testify to it.[7] Such differences in response
may be a result of the canonical traditions they inherited, which could easily
incline Jews one way or the other: either to resist with or without the attendant

---

3.   *Antiquitates*, 4.114–6.

4.   See also: JMG Barclay, *Jews in the Mediterranean Diaspora: From Alexander to
      Trajan (323 BCE–117 CE)* (Edinburgh: T&T Clark, 1996), 3; and also the
      discussion in B Halpern-Amaru, 'Land Theology in *Josephus' Jewish
      Antiquities*', *Jewish Quarterly Review*, 71 (1980–1): 201–29.

5.   Philo, *De Vita Mosis* 2.232. See the enlightening essay of S Pearce, 'Jerusalem as
      "Mother-City" in the Writings of Philo of Alexandria', in *Negotiating Diaspora:
      Jewish Strategies in the Roman Empire*, edited by JMG Barclay (London & New
      York: T&T Clark International, 2004), 19–36.

6.   *CPJ*, 152.23–5.

7.   See the discussion in the many essays in *Exile: Old Testament, Jewish and
      Christian Conceptions*, edited by JM Scott (Leiden: Brill, 1997).

action of returning, or to assimilate to the dominant culture. Hence, it is instructive to look at some of these. The strain which speaks of resistance may be represented by Psalm 137:

> By the rivers of Babylon we sat and wept when we remembered Zion. There on the poplars we hung our harps. For there our captors asked us for songs, our tormentors demanded songs of joy; they said, 'Sing us one of the songs of Zion!' How can we sing the songs of the LORD while in a foreign land? If I forget you, O Jerusalem, may my right hand forget its skill. May my tongue cling to the roof of my mouth if I do not remember you, if I do not consider Jerusalem my highest joy.

This psalm speaks of the Jewish Diaspora as an enforced removal, something undesirable and even tragic. Such a perspective is also found in the deuteronomistic and prophetic traditions. Jerusalem is presented as centripetal, and the implication of this is that every diaspora Jew should seek not only the welfare of *Eretz Israel* but also to return to it since it is not possible to sing the songs of Yahweh in a strange land. In fact, the psalm ends with a pronouncement of vengeance not only on those who destroyed Jerusalem but also those who taunted it at its destruction. With this nexus of ideas being enshrined in the canonical traditions, it is not surprising that the ardent zeal for Jerusalem's welfare and a sense of not belonging to a larger ethos did lead to the suicidal wars with the Roman Empire. These include not just the two wars fought in Jerusalem (66–70 CE and 132–5 CE) but also the Jewish revolt in Alexandria in 115–17 CE. Such revolts led, understandably, to the labelling of Jews as belligerent and antisocial.[8] Witness the remarks, and especially the sarcasm of the final sentence, found in Philostratus' *Life of Apollonius of Tyana* 5.33:

> For the Jews have long been in revolt not only against the Romans, but against mankind too. Those who have devised an anti-social way of life, who do not share with the rest of men in table-fellowship or libations or prayers or sacrifices

---

8.   Do note that Josephus has to write the *Bellum Iudaicum* to convince the Romans that the Jewish revolt of 66–70 CE was started by a radical group which was not representative of the Jewish race.

are more widely separated from us than Susa or Bactra or the
Indians who lie beyond these. So it was inappropriate to
punish them for revolting from us, when we would have
done better not to acquire them at all.

The above statement may be considered mild when compared with the
next, which is taken from Josephus. He puts what would have circulated in his
time into the mouth of Artaxerxes, who was informed by Haman that the Jews
were:

An unfriendly nation mingled with all mankind, which has
peculiar laws, is insubordinate to kings, is indifferent in its
customs, hates monarchy, and is disloyal to our
government.[9]

There might be a grain of truth to some elements of this charge, albeit
skewed in a discriminatory direction.

The pogrom of 38 CE, which took place in Alexandria, and through which
Jews were subjected to all forms of attacks and indignities, definitely
reminded diaspora Jews of how precarious their social position was,
prompting recall of the strain of response counselled in Psalm 137.[10]

On the other hand, as if it were offered as a counterpoint, we have the
counsel of Jeremiah, given to the exiles in Babylon (Jeremiah 29:5–7):

Build houses and settle down; plant gardens and eat what
they produce. Marry and have sons and daughters; find

---

9.   *Antiquitates*, 11.217.

10. Hypotheses about how this originated are many. Some scholars point to anti-
     Semitic feelings as the culprit: see, for example, V Tcherikover, *Hellenistic
     Civilization and the Jews* (Philadelphia: Jewish Publication Society, 1959), 309–
     32 and Z Yavetz, *Judenfeindschaft in der Antike* (München: Beck, 1997), 102–3.
     Others conjecture that the violence was directed against Jews only because they
     received special privileges from Rome. Thus, the real opposition was against the
     Romans: see, for example, EM Smallwood. *The Jews under Roman Rule: From
     Pompey to Diocletian* (Leiden: Brill, 1981), 233–5; Barclay, *Jews*, 48–9. But for
     a novel thesis and a good account of the events, see Gruen, *Diaspora*, 54–68. He
     concludes that the violence came actually from the marginalised indigenous
     Egyptians and was not directed at the Jews because of anti-Semitic feelings.
     Rather, it arose because of social unrest. Thus, Jewish relations with the ruling
     Greek elite during this period, is judged by him to be healthy.

wives for your sons and give your daughters in marriage, so
that they too may have sons and daughters. Increase in
number there; do not decrease. Also, seek the peace and
prosperity of the city to which I have carried you into exile.
Pray to the LORD for it, because if it prospers, you too will
prosper.

Recalling the words of Genesis 1:22, 28,[11] this counsel encourages the
exiles not just to survive but also to thrive and multiply. Instead of remaining
silent and passive, they should 'perform the Lord's song' through prayer and
action that would result in adding to the welfare of the cities to which they
were exiled. There is no note of vengeance struck. Instead, it is the prosperity
of the host-city that should be sought. Such counsel may, indeed, be regarded
as a *modus vivendi*, offered to help an adversely disadvantaged minority cope
with a difficult situation. But to be fair, it should be noted that it was also
performed in the hope for the return to *Eretz Israel* after the envisaged exile of
seventy years had been completed (vv 10–14). The strategy ensured that when
the restoration came about, there would be multitudes returning to build the
nation again. Foreign cities would then be regarded as staging grounds for
Yahweh's fulfilment of his promises of restoration.[12]

Interestingly, when return was possible, not all exiles took up the
opportunity. This was true even during the period when Israel had some sort
of autonomy in the affairs of the land, such as during the Hasmonean dynasty.
Jews who settled down in many Gentile cities remained happy where they
were although they continued to regard Jerusalem as their *mētropolis* (mother-
city). In fact, there are recorded instances of Jews leaving Judaea for other
lands.[13] This duality of Jewish experience—of having a widespread and

---

11. See WL Holladay, *Jeremiah 2: A Commentary on the Book of the Prophet
     Jeremiah Chapters 26–52* (Minneapolis: Augsburg Fortress, 1989), 138.

12. Some may take the case of Daniel as standing in the middle ground between the
     two poles mentioned. But since in the book there is a longing to return, we can
     classify its attitude towards the Diaspora as probably belonging to that of Psalm
     137, that is, Daniel might be serving the potentates but his interest was not in
     Babylon.

13. Josephus, *Contra Apionem* 1.194; 186–7. The authenticity of such statements is
     naturally debated amongst scholars. See Tcherikover, *Hellenistic Civilization*,
     56–7; J Mélèze-Modrzejewski, *The Jews in Egypt: From Rameses II to Emperor
     Hadrian* (Philadelphia: Jewish Publication Society, 1995), 73–4, 83, 99 and the
     concise discussion in IM Gafni, *Land, Center and Diaspora: Jewish Constructs*

thriving diaspora existing alongside a large Jewish community which resided in *Eretz Israel*—was a distinctive feature of Second Temple Jewish history, which would not be repeated until modern times.[14] But such a duality, it must be emphasised, was a new phenomenon in the life of this people then. In such a situation, we would expect not only would obedience to Torah be constantly exhorted, social acumen would also be highly prized. Understandably, there would be much experimentation, learning by trial and error, and much theological and philosophical reflection in the attempt to negotiate diaspora.[15]

Why should they not have returned? Practical reasons may be at work: the Jeremian advice has been taken up enthusiastically to the extent that *Eretz Israel* was judged to be too small to contain the entire Jewish people. But practical reasons were not the only ones to account for this phenomenon. There is evidence to suggest that the diaspora experience was interpreted in some Jewish circles to be something positive, and their staying put in different localities amounted to going beyond the counsel of Jeremiah. As it was pointed out earlier, dispersion could mean colonising, either in the sense of a universal mission through proselytising, or planting communities all over the world with a view to claiming it as an inheritance promised by Yahweh.[16] Consequently, diaspora is no longer viewed as a staging ground for a return to *Eretz Israel* but, rather, as a necessary process in the inheriting of the whole world. Indeed, it would be highly fascinating to conduct a study on how Jews coped with or negotiated diaspora when there was a mother-city they could always turn to. But this is beyond the scope of this paper.[17]

What becomes clear from this quick survey of broad attitudes of Jews with respect to the diaspora experience is that while the revolts against the Empire in 66–70 CE and 132–5 CE did become for many Roman historians the lens

in *Late Antiquity* (Sheffield: Sheffield Academic Press, 1997), 27–8. For a good discussion in Hebrew on the causes of Jewish emigration from Judaea, see A Kasher, 'Jewish Emigration and Settlement in the Hellenistic-Roman Period' [Hebrew], in *Emigration and Settlement in Jewish and General History*, edited by A Shinan (Jerusalem: Mercaz Zalman Shazar, 1982), 65–91.

14.   Gafni, *Land*, 19.
15.   See the many essays in *Negotiating Diaspora*, edited by Barclay, especially the introductory essay by the editor, 1–6.
16.   See Gafni, *Land*, 27–40.
17.   See S Pearce, 'Jerusalem', in *Negotiating Diaspora*, edited by Barclay, 19–36. See also the essays in *Jewish Local Patriotism and Self-Identification in the Graeco-Roman Period*, edited by S Jones and S Pearce (Sheffield: Sheffield Academic Press, 1998).

through which to stereotype the Jews,[18] this must be counter-balanced by a consideration of Jewish attempts to remain where they were scattered, participating in and seeking the welfare of these cities before those unfortunate events took place. What follows is an attempt to assemble and analyse the fragmentary evidence for Jewish contributions to life in different localities before the great revolts. This will give a much-needed corrective to the lopsided picture mentioned earlier.

2. Jewish participation in civic life

Side-stepping the thorny question of whether Jews were citizens or full members of different localities in the Diaspora, especially Alexandria,[19] we will instead look at data which might indicate active participation.[20] From the extant evidence, the picture which emerges is that of confident Jewish communities, and not ghettos, adroitly interacting with and participating in the larger society without compromising the twin fundamentals of Jewish self-understanding, which are monotheism and election.

Notwithstanding the pogrom in Alexandria in 38 CE, documentary and epigraphic evidence suggests that the Jewish community participated actively in the life of this *polis*. According to the *Letter of Aristeas*, the translation of Old Testament Scriptures into Greek is said to have been done by Jews who were steeped in the literature of the Greeks.[21] Such familiarity could hardly come about if they were aloof and indifferent to what was going on in the larger society. In fact, Philo also writes about Jews attending the theatre, being

---

18. See the many references in the magisterial study of Smallwood, *Jews under Roman Rule*, 123, note 15.

19. See the lucid summary of the issues in Barclay, *Jews*, 60–71. Undoubtedly, this will have an implication for our understanding of Jewish participation in civic life but such participation may be indicated not just by legal status but also forms of interaction and things the Jews did. Indeed, the significance and strength of the former depends on the latter.

20. Gafni considers whether local patriotism might be manifested in his *Land*, 43–50: through (i) Jews referring to themselves as people of a certain city; (ii) general statements which indicate attachment; and (iii) their referring to certain cities as being their *patrides*. Without dismissing the importance of all this, we nonetheless take a different tack. We will be looking for concrete examples of Jewish participation in civic life.

21. *Letter of Aristeas*, 121

mesmerised by the lines from Euripides.[22] Indeed, from their own ranks there arose a playwright, a man by the name of Ezekiel, who wrote a tragic drama on the theme of the Exodus.[23]

Of course, the most famous Alexandrian Jew to biblical scholars is the man Philo, who remains as the quintessential example of a Jew who was highly acculturated without sacrificing his distinctive Jewish characteristics. Not only was he thoroughly acquainted with Greek philosophy, he could sophisticatedly align it with the Jewish faith in his attempt to demonstrate the priority and pre-eminence of the latter. There is evidence to suggest that Philo regarded Alexandria as his *patris* and did not see this to be in contradiction to his affection for Jerusalem as his *mētropolis*.[24] Philo's writings also indicate familiarity with the skills and training programmes of the gymnasium, implying that he himself could have visited the place, which is severely castigated in the Maccabean literature (1 Maccabees 1:13–15; 2 Maccabees 4).

The significance of Jewish participation in Greek gymnasia needs elucidation. The gymnasium represented the climax of higher education of Greek youths in the cities of the Mediterranean world. Youths from the Greek upper classes were handpicked to form what was called the corps of *ephebes*. From this corps, future politicians and civic leaders of different institutions would be picked.[25] Would such a distinctively Greek institution take in foreigners, such as Jews? Two ephebic lists from Cyrene, revealing who the successful graduands were, were found to contain Jewish names: one from the end of the first century BCE and the other from the beginning of the first century CE. The relevant extracts are:

> Iason, son of Karnis
> Iesous, son of Antiphilos
> Ithannyras, son of Apollodoros
> Orion, son of Orion[26]

---

22. Philo, *Quod omnis Probus Liber sit*, 141.

23. H Jacobson, *The Exagoge of Ezekiel* (Cambridge: Cambridge University Press, 1983). See the astute analysis in Barclay, *Jews*, 132–8.

24. Philo, *In Flaccu*, 46. See Gruen, *Diaspora*, 346, note 95.

25. See HI Marrou, *A History of Education in Antiquity* (London: Sheed and Ward, 1956) 102–15; and D Magie, *Roman Rule in Asia Minor to the End of the Third Century after Christ*, volume I (Princeton: Princeton University Press, 1950), 62.

26. *CJZC*, no 6, col. II (first century BCE).

Chaireas, son of Ioudas[27]

What is so peculiar about these lists is the occurrence of names which are distinctively Jewish. The names Iesous and Ioudas appear to have never been used by Greeks. They are certainly the Greek transliteration of the Hebrew *yēšûaʿ* and *yᵉhûdâ*. In addition to these two lists, another was found at Iasos, dating to the early imperial period. This list contains the name Ioudas, which is plausibly a Jewish name.[28] The inclusion of Jews in these ephebic lists demonstrates that they were numbered among the elite. Jews did not shy away from enrolling in the gymnasia even when it was clear that their being circumcised might expose them to ridicule in a place where males trained naked.[29] We thus have evidence to show that it is not just in Alexandria that Jews participated actively in civic life.

There is another practice which demonstrates that Jews attempted to fit into the larger ethos. Dedicatory inscriptions have been discovered which indicate that Jews had no compunction adopting customs and conventions of their host cities. Such inscriptions were often intimately related to pagan religions or the imperial cult. However, this was done without sacrificing the Jewish belief in Yahweh as the one true God. We have ample evidence for this practice in Ptolemaic Egypt. During this period, Jews often dedicated their *proseuchai* to rulers. As Barclay observes, standard Ptolemaic loyalty formula was used but the usual ascription of the status of deity to the rulers was omitted. Furthermore, the *proseuchai* were said to be dedicated on behalf of (*huper*) the potentates, rather than to them.[30] Two examples will suffice, one coming from the city of Schedia, near Alexandria, and the other from Alexandria itself:

---

27.   *CJZC*, no 7c, line 13 (first century CE).
28.   See Tcherikover, *Hellenistic Civilization*, 350; PR Trebilco, *Jewish Communities in Asia Minor* (Cambridge: Cambridge University Press, 1991), 177; and MH Williams, *The Jews Among the Greeks and Romans: A Diasporan Sourcebook* (Baltimore: John Hopkins University Press, 1998), 113–14.
29.   See *Antiquitates*, 12.240–2. Some Jews resorted to *epispasm* to undo their distinctive hallmark of being circumcised. See 1 Maccabees 1.15; *T Moses* 8.1–5.
30.   Barclay, *Jews*, 31–2.

> On behalf of (*huper*) King Ptolemy (III) and Queen
> Berenike, his sister and wife, and their children, the Jews
> have dedicated the prayer-house.[31]

> On behalf of the Queen and the King, for the great God
> who listens (to prayers), Alypos has made the prayer-house.
> Year 15, Me[cheir?].[32]

The order of the dedicatees in the second inscription is most interesting,
with the Queen preceding the King. Most probably, this reflects the situation
when Cleopatra VII was the *de facto* ruler although her son Caesarion, by
Julius Caesar, was also acclaimed as King.

A similar act was performed by Jews of Asia Minor and Cyrene, when
they passed a resolution to honour Augustus Caesar. What this resolution was
is not entirely clear but it certainly was issued to show support of Augustus's
rule and to obtain imperial favour especially on the thorny matter of the
collection of Jewish taxes for the Temple in Jerusalem. Augustus's response
addressed not just these diaspora Jews but also the Jewish nation in Palestine
(*to ethnos to tōn Ioudaiōn*). This is because the community in Palestine was
the recognised stock of the Jewish people. His words are recorded in
Josephus:

> Caesar Augustus, Pontifex Maximus with tribunican power,
> decrees as follows. Since the Jewish nation has been found
> well disposed to the Roman people not only at the present
> time but also in time past, and especially in the time of my
> father the emperor Caesar, as has their high priest
> Hyrcanus, it has been decided by me and my council under
> oath, with the consent of the Roman people, that the Jews
> may follow their own customs in accordance with the law
> of their fathers . . . and that their sacred monies shall be
> inviolable and may be sent up to Jerusalem . . . As for the
> resolution which was offered by them in my honour
> concerning the piety which I show to all men, and on
> behalf of Gaius Marcius Censorius,[33] I order that it and the
> present edict be set up in the most conspicuous (part of the

---

31.   *CIJ*, II, no 1440 (third century BCE).
32.   *CIJ*, II, no 1432 (first century BCE).
33.   Consul in 8 BCE and proconsul of Asia in 2–3 CE.

temple) assigned to me by the federation of Asia in Ancyra.[34]

In the same vein, we may also point to the sacrifices offered by the Jewish priests in Jerusalem in honour of the Caesars.[35]

Such gestures more than spoke of just prudence or an attempt at ingratiating a community with a powerful lord. As Gruen observes:

> Homage to the royal house had symbolic significance in a double direction. It brought the Jews into a Ptolemaic context; but it also brought the Ptolemies into a Jewish context. The king could provide benefits—as he did when granting *asylia* to the *proseuche*. But the Jews provided benefits as well by associating the king with the supreme being, the *theos hypsistos*, to whom the synagogue was dedicated.[36]

This commingling of interests and the collusion of contexts were probably at work in a benefaction performed by a Gentile for the Jews. In Acmonia in the first century CE, Julia Severa, a chief priestess (*archiereia*) of the imperial cult, became the patron of the Jewish community there by building a synagogue for it.[37] We know of her through an inscription put up as a result of the refurbishment of the synagogue by the patrons P Tyrronius Cladus the *archisynagogos*, Lucius son of Lucius the *archisynagogos*, and Pophilius˙ Zotikos the *archon*.[38] This might have been done in the eighties or nineties but the act of Julia Severa's patronage was certainly pre-seventies. Numismatic evidence indicates that Julia Severa was active in the fifties and

---

34. *Antiquitates*, 16.162–5.
35. Philo, *Legatio ad Gaium*, 280.
36. Gruen, *Diaspora*, 122.
37. I Levinskaya notes that Julia Severa was related to the Galatian dynasty and connected with the influential Italian family of Turronii in her *The Book of Acts in its Diaspora Setting* (Grand Rapids: Eerdmans, 1996), 123, number 22. There is some debate on whether or not she was a Jew. The evidence that she was a Gentile seems to me overwhelming. See the discussion in Trebilco, *Jewish Communities*, 59; and ARR Sheppard, 'Jews, Christians and Heretics in Acmonia and Eumeneia', in *Anatolian Studies*, 29 (1979): 169–80.
38. *CIJ*, 766.

sixties.[39] It is certainly highly significant that the Jews were willing to accept the patronage of a pagan priestess. Such patronage could take place not only if Jews were fully involved in the life of the polis but also if they were recognised as such by the larger pagan society. In fact, some scholars have entertained the possibility that P Tyrronius Cladus, an *archisynagogos* for life, might have been a Gentile since he has the same *nomen* as C Tyrronius Rapon, who had been a high priest together with Julia Severa.[40] If this was indeed the case, we then have a case of some Jews honouring a Gentile with the title of *archisynagogos*, which supports the point that is made here. However, since this datum is outside the chronological boundaries set by the paper, this tantalising possibility will not be discussed.[41] All the foregoing need not imply that the Jews in Acmonia had apostatised or syncretised. What might be a better explanation is that they have managed to negotiate the intricacies of diaspora and learned to live and let live, to contribute and also to receive. Of course, one can envisage that Jews from other diaspora communities, and especially the community which was in Palestine, might view this act with disquiet but it certainly indicates that, in at least one city, relations between Jews and pagans were such that the former did not deem the latter's contributions so idolatrously tainted as to be rejected.

What we have established thus far is that Jews were very much aware of the kind of cultural ethos they were encountering and were also either contributing to it, being part of it or milking it. Their very best children joined gymnasia to be trained in the same way as the children of the Greek elite. Dedicatory formulas were used in the erection of their synagogues, without, of course, adopting phraseology which crosses the boundaries erected by a monotheistic faith. What emerges from all this is not a picture of Jewish communities having withdrawn into a ghetto. Instead, it is that which shows their confidently interacting with the larger ethos.

3. Jewish contributions to civic life

The evidence adduced thus far demonstrates that many Jewish communities were actively participating in the cities in which they were located. However,

---

39. See B Lifshitz, *Donateurs et fondateurs dan les synagogues juives* (Paris: Gabalda, 1967), 36.

40. S Mitchell, *Anatolia: Land, Men and Gods in Asia Minor*, Volume 2 (Oxford: Clarendon, 1993), 9; see also, T Rajak and D Noy, 'Archisunagogoi: Office, Title and Social Status in the Greco-Jewish Synagogue', *Journal of Roman Studies*, 83 (1993): 88.

41. But see the interesting discussion in Rajak and Noy, 'Archisynagogoi', 88–9.

there is also evidence to show that Jews made important contributions. For the purpose of description and analysis, these may be broken down into the following categories: moral, military, administrative and fiscal, and benefactions.

3.1 Moral contributions

It is well known that there were certain Gentiles who were called 'Godfearers'. These were people who were sympathetic to the Jewish faith, followed the commandments, especially those of a moral nature without being full members of a Jewish community, that is, they have yet to be circumcised. What attracted them was certainly the morality, which they perceived to be superior to what was offered by other competing religions or philosophies. This phenomenon has been widely discussed in scholarly research and need not be taken up further in this paper.[42]

What is seldom noticed is the evidence from Josephus, which purportedly speaks of kings thinking highly of the integrity of Jews and hence, sending them to outposts they considered restive and potentially rebellious. The passage from *Contra Apionem* is instructive:

> Ptolemy (I) son of Lagos held the same opinion of the Jews who dwelt in Alexandria as Alexander, for he entrusted to them the fortresses throughout Egypt, in *the belief that they would be faithful and excellent guards* [my emphasis]. And when he wanted to exert firm control over Cyrene and the other cities of Libya, he sent a detachment of Jews to them to act as military colonists.[43]

---

42.   See JM Reynolds and R Tannenbaum, *Jews and Godfearers at Aphrodisias* (Cambridge: Cambridge Philological Society), 48–66; SJD Cohen, 'Crossing the Boundary and Becoming Jew', *Harvard Theological Review*, 82 (1989): 13–33; and the treatment of M Goodman, *Mission and Conversion: Proselytising in the Religious History of the Roman Empire* (Oxford: Clarendon Press, 1994). For a good summary of the issues, see S McKnight, 'Proselytism and Godfearers', in *Dictionary of New Testament Background,* edited by CA Evans and SE Porter (Downers Grove and Leicester: IVP, 2000), 835–47.

43.   *Contra Apionem*, 2.44.

It is true that Josephus will seek every opportunity to speak well of the Jews in the interest of defending his own race[44] but this should not be taken to mean that the datum here has been spun out of whole cloth. This is so because Josephus would have known that any fabrication of the evidence would certainly not have won the argument with Apion. We can thus safely conclude that it is historically reliable that Jews were made military colonists in many outposts because of their high moral reputation.

For a non-Josephan indication that Jews contributed to the moral landscape of the Ptolemaic kingdom, we may cite 2 Maccabees 1:10. In this passage, a certain Aristobulus, who was an accomplished scholar in things Judaistic and Greek, is described as the teacher of Ptolemy the King, that is, Philometor. What he was teaching Philometor is anyone's guess but one good possibility is that it concerned things Judaistic. Aristobulus would most probably be engaged to teach moral philosophy. Unfortunately, the historical value of this datum has been questioned and some scholars argue that the address to the king is simply a literary convention.[45]

It is not just the Ptolemies who thought highly of Jewish integrity. Antiochus III the Great, the father of Antiochus Epiphanes, held a similar opinion. His letter to his satrap in Lydia is attested in Josephus and most scholars regard it as authentic.[46] This letter mentions explicitly the connection between Jewish integrity with Jewish faith:

> King Antiochus to Zeuxis, his father, greeting . . . Learning
> that the people in Lydia and Phrygia are revolting, I have
> come to consider this as requiring serious attention on my

---

44.   See T Rajak, *Josephus: The Historian and His Society* (London: Duckworth, 1983), 183–222; and GE Sterling, *Historiography and Self-definition: Josephos, Luke-Acts and Apologetic Historiography* (Leiden: Brill, 1992), 308–10.

45.   See Barclay, *Jews*, 113, 151–2.

46.   Supporting its authenticity are E Schürer, *The History of the Jewish People in the Age of Jesus Christ*, revised and edited by G Vermes, F Millar, M Black and M Goodman, volume III (Edinburgh: T&T Clark, 1986), 17, number 33; E Bickerman, 'Une question d'authenticité: Les privilèges juifs', in his *Studies in Jewish and Christian History*, Part Two (Leiden: Brill, 1980), 24–43; and Williams, *Diasporan Sourcebook*, 7. The contrary view is represented by A Schalit, 'The Letter of Antiochus III to Zeuxis', *Jewish Quarterly Review*, 50 (1959–60): 289–318; and JD Gauger, *Beiträge zur jüdischen Apologetik: Unterschungen zur Authentizität von Urkunden bei Flavius Josephus und im I. Makkebäerbuch*, (Bonn: P Hanstein, 1977), 1–151. A judicious middle-of-the-road position is taken up by Barclay, *Jews*, 261–2.

part, and, on taking counsel with my friends as to what should be done, I determined to transport two thousand Jewish families with their effects from Mesopotamia and Babylonia to the fortresses and most important places. For I am convinced that they will be loyal guardians of our interests because of their piety to God (*dia tēn pros ton theon eusebeian*),[47] and I know that they have had the testimony of my forefathers to their good faith and eagerness to do as they are asked.[48]

Transportation of two thousand Jewish families as the solution to the grave matter of revolts in Lydia and Phrygia certainly indicates the sort of confidence and respect Antiochus the Great had for the Jews. He knew he would not be adding fuel to fire. What is of great interest is that the reason he gave for so doing mentions his belief that the piety of the Jews would make them loyal guardians of Seleucid interests. While not strictly to be classified as military colonists in this instance, these Jews were certainly regarded as stabilising elements.

One of the cities in which these Jews settled would have been Apamea because it was the chief city of Phrygia.[49] There is evidence that by the turn of the era, Apamea would have contained a sizeable Jewish community.[50] Very interestingly, coins minted in this city towards the end of the second century CE bear image of Noah in his ark. These are the only ancient coins ever discovered which feature a scene from the Bible. The letters NΩE are inscribed on the ark to make it doubly sure that it is Noah who is being referred to and not another legendary figure. Two successive scenes in Noah's life are featured: to the left is a depiction of Noah and his wife in the ark, which, following Greek style, is depicted like a box. To the right, Noah's departure with his wife is depicted, with their right arms raised, which

---

47.   Note variant. Some manuscripts insert *autōn* after *theon*.
48.   *Antiquitates*, 12.148–50.
49.   See Trebilco, *Jewish Communities*, 86.
50.   Cicero, *Pro Flacco*, 28.66–9 mentions that a hundred pounds of gold contributed by the Jewish community as a Temple tax were seized by L Valerius Flaccus. This amount suggested was equivalent to about 135,000 drachmae and indicated the sizeable population of Jews in that city.

symbolise the posture of prayer for deliverance.[51] Five coins of such nature were discovered, spreading across the reigns of a few Emperors.[52] The coin of particular interest that is catalogued in ER Goodenough's *Jewish Symbols in the Greco-Roman Period* bears the words: ΕΠ. Μ. ΑΥΡ. ΑΛΕΞΑΝΔΡΙΟΥ Β. ΑΡΧΙ. ΑΠΑΜΕΩΝ which mean 'issued under Markos Aurelios Alexander, son of Alexander, high priest of Apamea'.[53] This is to be dated to 244–8 CE.

What needs to be taken into consideration carefully are two additional data regarding Apamea. The region of Phrygia had some local flood traditions[54] and Apamea had its own variation of them.[55] Furthermore, the city of Apamea had a nickname, which was *kibōtos* (ie, the box). But in these flood traditions, this word is never used since escape is made on foot. Only the Deucalion flood story from Greece mentions an ark but the word used is *larnax*.[56] All this strongly suggests that even if the nickname originally referred to the commercial importance of the city,[57] this was reinterpreted with reference to the story of Noah. One of the flood legends in Phrygia which would most probably have influenced the Apameans spoke of two survivors of a great flood by the names of Philemon and Baucis, who escaped on foot.[58] These were now replaced by Noah and his wife. What is significant here is that Noah's wife had somewhat of a pedestrian role in the biblical tradition and she is not named in the Genesis flood account (Genesis 6:18; 7:13; 8:15, 18).[59] But she is featured in this coin, prompting the hypothesis that what brought about this was most probably a local legend about a couple escaping from the flood, which has now been appropriated and reinterpreted by the Jews.

---

51. See A Grabar, 'Images bibliques d'Apamée et fresques de la synagogue de Doura', *Cahiers Archéologiques* 5, 11.

52. Grabar, 'Images', 11.

53. ER Goodenough, *Jewish Symbols in the Greco-Roman Period*, volume III (New York: Pantheon, 1953), number 700.

54. See Trebilco, *Jewish Communities*, 88–9.

55. See Plutarch, *Vitae Parallelae* 5.

56. In Apollodorus, *Bibliotheca*, 1.7.2 and Ovid, *Metamorphoses*, 1.125–415, we are told that Prometheus informed his son, Deucalion, that Zeus was about the flood the earth. Deucalion built a *larnax* to escape the calamity together with his wife Pyrrha.

57. See BV Head, *Historia Numorum: A Manual of Greek Numismatics* (Oxford: Clarendon Press, 1911), 666.

58. Ovid, *Metamorphoses*, 8.618–724.

59. See Trebilco, *Jewish Communities*, 93.

That this interpretation is on the right track is confirmed by the evidence in the Sibylline Oracles, especially 1.261–267, which locates Ararat in Phrygia. Usually, the location for Ararat is identified as being in Armenia and thus, the Oracle's locating of Ararat in Phrygia may be deemed to be highly significant.[60] All this opens the possibility of conjecturing that Jews could have exploited the local traditions and sought to persuade their Apamean neighbours that their flood hero was none other than the biblical Noah, who was also probably believed to have preached and settled in that city.

> [261] There is a certain tall lofty mountain on the dark
> [262] mainland of Phrygia. It is called Ararat.
> [263] When all were about to be saved on it,
> [264] thereupon there was a great heartfelt longing.
> [265] There the springs of the great river Marsyos[61] had
> sprung up.
> [266] In this place the Ark remained on lofty summits
> [267] when the waters had subsided

This particular portion of the Sibylline Oracles has been dated by Collins to around 30 BCE.[62] Thus, even though the coins may be dated to the close of the second century CE, we may posit that the dialogue between Jewish and Apamean flood traditions would have begun some time before that. In short, it is arguable that the Jews had reinterpreted the local flood tradition to make it conform to the Biblical account. This reinterpreted account was accepted by the Apamean community. The significance of this is that the founding narrative of a Gentile community, which would have played a critical role in its self-understanding, was now Judaised. All this can only mean that the Jews in this city were certainly highly respected and influential long before the coin

---

60. See *Antiquitates*, 1.90. Trebilco even conjectures that the provenance for Sibylline Oracles Books I & II might very well be Phrygian (see his, *Jewish Communities*, 95).

61. A local tributary of the river Maeander was named the Marsyos, alluding to the tale of satyr who invented the *aulos* (a double oboe) whose loss to Apollo in a musical challenge led to his being flayed alive (Apollodorus, *Bibliotheca* 1.4.2). The spring from which the Marsyos flowed was located within close proximity to Apamea.

62. JJ Collins, 'Sibylline Oracles', in *Old Testament Pseudepigrapha*, edited by JH Charlesworth (New York: Doubleday, 1983), 331.

being referred to was minted. However, as Trebilco notes, there is also a 'give
and take' process involved, in that whilst the Apamean community accepted
the Jewish story of the flood, the Jews showed deference to the Apamean
tradition by depicting a couple on the coin.[63]

3.2 Military contributions

Although there is attestation of the transportation of Jewish families to volatile
outposts of the Seleucid kingdom, there is no explicit mention of any Jew
serving in its armies. All the evidence we have for Jews serving in armies
comes from the Ptolemaic kingdom. Williams notes that Jews served in
different capacities in the Ptolemaic armies.[64] But we shall concentrate on the
evidence that shows Jews serving in prominent military positions.

Josephus attests that during the reign of Ptolemy VI Philometor, who was
well disposed towards the Jews, Onias and Dositheos were made generals and
held chief military posts. Not only that, they played critical roles in the
resolution of the internecine wars going on then.[65] Similarly, under Cleopatra
III, the daughter of Ptolemy VI Philometor, Chelkias and Ananias rose to
great military heights and became trusted generals of the potentate[66] in the
dynastic strife with her own son, Ptolemy Lathyrus. Note the following
account:

> For Queen Cleopatra (III), who was at war with her son
> Ptolemy, surnamed Lathyrus, appointed as her generals
> Chelkias and Ananias, sons of the Onias who had built the
> temple in the nome of Heliopolis, which was similar to the
> one at Jerusalem, as we have related before. And having
> entrusted her army to them, Cleopatra did nothing without
> their approval, as Strabo of Cappadocia also testifies, when
> he writes as follows: 'For the majority, both those who
> came back from exile and those who were later sent to
> Cyprus by Cleopatra, immediately went over to Ptolemy.
> And only the Jews of the district named for Onias remained

---

63. Trebilco, *Jewish Communities*, 94.
64. Williams, *Diasporan Sourcebook*, 88.
65. *Contra Apionem*, 2.49–52.
66. They were sons of Onias. So influential were they that they (principally Ananias)
    were able to counter the proposal of many of the potentate's advisers to annex
    Judaea and thus stopped her from so doing (see *Antiquitates*, 13.352–5). Indeed,
    Barclay suggests that a crucial component of Cleopatra's power-base was the
    force commanded by them (see his *Jews*, 9).

faithful to her, because their fellow citizens, Chelkias and
Ananias were held in special favour by the queen.'[67]

In a fragmentary inscription from the Helipolite nome, the son of Chelkias
is mentioned, most probably, as a *strategos* (general) who has distinguished
himself in the service of the *plethos* (the Jewish community), and was thus
awarded a golden crown:

> (son) of Chelkias, *strategos* (?) . . . of the *plethos* of those
> in the sacred precinct . . . to those who honoured . . . to him
> on account of . . . it was decided . . . *strategos* . . . with a
> crown . . . by the kings (?).[68]

If one is not satisfied with any evidence stemming from Josephus, there
are actually interesting papyri that one can turn to which point in the same
direction. *CPJ*, I number 21, dating to 210 BCE, mentions three Jewish
thieves who belonged to the Epigone. The Epigone were the military
reservists. Jews also served as *taktomisthoi*, high-ranking officers who
probably had the role of a paymaster. *CPJ*, I number 24, dating to 174 BCE,
mentions a loan being given by Ioudas, a Jew of the Epigone, to Agathokles, a
Jewish *taktomisthos*. The witnesses to this loan included two Jews of the First
Hipparchy of Dositheos, a cavalry unit. They are described as having land-
holdings of over fifty acres each, prompting the suggestion that these were
high-ranking cavalry officers.

All in all, we have very impressive evidence for Jewish involvement in the
military, especially during the period of Ptolemaic Egypt. Some of them were
promoted to positions beyond the rank and file, and became trusted generals
of potentates. Their roles were so critical that sometimes their success or
failure meant either peace or further strife in the region in which they were
settled.

3.3 Administrative and fiscal roles

We certainly have evidence to show that Jews were involved in the smooth
running of cities. Some of these held very influential and powerful positions.

CPJ, I number 25 speaks of a certain Jew who was a policeman.
Unfortunately, his rank is not given. However, an interesting inscription has

---

67. *Antiquitates*, 13.285–7.
68. *CIJ*, II, no 1450. See Schürer, *History*, Volume III: 48, 136.

come to light, which mentions a certain Ptolemy, who together with the Jews of Athribis, dedicated a *proseuche* to King Ptolemy and Queen Cleopatra:

> On behalf of King Ptolemy and Queen Cleopatra, Ptolemy, son of Epikydes, the chief of police, and the Jews in Athribis (have dedicated) the prayer-house to the Most High God.[69]

The ethnicity of this Ptolemy has certainly been disputed[70] but there is no cogent reason why he could not have been a Jew, since the dedication was jointly given by him and the Jews.

It is not just in the police force that one finds Jewish contribution. Many papyri from Egypt bear witness to the fact that Jews took on administrative and fiscal roles in the polis.[71] Some of them were even in the top echelons of civil service. Below is an interesting letter written by Heriodes to a certain Onias.[72] The opening lines mention the health and affairs of the reigning potentates, suggesting that this Onias was a high-ranking officer:

> Heriodes to Onias, greetings. King Ptolemy (VI) is well and King Ptolemy his brother and Queen Cleopatra his sister and their children and their affairs are as usual. If you are in good health and the rest of your affairs in order, that would be as we wish. We ourselves are going along well enough. The copy of the letter to Dorion, the *hypodioketes* (lit. 'under-manager') is appended for you. Understanding, therefore, that it is incumbent upon all alike who are concerned with administration to show consideration for those engaged in sowing, please make every effort and take every precaution that neither those who are incapable of farming are impressed nor those who are capable are sheltered on any pretext whatsoever. Let everything be done in the manner set out in the document that has been sent to you by us.[73]

---

69. *CIJ*, II, no 1443.
70. GHR Horsley, *New Documents Illustrating Early Christianity 4* (Macquarie: Macquarie University Press), 201, argues that he was a Gentile.
71. *CPJ*, I, nos 69, 100, 101, 107; II, no 240.
72. There is no evidence that the name Onias was ever used of a Gentile.
73. *CPJ*, I, no 132.

Mention must be made of the office of the *alabarch*. While it is not entirely clear what this involves, it is agreed by all scholars that it is a high office. Most probably the office supervises the collection of custom duties on the Eastern Nile.[74] Josephus mentions a certain Demetrius[75] who held this office but his predecessor was Alexander, the brother of Philo. With this reference, we come to the most distinguished Jewish family in Alexandria of the Roman period.

It is certainly true that Philo and his brother, Alexander, represented the upper class in Alexandria. But both were devout and loyal to their Jewish traditions, the latter having sent massive donations for the building and refurbishment of the Second Temple.[76] Alexander was *alabarch*, but even more, his relations with the imperial court were such that he was made overseer of the Egyptian property of Antonia,[77] the mother of the future emperor, Claudius. He was rich enough once to grant a loan of 200,000 drachmae.[78] In modern parlance, he may be described as being extremely well connected.

One would have thought that such heights reached by Alexander could not be surpassed. But astonishingly, Alexander's impressive achievements were outshone by his brilliant and illustrious son, Tiberius Julius Alexander. He had the accolade of holding very key positions right through the reigns of several Emperors, from Claudius to the Flavians. Thus, even when the Empire changed hands, and especially during the turbulent years of the four Emperors, Tiberius emerged unscathed. Instead, his political clout appeared to have grown from strength to strength. In 42 CE, he was made *epistrategos* of the Thebaid. In 46–48 CE, he was appointed procurator of Judaea, succeeding Fadus.[79] In 63 CE, he had the highly significant role of being the advisor in Rome's war with King Tiridates of Armenia.[80] And in 66–69 CE, he was given the highest equestrian office of governor of Egypt.[81] Moreover, so powerful was he that he was a key player during the in-fighting of imperial

---

74. Williams, *Diasporan Sourcebook*, 192, no 50; Barclay, *Jews*, 68 note 43.
75. *Antiquitates*, 18.259; 20.147.
76. *Bellum*, 5.201–5.
77. *Antiquitates*, 19.276–7.
78. *Antiquitates*, 18.159–60.
79. *Antiquitates*, 20.100–3.
80. Tacitus, *Annals*, 15.28. The implication of this is that he was chosen as Titus' lieutenant not merely because he was a Jew.
81. *Bellum*, 2.309.

rivals at the end of the Julio-Claudian dynasty. For all his services to the
Flavians, especially during the power struggle to be the Emperor of Rome, he
was appointed the Prefect of the Praetorian Guard in Rome. A papyrus
fragment testifies:

> of Tiberios Ioulios Alexander, the former Prefect (of
> Egypt), who also became Praetorian Prefect.[82]

Perhaps his name says it all, Tiberius Julius Alexander's loyalty to his
ancestral traditions or his roots appeared to have taken second place in
deference to his imperial masters. Significantly, three of Philo's philosophical
tractates mention him as expressing objections to the notion of divine
providence and justice.[83] In the course of his governorship, he had to
suppress an uprising by his own people in Alexandria. A little later, he was
Titus's second-in-command at the siege of Jerusalem,[84] a city which his uncle
has called *metropolis* and which his father had contributed many financial
resources. Indeed, there is evidence to suggest that in the course of his service
to the Empire, he might even have compromised his strict monotheistic
upbringing. He had the task of setting up a relief of Claudius, which involved
offering worship to the Egyptian deities Khonsou and Seb.[85] In fact,
Josephus, while remaining rather reticent about Tiberius Julius Alexander's
relationship with Judaism none-the-less admits that he 'did not remain faithful
to his ancestral customs'.[86] Whether or not future scholars will be kinder in
their assessment of a man caught between the Scylla of tradition and the
Charybdis of politics, there is no taking away from him his high
achievements.[87]

To round off this section and to forestall the impression that it is only in
Alexandria that Jews could attain high office, it may be mentioned that in
Cyrene, Jews had somewhat similar opportunities and made contributions.

---

82. *CPJ*, II, no 418b.

83. *De Providentia*, 1 and 2; *De Animalibus*.

84. *Bellum*, 5.45–6, 510; 6.237–42.

85. *OGIS*, 663.

86. *Antiquitates*, 20.100.

87. See EG Turner, 'Tiberius Iulius Alexander', *Journal of Roman Studies*, 44
    (1954): 54–64; V Burr, *Tiberius Iulius Alexander* (Bonn: Rudolf Habelt, 1955);
    RA Kraft, 'Tiberius Julius Alexander and the Crisis in Alexandria According to
    Josephus', in *Of Scribes and Scrolls: Studies on the Hebrew Bible,
    Intertestamental Judaism and Christian Origins*, edited by HW Attridge, JJ
    Collins and TH Tobin (Lanham: University Press of America, 1990), 175–84.

Eleazar of Cyrene held the post of a *nomophulax* in the mid-first century. This position entailed considerable responsibilities in the areas of finance, record-keeping and law enforcement.[88] It thus required not just skill and education but also the confidence of the leaders of the city.

3.4 Benefactions

Any discussion of a people's contribution to society cannot be complete without delving into the matter of benefactions or monetary contributions to civic projects. Strangely, the evidence for this is rather silent when compared to Jewish benefactions offered to the *mētropolis* or to synagogues all over the Empire. There might be two possible explanations for this state of affairs. Either it is due to an accident of history or it may be a result of diaspora Jews channelling their surplus resources to the Temple in Jerusalem.[89] Nevertheless, we have a very interesting recorded instance of a benefaction made to a host-city. An inscription from the mid-second century BCE testifies to a certain contribution of 100 denarii, given to a festival of Dionysius: 'Niketas, son of Iason, a Jerusalemite—100 denarii.'[90]

The ethnicity of Niketas is disputed but his father's name, Jason, was commonly used by Jews. Furthermore, his place of origin indicates that the assumption that he was a Jew is eminently cogent.

We have more evidence of Jewish monetary contributions to civic projects after the Jewish War and the Bar Kokhba revolt.[91] But in the period under consideration, it may be hypothesised that with Jews holding key positions in many cities, some sort of benefactions would have been performed as it was expected of many such holders of office in those days.[92]

4. Conclusions

With all these impressive participation in and contribution to civic well-being in the Diaspora, one would have thought that Jewish existence in it would be peaceful. Indeed, this was certainly true for many cities and for most times.

---

88. See S Applebaum, *Jews and Greeks in Ancient Cyrene* (Leiden: Brill, 1979), 186–90.
89. *Antiquitates*, 14.110–13; *CIJ*, II, no 1256; *Antiquitates*, 20. 51–3.
90. *CIJ*, II, no 749.
91. Gruen, *Diaspora*, 130; Trebilco, *Jewish Communities*, 81–3, 174–6.
92. See the evidence in P Garnsey and R Saller, *The Roman Empire: Economy, Society and Culture* (London: Duckworth, 1987) especially 33; See DD Walker, 'Benefactor' in *New Testament Background*, edited by Evans and Porter, 157–9.

However, for Palestine, the case would have been slightly different. The Jews living in it fought two suicidal wars against the Romans within a mere time interval of sixty-two years. In fact, they were not alone in this bellicose enterprise. Jews from many parts of the Diaspora came to the aid of their brothers living in Palestine and took up their cause.[93] As a result, there were reprisals in cities scattered across the Roman Empire where Jewish communities were found.[94] Of course, the Jews who belonged to the upper echelons of society in the Diaspora would most probably have viewed all this with great misgiving and attributed it to the unrestrained radicalism of some hotheads. But once the first sword was unsheathed, there could be no turning back. One event led to another as though they were obeying some sort of iron law of cause and effect. Even if some Jews sought to live peacefully, other ethnic groups might not reciprocate, as it was easy to believe Jews of one city would share the same agenda as Jews of the mother city. That said, it must be emphasised that Jewish privileges in the Diaspora were not rescinded by the Flavian Emperors even though many requests of this nature were made.[95] Official policies did not always see eye to eye with popular sentiments. Indeed, we have evidence to show that at least one Jew continued to hold high office. It may very well be that the factor which prevented official policies from becoming thoroughly oppressive was the consistent Jewish contribution to the welfare of cities in the Roman Empire.

In case one thinks Jewish wars or revolts were started only by Palestinian Jews who happened to be belligerent and bellicose, let it be reiterated that a Jewish revolt in the Diaspora was also seen in Alexandria, having been staged elsewhere in the Roman Empire before arriving on its doorsteps. This could have arisen again because the smouldering animosity, being left unchecked, was fanned into flames by the strong winds of messianic liberation or from perceived injustice and prejudice.[96]

---

93. See *Bellum*, 1.5, but see M Goodman, 'Jews in the Decapolis', in *Aram*, 4 (1992): 45–56, who mentions the case of Scythopolitan Jews who sided with their Gentile neighbours against the Jewish rebels.

94. See *Bellum*, 2.457 where according to Josephus 20,000 Jews were killed as a reprisal to the killing of Roman troops in Jerusalem. See the hint of a division in the Jewish communities there over the Jewish War in *Bellum*, 2.267, 287; *Antiquitates*, 20.178. For the impact the Revolt had on other cities, see *Bellum*, 2.457–86; *Antiquitates*, 12.121–4.

95. *Bellum*, 7.106–11.

96. The catalyst of the Revolt of 115–117 CE in Alexandria certainly came from a certain Loukas, who was somewhat a messianic figure. See Barclay, *Jews*, 78–80.

What this paper has sought to do is to show that there is more to the tale of Jewish revolts or pogroms against them. The other part of the tale must be told in order that a lop-sided perspective be corrected. This is about Jewish participation and contribution. The different aspects of Jewish contribution we have pointed out are not trivial things. Their importance may lead one legitimately to conclude that the Jewish response to the Diaspora was a complex one. Not only this, responses to Jewish presence in the Roman world were also complex. Local conditions and inherited traditions all have a part to play.

All this raises an important question. If, for the sake of analysis, we can categorise Jewish responses to diaspora into two, are they to be viewed as being antithetical to each other or are they two aspects of one hope? This is a significant question as Jewish scriptures contained much that viewed the Jewish Diaspora as a form of judgment for disobedience and returning to the homeland as the blessing of the *eschaton*. If they are to be viewed as antithetical, it will be between a realistic pragmatism and an idealistic liberation, or to use scriptural traditions, between Jeremiah 29:5–7 and Psalm 137. However, this manner of pitting scriptural traditions omits one great procrustean bed and this is the Abrahamic tradition which lies behind the deutero-nomistic perspective, and in which the expectation that the Jews would inherit the earth and be a blessing to all are sounded. If this may legitimately be factored in the quest for a rationale to explain the varied responses to diaspora, then the complex reactions we have studied may very well be two aspects of the one hope. This explains why diaspora Jews were happy to remain where they were even when a thriving Jewish community in Palestine existed. It also explains why when the centre of Judaism was threatened, other Jews joined in the fray. In fact, even before this, Jews were helping each other out in embassies to Roman Emperors for the welfare of Zion.[97] When the Temple was destroyed and the land overrun, diaspora Jews continued with their day-to-day living, believing that by so doing, they were also aiding the fulfilment of the one hope—the restoration of Zion and the inheritance of the world.[98]

---

97. See the appeal of Roman Jews to Augustus, made on behalf of their Palestinian comrades, for the purpose of ending the Herodian rule (*Antiquitates*, 17.300-1). See also Philo, *Legatio Ad Gaium*, 213–17.

98. See *Contra Apionem*, 2.102–9, 193–8.

5

Jesus, Paul and Peter and the Roman State

Paul Barnett

The creation of an Islamic theocracy in Iran following the overthrow of the Shah in 1979 and the rise of the Jihadist movement have raised critical questions about the state and the Christian's relationship to the state. Clearly the nature of 'the state' is the big issue of our times. Does the New Testament shed light on this issue? In fact it does shed considerable light since this was a major concern to Jesus and his apostles Paul and Peter.

There were two streams of thought in New Testament times that create the context for Jesus' teaching about theocracy. One was the Zealots' vision for a renewed Davidic theocracy and the other was the Roman Caesar's demand to be recognised as a universal king.

1. Jesus and the Zealots

The Davidic kingdom was a theocracy. In that kingdom (at least considered in ideal terms) the king ruled the people for the covenant LORD through the divinely given Torah Law. Within that kingdom the Temple and its priests and rituals were of utmost importance. Those ideal terms, however, rarely coincided with reality. The kings themselves were the problem in the main, as witnessed by the continuing conflicts between those kings and the prophets who admonished them for their failures to uphold the Sinai covenant.

Theocracy in Israel did not last for very long, in fact for only those years when the great powers of the Fertile Crescent and the Mediterranean region were weak and Israel was strong. The successive rise of and invasion by Babylonians, Persians, Greeks and Romans meant that Israel existed as a minor satrapy in those great kingdoms, whether Babylonian, Persian, Greek or Roman. By New Testament times, then, theocracy in Israel belonged to the distant past. In any case, Israel now largely existed in its scattered Diaspora with perhaps as few as ten per cent of Jews living in their historic homeland.

Nonetheless, theocracy remained a fiercely held ideal, most obviously from the time of Judas Maccabeus' revolt against the Hellenising programmes of King Antiochus IV in Antioch. The language of zeal and zealotry now begins to be used in Israel, based on the extreme actions of Phinehas (Numbers 25:6–9) and Elijah's slaughter of the prophets of Baal on Mount Carmel (1 Kings 18:36–40). Judas Maccabeus' revolt against Antioch marks the beginning of the 'zealot' mindset that was to dominate Jewish thinking in the next two centuries, including the era of the New Testament in which Christianity was born.

There are some points of contact between the Zealots of Israel and the modern Islamic Jihadists, in particular the willingness to lay down one's life for a religious cause. Clearly, then, Jesus' attitude to zealotry and the apostles' attitude to zealotry are important for the concerns of the times in which we live.

In Jesus' day the zealot hope was expressed in the slogan 'No master except God'.[1] The catalyst was the Roman demand that individual Jews submit to a census for the payment of personal tax to the pagan overlord. Hence the cry of Judas the Galilean in 6 CE: 'No master except God'.[2] Zeal for the name of Yahweh meant killing or being killed in his name. That 'Name' and its honour were more valuable than one's own life, anticipating in some respects the attitudes of contemporary suicide bombers.

2. Jesus, the Zealots and the Roman Caesar

2.1

Jesus' teaching specifically opposed the zealot paradigm, which was to 'hate the enemy and love the friend'. This paradigm was fundamental within extreme Jewish groups, whether Qumran covenanters[3] or the followers of various warlords like Judas the Galilean, Simon bar Gioras or John of Gischala. Let us be reminded of Jesus' teaching:[4]

> You have heard that it was said, 'You shall love your neighbour and hate your enemy.' *But I say to you* [my emphasis], Love your enemies and pray for those who persecute you, so that you may be sons of your Father who

---

1.　I am employing the term 'zealot' in a generalised way. To be precise the zealot *faction* arose only within the period of the war 66–70 CE. Nonetheless, there were individuals who were referred to as 'zealot' (See, for example 'Simon who was called "zealot"' [Luke 6:15].)

2.　Josephus, *Jewish War*, 2.118.

3.　See *Qumran Community Rule*, 1:4.

4.　The Revised Standard Version is used throughout in Biblical references.

is in heaven; for he makes his sun rise on the evil and on
the good, and sends rain on the just and on the unjust
(Matthew 5:43–45).

Love, not hate, lay at the heart of Jesus' teaching.

Jesus' attitude to the 'men of violence' of his times is clearly stated in
these words: 'From the days of John the Baptist until now the kingdom of
heaven has suffered violence and men of violence take it by force (Matthew
11:12).' Jesus' words offer commentary on the violence dear to the heart of
the 'zealots' of Jesus' times.

The attempts of Robert Eisler and SGF Brandon to identify Jesus as a
zealot or zealot sympathiser have rightly been discredited. Jesus' teaching was
in direct contradiction of the zealot ideal and the zealot method.

2.2

Ironically, however, the Romans executed Jesus for fulfilling a role he had
strenuously opposed. It began with the accusation of the Temple authorities.

> Then the whole company of them arose, and brought him
> before Pilate. And they began to accuse him, saying, 'We
> found this man perverting our nation, and forbidding us to
> give tribute to Caesar, and saying that he himself is Christ a
> king' (Luke 23:1).

This is, indeed, ironical. These were the very crimes of his fellow Galilean
Judas two decades earlier. That Judas forbade paying taxes to the Romans and
he claimed to be a king. Moreover, as we have seen, he had a 'kingdom'
message. It was 'No master except God'.

The Romans found Jesus the Galilean guilty of claiming to be 'king of the
Jews' and he was crucified for that crime, that is, of treason against Rome. It
was a spectacular miscarriage of justice. The Temple authorities wanted Jesus
out of the way because he had a large and growing following. Though Pilate
was a tyrant and a brute, the chief priests had a hold over him.[5] So Jesus was
removed on the pretext that he was a zealot king with a theocratic programme
that was inimical to the *Pax Romana*. But it could not have been further from
the truth.

---

5.   Philo, *Embassy to Gaius*, 301–02.

The truth was that Jesus identified himself as the fulfilment of the prophecies of the oracles of God. Specifically Jesus identified himself as the Son of Man (prophesied by Daniel) and the vicariously suffering Servant (prophesied by Isaiah). Paradoxically, the one was the most exalted of figures and the other the most humiliated. The only pathway to glory, he said, was through suffering for others. Only at the last did Jesus publicly disclose himself as the Lord's anointed, his Christ (fulfilling the prophecy of Nathan). Only to his immediate circle did Jesus reveal himself to be 'the Son' of Abba, his Father-God.

The Jewish authorities did not or would not penetrate into the true persona of Jesus, who unimaginably amalgamated within himself the disparate strands of Old Testament hope. And so he was accused, condemned and crucified as a bloody local warlord, a new Judas the Galilean.

2.3

Here, though, we must note carefully Jesus' recorded reaction to this injustice. The Johannine tradition is particularly important in bringing out the involvement of the Roman authorities in the arrest and trial of Jesus. According to John Jesus was arrested by a significant cohort of Roman troops, with Temple police playing a subsidiary role. Again, according to John, Jesus submitted to more extensive Roman interrogation than we would have guessed from the Synoptic accounts.

In the course of those interrogations Jesus makes important and revelatory replies:

> Jesus answered,
> 'My kingship is not of this world; if my kingship were of
> this world, my servants would fight . . .' (John 18:36).
> Pilate . . . said to him,
> 'Do you not know that I have power to release you, and
> power to crucify you?
> Jesus answered him,
> 'You would have no power over me unless it had been
> given you from above . . .' (John 19:10–1).

From this exchange between Jesus and the Prefect we note:

a) Jesus is no theocratic king; God's kingdom is not a theocratic kingdom.

b) Jesus rejects the zealot ideal of violence; his is a heavenly kingship.

c) Pilate holds his imperium from Caesar, including the *ius gladii*, the authority to execute. But Jesus teaches that Caesar and therefore his delegates have their authority *from God* himself. Implicit in John's Gospel is the divine indictment of Pilate who failed to provide a duty of care to a powerless and innocent provincial like Jesus.

d) Consistently, Jesus does not threaten revenge against those who wrongfully and illegally torture and execute him. Luke records Jesus' words, 'Father, forgive them, for they do not know what they are doing'. Accordingly, Jesus' manner of death and his attitude to Jewish and Roman authorities do not subvert or overthrow the divinely appointed lines of government but uphold it.

These four elements—Jesus' heavenly, not theocratic kingship; his recognition that God (the ultimate authority) bestows mediating authority to those like Pilate who hold office and his forgiving, non-subversive attitudes towards authority—will reappear in the New Testament letters of Paul and Peter. Furthermore, these will be critical in the centuries following, ahead of the Constantinian settlement.

2.4

We come now to Jesus' famous reply to the entrapment question about paying taxes. This bears on both the vision of a Jewish theocracy (signalled by the zealot ban on tax paying) and the Roman demand on Caesar's theocracy (acknowledging his unrivalled kingship).

Of course, the question was not merely about the rights and wrongs of taxation, the rate of taxation or whether direct or indirect tax is better. True, taxes were high; the local people lobbied Tiberius in 17 CE for their reduction. Furthermore, Roman provincial administration was proverbially corrupt. Tiberius himself cynically observed that governors were like blood sucking flies. The real issue, though, was the hated 'poll tax' which symbolised the subservience of Yahweh's people to the hated heathen Romans. This is an important passage with far-reaching consequences.

> And they sent to him some of the Pharisees and some of the
> Herodians, to entrap him in his talk. And they came and

> said to him, 'Teacher, we know that you are true, and care
> for no man; for you do not regard the position of men, but
> truly teach the way of God. Is it lawful to pay taxes to
> Caesar, or not? Should we pay them, or should we not?'
> But knowing their hypocrisy, he said to them, 'Why put me
> to the test? Bring me a coin, and let me look at it.' And
> they brought one. And he said to them, 'Whose likeness
> and inscription is this?' They said to him, 'Caesar's.' Jesus
> said to them, 'Render to Caesar the things that are Caesar's,
> and to God the things that are God's.' And they were
> amazed at him (Mark 12:13–17).

The answer was clever, extricating him from the apparently inescapable
trap. To have said 'yes' would have identified him as a 'zealot' and to have
said 'no' as a Roman collaborator. Jesus was neither a zealot (and an advocate
of theocracy) nor an unquestioning devotee of the hegemony of the Roman
Caesar.

Beyond its cleverness, however, Jesus' answer articulated his unique view
of the state—even the pagan state—in the purposes of God. So what was that
answer?

First, he actually directed the payment of taxes to the heathen occupier. In
a single stroke, Jesus repudiated zealotry and theocracy. We infer from Jesus,
then, that the believer can live under the rule of the unbeliever.

But second, Jesus directed the people to 'render to God the things that are
God's. This was likely in reaction against the iconic and idolatrous character
of the coin, showing the effigy of the emperor (Tiberius) and the words,
'Tiberius Caesar, son of the deified Augustus, Pontifex Maximus'. In other
words, the coin portrayed the emperor as a demi-god. Jesus' words, 'render to
God the things that are God's' clearly prohibited any veneration of a mere
man like this. Let the emperor know his place.

In effect, then, Jesus attributes all authority to God, demanding due
recognition of his deity and sovereignty. Beneath that sovereignty, however,
Jesus located a rightful role 'Caesar', that is, for the state. In the divine order,
Caesar is to provide an infrastructure for the welfare of his citizens. Clearly,
though, Caesar's state must not be an oppressive totalitarian state, whether a
heathen totalitarian state or a religious totalitarian state. 'Caesar' must know
his place.

In passing, the context of the Book of Revelation indicates that the Caesar
of that time, 90s CE, did not know his place. That Caesar was, so far as we

can tell, Domitian. This was the emperor who insisted on being called
'*Dominus et Deus*'.

> And the beast [the emperor] was given a mouth uttering
> haughty and blasphemous words, and it was allowed to
> exercise authority for forty-two months; it opened its mouth
> to utter blasphemies against God, blaspheming his name
> and his dwelling, that is, those who dwell in heaven. Also it
> was allowed to make war on the saints and to conquer
> them. And authority was given it over every tribe and
> people and tongue and nation, and all who dwell on earth
> will worship it, every one whose name has not been written
> before the foundation of the world in the book of life of the
> Lamb that was slain (Revelation 13:5–8).

That 'Caesar' was demanding reverence and worship of himself, a worship
that should only have been 'rendered' to God himself.

Clearly, therefore, Jesus' words 'render to Caesar' are sharply qualified
and conditional. All Caesars including leaders in modern democracies should
heed his words.

Where a ruler takes to himself a divine right and acts as a demi-god that
ruler becomes anti-Christ and the 'Beast' of Revelation 13. His city becomes
'Babylon', a place of captivity and suffering for the people of God (and
others).

Let me now draw a line under this section about the immediate era of
Jesus. He opposed both the theocracy of the zealots and the theocracy of the
Caesar cult.

3. Apostolic catechesis based on Jesus' words and works

There is strong evidence of an early catechesis in relation to disciples and the
state. This evidence emerges from Romans 13:1–7 and 1 Peter 2:13–17.

In Romans 13:1 Paul enjoins 'be subject (*hupotassesthō*) to governing
authorities' and in 1 Peter 2:13 Peter says 'be subject (*hupotagēte*) to every
human institution'. The similarity is clear. In Romans 13:3 Paul observes
'rulers are not a terror to good conduct (*tō agathō*) but to bad (*tō kakō*)' and in
1 Peter 2:14 Peter states that kings and governors are 'sent to punish those
who do wrong (*kakopoiōn*) and praise those who do right (*agathopoiōn*)'.
Again the similarity is evident. In Romans 13:7 Paul encourages 'honour

(*timē*) to whom honour is due' and in 1 Peter 2:17 Peter says 'honour (*timēsate*) all'. Once more the similarity is clear. Nonetheless, these texts from Paul and Peter are not identical.

The similarities point to some connection between the texts but the dissimilarities imply that they are depending on a common source rather than one upon the other. In other words, a catechetical source had been created in the few decades between Jesus and the writing of these texts that called for a distinctive ethical attitude to the Roman state. That source did not arise from within Judaism since anti-Roman feeling ran high among the Jews at that time. On the contrary, this tradition sprang from Jesus' distinctive attitudes, on one hand against zealotry, and on the other, his recognition of the role of Caesar, pagan though he was.

Significantly, there are further connections between these two state-related passages. I refer to the almost identical demands of these respective letters— Romans and 1 Peter—for non-retributive behaviour against official persecution.

In the passage in Romans immediately preceding his injunctions regarding the state Paul writes, 'repay no one evil for evil (*mēdeni kakon anti kakou apodidontes*)' whereas Peter wrote 'do not repay evil for evil (*mē apodidontes kakon anti kakou*)'.[6] The words are strikingly similar, yet not identical. Once again the juxtaposition between similarities and dissimilarities points to an earlier independent common catechetical source that was formulated soon after Jesus.[7]

In addition to the injunction 'not returning evil for evil' (*mēdeni kakon anti kakou apodidontes*), Paul also exhorts in the same passage to 'bless those who persecute you, bless and do not curse' (*eulogeite tous diōkontas, eulogeite kai mē katarasthe*).[8] Clearly this non-retributive behaviour urged by Paul springs from the teaching of Jesus in the Gospel tradition.[9]

In 1 Peter, however, the non-retributive attitude is inspired by Jesus' own example where he suffered unjustly:

> Christ also suffered for you, leaving you an example, that
> you should follow in his steps. He committed no sin; no

---

6. Romans 12:17, 1 Peter 3:9.
7. See 1 Thessalonians 5:15: 'See to it that no one renders to anyone evil for evil' (*orate mē tis kakon anti kakou tini apodō*).
8. Romans 12:17 and 14.
9. Matthew 5:38; Luke 6:29, 35 for Romans 12:17 and Matthew 5:44; Luke 6:26 for Romans 12:14.

guile was found on his lips. When he was reviled, he did
not revile in return; when he suffered, he did not threaten;
but he trusted to him who judges justly (1 Peter 2:21–23).

Christ's manner of dying—non-subversively—inspired Peter's injunction:

Be subject for the Lord's sake to every human institution,
whether it be to the emperor as supreme, or to governors as
sent by him (1 Peter 2:13–14).

The Lord's own non-retributive 'subjection' to the emperor's governor
Pilate provided his own 'example' of 'rendering to Caesar the things that are
Caesar's'. In other words, Jesus did not subvert but upheld the Roman state,
both by teaching and his own powerful example.

Peter's important emphasis on Christ as *exemplar* of faithful, non-
retributive sufferings under injustice is balanced by his emphasis on his role
as the Deuteronomic-Isaianic *sin-bearer*.

He himself bore our sins in his body on the tree, that we
might die to sin and live to righteousness. By his wounds
you have been healed (1 Peter 2:24).

For Christ also died for sins once for all, the righteous for
the unrighteous, that he might bring us to God . . . (1 Peter
3:18).

Overall in 1 Peter, however, the greater emphasis appears to be on Christ
the exemplar, who by deed and word shows believers how to live but also to
suffer and die in a hostile society.

It is clear, therefore, from these passages in Romans 13:1–7 and 1 Peter
2:13–17, 21–23; 3:9 that Jesus' teaching and example (in relation to both the
zealot theocracy and the Roman state) profoundly influenced the catechetical
instruction of disciples in the Pauline and Petrine churches. This catechesis,
however, predated the writing of these letters, springing from Jesus himself
soon after his historical lifespan.

This instruction of the Lord, mediated through his apostles, was to prove
hugely important in the following centuries when believers were to suffer
under various emperors. While important this teaching is, nonetheless, negative and defensive. Is there more that can be said? In particular, do these

apostolic writings prompt the disciples of Christ to 'Seek the welfare of the City'.

4. Caesar and the city

Two key passages (once more) are Romans 13:1–7 and 1 Peter 2:13–17 which are overwhelmingly positive. Paul speaks of the ruler as 'God's servant (*diakonos*) for your good' (verse 4) and as a 'minister (*leitourgos*) of God' who is to be 'respected' and 'honoured' (verse 7). Thus Paul enjoins 'pay all of them their taxes for they are attending to' these matters (verse 7).

Peter's sentiment is similar:

> Be subject for the Lord's sake to every human institution,
> whether it be to the emperor as supreme, or to governors as
> sent by him . . . Honour all men. Love the brotherhood.
> Fear God. Honour the emperor (1 Peter 2:13-14, 17).

It is of utmost importance to note that Paul and Peter are not making these requests of believers living in a Christian theocracy like those in the centuries following Constantine. The emperor at the time Paul wrote Romans and Peter wrote his First Letter was the infidel, Nero.

Indeed, in the centuries before Constantine Christian leaders repeatedly called on Christians to submit to and be loyal to the Emperor.

It needs to be pointed out, however, that submission to Caesar is voluntary and discretionary. Believers don't give Caesar a blank cheque. There have been many occasions when Christians have opposed the State and its leader. This prophetic opposition to a corrupt king has its roots in the Old Testament and in John the Baptist's opposition to his tetrarch's marriage. It has risen to the surface many times in the centuries since, whether by John Chrysostom or Thomas Becket.

Seeking the welfare of the city specifically means giving a voice to the voiceless and power to the weak and marginalised. It is by no means necessarily the same thing as compliance to Caesar. Caesar may be acting against the weak, and has often done so.

5. Seeking the welfare of the city

There are echoes in 1 Peter from another letter written centuries earlier, written by the prophet Jeremiah to the exiles from Jerusalem now captive in Babylon. Jeremiah's letter mentions 'exiles' and 'Babylon', references that also appear in 1 Peter (1:1, 17; 5:13):

These are the words of the letter which Jeremiah the
prophet sent from Jerusalem to the elders of the *exiles* [my
emphasis], and to the priests, the prophets, and all the
people, whom Nebuchadnezzar had taken into *exile* [my
emphasis] from Jerusalem to *Babylon* [my emphasis] . . . It
said: 'Thus says the LORD of hosts, the God of Israel, to
all the exiles whom I have sent into exile from Jerusalem to
Babylon: Build houses and live in them; plant gardens and
eat their produce. Take wives and have sons and daughters;
take wives for your sons, and give your daughters in
marriage, that they may bear sons and daughters; multiply
there, and do not decrease. But seek the welfare of the city
where I have sent you into exile, and pray to the LORD on
its behalf, for in its welfare you will find your welfare . . .'
(Jeremiah 29:1–7).

Remarkably, despite their *exile* in *Babylon* Jeremiah calls for positive
attitudes and actions towards the city where God's people are in captivity. He
urges 'seek the welfare of the city' and to 'pray to the LORD on its behalf'.
Similar attitudes are implicit in Peter's words to these 'aliens and exiles' in
Babylon, that is to say, the disciples of Christ (2:13–17).

Despite their present sufferings of persecution that show signs of
becoming even more intense, they are witnesses to Christ by imitating his
patience and non-vengeance. More than that, they are to 'be subject' to—that
is, co-operate positively and voluntarily with—appointed authorities. Likewise, they are to avoid any form of anti-social behaviour.

In other words, like Jeremiah the apostle Peter is calling on believers to
make their home in a place that is not ultimately their home. Although the
world beyond (the kingdom of God) is that home, in the meantime they—and
we—are to seek the welfare of this city, even though it is the city of Babylon
and not the city of God.

6. Seeking welfare in the centuries following

It is well known that in the following centuries Christians were noted for their
works of charity, including towards those who were not of the 'household of
faith'. It is worth recollecting some examples of this 'welfare'.

Justin, writing earlier in the mid-second century, notes that a collection was made during the weekly assembly of Christians for distribution by the 'president' for a rather broader group.

> This collection was for the succour of the orphans and widows, and those who through sickness or any other cause, are in want, and those who are in prison, and the strangers sojourning among us, and in a word takes care of all who are in need (*Apology* 1.66).

The same development is on view half a century later in Tertullian's comment:[10]

> Even if there is a chest of a sort, it is not made up of money paid in entrance fees, as if religion were a matter of contract. Every man once a month brings some modest coin—or whenever he wishes, and only if he does wish, and if he can; for nobody is compelled; it is a voluntary offering. You might call them the trust funds of piety. For they are not spent upon banquets or drinking parties; but to feed the poor and to bury them, for boys and girls who lack property and parents, and then for slaves grown old and ship-wrecked mariners; and any who may be in mines, islands or prisons, provided it is for the sake of God's school, become the pensioners of their confession (*Apology* 3.9:1–6).

As well, the churches were concerned for others distant from themselves, following the example of Paul's collection from the Gentile churches for Jerusalem. These post-apostolic Churches did not confine their generosity to their own members, but were aware of the needs of the fellow-believers in other places. The Church of Rome was noted for its generosity, both to its own needy members, but also to those further afield. Dionysius, Bishop of Corinth wrote to his counterpart in Rome *c* 180 CE:

> This has been your custom from the beginning, to do good in manifold ways to all Christians, and to send contributions to many churches in every city, in some cases

---

10.   The following texts of the church fathers are from the *Loeb Classical Library*.

> relieving the poverty of the needy, and ministering to
> Christians in the mines, by the contribution you have sent
> from the beginning . . . (Eusebius, *HE* 4. 23.11).

At the time of the plague in Carthage Cyprian, the Bishop of Carthage,
addressed the Christians:

> There is nothing remarkable in cherishing merely our own
> people with the due attention of love . . . we should love his
> enemies as well.

Pontianus, Cyprian's biographer, added: 'Thus the good was done to all
men, not merely the household of faith'.[11]

Such a caring attitude by Christians towards pagans may have contributed
to their growing sense that this religion was relevant to them and destined
soon to become the new religion of the Roman world. Within fifty years or so
this began to be an accomplished fact.

In 360 CE Constantine's nephew Julian became emperor. He is famously
known as Julian 'the apostate' whose short tenure is noted for his brief but
futile attempts to take the Roman world back to the paganism it left behind
with the conversion of Constantine. Although intelligent and a capable soldier
Julian's surviving writings disclose a rather eccentric and impractical
personality. Of special interest are Julian's attempts—also futile—to have that
paganism express various forms of welfare replicating those that had been
established by the Christians. Julian was specially galled by the ways the
Christians assisted those who were not of their own persuasion. Accordingly
Julian wrote to the High Priest of Galatia decreeing what had to be done:

> In every city establish frequent hostels in order that
> strangers may profit from our benevolence; I do not mean
> this for our own people only, but for others also who are in
> need of money. I have but now made a plan by which you
> may be well provided for this; for I have directed that
> 30,000 *modii* of corn shall be assigned every year for the
> whole of Galatia, and 60,000 pints of wine. I order that one
> fifth of this be used for the poor who serve the priests and
> the remainder be distributed by us to strangers and beggars.

---

11.   Quoted in R Stark, *The Rise of Christianity* (San Francisco: Harper, 1997), 87.

> For it is disgraceful that, when no Jew ever has to beg, and
> the impious Galileans [Christians] support not only their
> own poor but ours as well, all men see that our people lack
> aid from us (*Epistle* 49).

At the same time, Julian was exercised by the fact that Christians were
teaching the children of the empire rhetoric and grammar based on the
classical pagan authors. Since Christians did not believe in the gods or hold
the beliefs of classical paganism it was absurd for them to be teaching what
they did not believe. Let them stop teaching pagans and go off to the churches
of the Galileans and there teach the Gospels (*Epistle* 42).

A number of basic Christian values combined to inspire a concern for
'welfare of the city' by the disciples of Jesus. There was the conviction that
their God and Father was the creator and sustainer of all people, whether
believers or not. Likewise the incarnation and the saving death and resurrection of the Son of God were seen to be a source of redemption for all
people. There was universal application of the Gospel. Jesus' miracles of
healing the sick and feeding the hungry showed the way for the believers' care
of one another in the churches, widows and orphans in particular.

From early times the churches appointed almoners to bring practical aid to
needy members. This 'hands on' concern was expressed on a massive scale in
Paul's 'collection' from the Gentile churches for the poor saints in Judea. As
well, there were hints that 'good' was to be done to 'all men' and not just
within the household of faith.[12]

In a word, the Christian gospel was inspired by 'love', the love of God,
and believers were to express that love in highly practical ways, not only to
fellow believers, but to all.

Beyond these values, however, we must note the distinctive teaching and
example of Jesus. He rejected the way of violence implicit in the zealots'
theocratic programme, on one hand, and the totalitarian theocratic claims of
Caesar, on the other. Rather, Jesus insisted on the ultimate authority of God
and his own rightful claim to be the messianic Son of Man. To God and his
Christ must be rendered veneration and service, to them and to them alone.
Caesar must know his place.

But Caesar does have a place, ruling over human societies for their good.
Let Caesar learn from King Christ who is a server and not an exploiter of
those under his rule, especially the vulnerable. The place Christ gives to

---

12.   See, for example, Galatians 6:10; 2 Corinthians 9:13.

Caesar, admittedly qualified, is articulated within the apostolic instructions in the following decades, as we have noted

These things combined to inspire the Christians of the next centuries in their service not only of their own people, but of all people. And this, as much as anything else, contributed to the astonishing events of the fourth century whose effects are still working themselves out.

7. Reflection

The above discussion calls for the following reflection on Christian engagement in society today:

a) Jesus does not call for a theocratic polity.

b) Since rulers receive their authority from God they must exercise it as servants of the people.

c) People, including Christian people, are to live respecting, honouring and co-operating with rulers, unless their rule has become a criminal rule.

d) There is a prophetic role for Christians and their leaders in confronting rulers who are not acting out of care for their people.

e) Where a ruler becomes an anti-Christ the city becomes 'Babylon'.

f) Christians should seek the welfare of the city, in particular the welfare of the weak and voiceless.

Historical and Theological Studies

6

All Authority is from God

Oliver O'Donovan

My purpose in this paper is to revisit this Christian proposition about secular authority: 'all authority is from God'. In a period when all thinking about politics, including Christian thinking, has come to be marked by a certain deep-rooted anti-authoritarianism, this focus of attention is likely to elicit a frisson of discomfort and suspicion. And there are theological reasons for this, since there is certainly a point at which the anti-authoritarianism of our times meets up with an important evangelical truth. The conquest of Christ over death and hell is at the same time a conquest of the principalities and powers who rule this earth. This is a theme I have argued myself; and it runs memorably through the work of my friend NT Wright, not least in his fine book on the resurrection: 'the triumph of Christ on Easter Sunday was, at the same time, a triumph over the imperial pretensions and powers of the Roman empire.'[1] Now, to this anti-authoritarian moment in the Christian proposition we shall have to allow the last word: 'the kingdoms of this world have become the kingdom of our God and of his Christ!' But it is too easy to lose the force of this proclamation by treating this last word of the apostolic Gospel as though it were the first word, and comprised every successive word in between the first and the last. It is possible to jump to the conclusion that secular authority exists, like Pharaoh, solely for God to show his might by liberating us from it; so that the first proposition of the Christian church about secular authority, that expressed in the text from Romans 13, 'all authority is from God', seems—at best—to have been a misunderstanding, at worst a serious evasion of the Gospel. We are familiar enough these days with the rhetorical denunciation of 'Christendom'—that age of church history in which this mistake was supposed to have been all determinative. But since Christendom was, on any reckoning, a long period, we are led by this train of thought to a question about Christian tradition that ought, if we are wise, to trouble us: did nobody, then, ever understand the Christian Gospel before

---

1. NT Wright, *The Resurrection of the Son of God* (London: SPCK, 2003).

ourselves? But perhaps it is we who do not understand it if we do not understand what it means that all authority is from God, and that the kingdoms of this world owe all the authority they ever had to him.

Before exploring the proposition more closely, let us say something about the scope of this discussion. It is, in the first place, an enquiry of normative reasoning, not of historical exegesis. I leave on one side exegetical questions about the context of this proposition in the Epistle to the Romans, for we might as easily have taken the saying of Jesus to Pilate, 'You could have no authority over me, if it were not given you from above (John 19:11)'. In the second place, it is a conceptual, not a casuistical enquiry. Our purpose is to 'unpack' the proposition, to 'think it through', to 'get below the surface', phrases which all suggest an uncovering of the presuppositions and implications that centre upon this proposition and constitute its sense as a testimony to human experience. We have to see how and in what sense the proposition commends itself to us as true, and only then to ask how it shapes the practical deliberations that are open to us. In the third place it is a universal enquiry, not confined to any given set of historical circumstances, for example, when the state happens to be friendly to Christianity. The truth of the proposition must be available to us when we have to encounter dissonance with the ruling values of the public culture and may face conflict. Whatever discussion may be had about the particular political background to the writing of Romans 13, here is a proposition that bears its universal claim upon its face. One does not say 'all authority is from God' in a qualified or hypothetical sense. When Socrates, facing death, said, 'No harm comes to a good man', he did not mean, 'No harm comes to a good man in fifth-century Athens'!

1. The paradox of political authority

Let us, then, explore the proposition more closely, beginning with a word-by-word reflection on its terms. 'All authority is from God.' What exactly do we mean by 'authority'? There is a paradox at the heart of the notion. Authority directs us, but directs us in a way that requires a response of freedom. Authority is not the same as physical force that pushes us around, reducing us to the impotence of mere objects. Those who push us around characteristically lack authority. Authority is responded to by obedience, which is a response we can make only as free subjects of our actions. But if authority directs us, it does so by way of command. And command implies two things: first, that the initiative in our action lies outside us, presented to us by some other agent; second, that the reasonableness of this initiative is not wholly apparent to us; the reasons are someone else's reasons, not our own.

Of course, to act in freedom is always to act with good reasons. Reason and freedom cannot be separated. And when we freely obey what authority commands of us, we act as we have good reason to act. We do not perform an irrational or reasonless action. The command of the authority is itself our reason for doing what we are commanded. Yet there are other reasons bearing on our action that we cannot know or grasp. We may often have to act, and may act with full conviction, without knowing everything that could be relevant to justifying our action. It is a distinctive feature of practical reasoning that reasons may be sufficient without being complete. In theoretical reflections we may say we are unsure until everything that possibly can be understood has been understood. But in moral deliberation philosophers refer to a 'moral certainty', that is, a sufficient reason that is enough to ground convinced action, even though it is incomplete. We know enough about climate change to know that we ought to cut carbon emissions urgently —even though we know that there is a great deal about climate change that we do not know. Authority is a special case of the sufficient reason, and obedience a special case of moral certainty. It has been said: authority is a reason for acting in the absence of reasons. This paradox is true provided we emphasise both sides of it. Acting under authority we act without knowing all possible reasons. Yet authority is a reason, and a sufficient one. The authority of the command makes it reasonable to obey.

We see here the advantages of using the term 'authority' as the central focus of political enquiry, rather than speaking all the time about 'the state'. Authority is an event, not an institution, a moral relation that comes about rather than an entity that merely subsists. 'The state' is, anyway, an ambiguous term. It can mean 'government' as a distinct function within society, as contrasted with agriculture, scholarship, industry and so on. Or it can mean the whole of society as politically organised. In the latter sense 'obedience to the state' means obedience of the part to the whole, a profoundly un-Christian notion. But if we are careful to use 'the state' in the former sense, we still have to face the question of *when* and *how* governing instances have authority and lay claim on obedience. If we are asking what makes obedience reasonable, the answer must do more than gesture at a given body; it must point to the *functions* of that body, its exercises of authority, which make it reasonable to obey it. Archbishop Janani Luwum of Uganda, who is honoured as a martyr in my church, had at some point to say to himself something like this: 'Yesterday it was our duty to obey the President; today it is not, because he has manifestly abandoned the ruling functions which gave his commands authority.'

'All authority is from God.' But by no means all authority is political authority. Political authority interests us especially here, as it interested St Paul in Romans 13; but we cannot understand political authority without grasping how it is like, and how unlike, other kinds of authority. Often in the Old Testament the supreme example of authority is taken to be wisdom. We are encouraged to do what the wisest and most well-informed persons counsel. We are not required to follow their precepts, but we are given strong incentives to do so, and to do so simply on their authority. 'My son, pay attention to what I say; listen closely to my words. Do not let them out of your sight, keep them within your heart (Proverbs 4:20)'. That such advice comes from such a source is sufficient reason to follow it. However, a major difference between types of authority comes into view here. The authority of the wise is based on reasons which can in principle be learned and appropriated. Indeed, that is part of the purpose of teaching their precepts to the young: 'Blessed is the man who finds wisdom, the man who gains understanding (Proverbs 3:13).' Most of us have to make our decisions about climate-change solely on the basis of what the experts have told us. The detailed science of the question is something we do not begin to understand. Yet I know no reason why I should not be able to master it if I had time and opportunity to do so; and if I did, I could be as authoritative on the subject as any scientist today. I might, of course, try to master the science and fail, from lack of intelligence, application or whatever cause; but that would be for the event to show. There is nothing that puts this science in principle out of my reach. The authority of the wise, then, is in principle communicable to others, and can be acquired by learning.

But there is a different kind of authority that cannot be acquired in this way: the authority of a parent over a child. This arises from a particular natural relation between the two that could not be different—or one might say, could only be different if they were two wholly different persons. I can say 'I might have been a scientist'. The words 'might have been' have a proper application in speculations about alternative things that might have befallen us. But we cannot assign any meaning to the words: 'I might have been my father's father, or my child's child.' For to be my father's father or my child's child is not something that could have befallen me.

The authority of the wise is an acquired authority, gained by achievement; it may be lost by acting unwisely. It is also a functional authority, which lasts just so long as it is obviously of use, but ceases when we are no longer in need of the guidance that the wise can give us. The authority of a parent subsists independently of achievement; it outlasts its functional usefulness indefinitely; and though a drunken and unwise father may lose his children's respect, he still claims a measure of authority from the sheer fact that he is their father and they his children.

Political authority is in many respects more like the authority of the parent. There is a simple givenness about it. It can persist in the face of startling failures of wisdom and virtue on the part of those who exercise it. A bad law does not delegitimise the government; if it did, there would be no legitimate government anywhere! Yet it does not resemble parental authority in all respects, but in some is more like the authority of the wise: it is limited to those matters and occasions for which it has a functional use, and does not, like the authority of the parent, rest on a natural relation. All this contributes to the rather puzzling appearance of political authority: having no natural basis on the one hand, no basis in achievement on the other, it seems to float in the air without support. It is ungrounded.

'All authority is from God.' While this applies to all kinds of authority in some sense, precisely the ungrounded character of political authority demands that we make this affirmation about it in a peculiarly strong way. Lacking a foundation in the created order of things, political authority is immediately dependent on divine providence. The Old Testament speaks of kings and judges and warriors as 'raised up' by God. Political authority is something that 'happens', rather than something that is. Its appearance, then, demonstrates the preserving intervention of God into the order of the world in a way that the natural authorities of wisdom and parenthood do. The paradox of political authority is grasped solely through the words 'from God'. Political authority is inexplicable in terms of simple inter-human relations; it is a sign of the active intervention of God in governing human affairs.

Yet it is not simply an intervention of the divine into the human, a kind of burning bush. It is more like the miracle of Aaron's rod. 'All authority is from God.' God has given human beings to exercise an authority over one another, an authority which is not theirs by any natural relation. There is no qualification to explain this, like wisdom, no natural priority, like parenthood. Anti-authoritarianism and egalitarianism are, as they were, the state of nature in which we boggle at the miracle. There is no natural sovereignty of one human being over another. How is it that God makes us 'like angels of God' to one another—able, by a simple act of will, to present one another with sufficient reason to act as we intend?

2. Political authority and God's governance

Let us, then, explore this paradox of political authority a little further. Does
the paradox consist, as some would say, in the power of government to
dispose of its subjects' lives? That power it certainly has—and has it,
irrespective of whether it customarily exercises the power of capital
punishment. Capital punishment has been out of use in Britain for nearly half
a century now, but in London the other day the Metropolitan police, in pursuit
of a suspected suicide bomber whom they thought was on the point of
committing an outrage, unhesitatingly shot their victim dead in front of a large
crowd of horrified onlookers, no questions asked. But there is no paradox in
the fact that organised force can overwhelm, destroy, or simply restrict
anybody's freedom. That armed police or an army can do such a thing is no
more puzzling than that a tsunami can do it. We cannot understand anything
about political authority if we discuss everything simply in terms of power. To
talk about political authority is to talk about something more than, and very
much more mysterious than, power.

It is to talk of right. And this is where the paradox arises. The puzzle lies
not in the exercise of power, but in the right to exercise power. But how does
one human being acquire the right to take another's life? There was under-
standable public dismay when it turned out that the victim of the police
marksmen in the incident I mentioned was not connected to the bombing plot
in any way; but nobody questioned the right of the police to do such a thing,
had the facts been as they had supposed them to be. Where can a right to
dispose of others' lives, even in such circumstances, come from? It can only
come from a prior relation between government and subject, a relation in
which government can claim its subjects' obedience. The right to power is
secondary; the right to obedience primary. Political authority claims the full
co-operation of our freedom in obedience, and that is a human claim, one that
no tsunami can ever make.

But here we touch the heart of the paradox. A right must be publicly
intelligible, open to reasoned discussion. A right that could never be
demonstrated would be no right at all. A right cannot be constituted merely by
asserting it, not even by government's asserting it—however much some
people seem to want to do that. Yet obedience to authority means taking
things on trust—acting in the absence of full reasons. How, then, can a 'right
to obedience' be made intelligible?

The central tradition of Western political thought has attempted to resolve
this paradox by stressing that the absence of full reasons is only one end of the
paradox; authority is a reason for acting in the absence of reasons. But what
kind of a reason is it? The Western tradition has seen it as an institution, that

is, a kind of procedural device put in place by human ingenuity. The simplest model is an accepted technique for reaching decisions which reasoning cannot settle. We put names into a hat and draw one out; we toss a coin; or we say, 'when the committee is evenly drawn on a question, the chairman has a casting vote'. Sometimes government has been conceived this way, as a simple decision-making body, where collective decision-making is obviously impossible.

But this simplest model obviously needs improvement, in order to accommodate a central perception about the authority of government: namely, that it depends not simply on an ability to resolve dilemmas decisively, but on an ability to resolve them justly. Justice brings us back to reasons again— reasons which we suppose to underlie all our dilemmas, but which may not be equally apparent to all of us all the time, either because we are not well enough informed or because our private interests are distorting our perception. Is it enough to say that government is an institution for enacting justice in the affairs of society?

It is certainly very important to say that. But it is still not enough. For it does not explain two important features of political authority. The first is its right to command sanctions. Justice is what we owe our neighbours, and that debt of justice is certainly well rendered by an institution that investigates disputes and reaches a judgment on them. But what could possibly turn such an institution into an authoritative institution, that can rightfully impose its judgments on us, willy-nilly? The central Western myth of the social contract has imagined citizens contracting with one another to make their lives subject to a form of government that they set up. But not only is it impossible to imagine such a contract—how would you make such a contract where there was not even the most vestigial notion of what contracting and promising meant?—it is not clear how such a contract could introduce a right of government. I may perhaps agree to surrender my goods and liberty and life to the judgment of the state; but can I agree to surrender yours? Or my grandchildren's? We might express this question as follows: How is justice sovereign? Since human beings have no natural sovereignty over one another, by what sovereignty are they authorised to dispose of one another's lives in the service of justice? That is the question to which it seems the Western tradition can offer no answer. The Christian answer is: 'all authority is from God'.

The other factor it does not explain is that not anybody can give judgment. The Deuteronomic law of the king insists that the king must be chosen from among the people, must be by an Israelite. And there is a very strong intuition that governments that do not have a vital organic relation with the people they rule lack authority, irrespective of how well they discharge their functions otherwise. Imperial rule was an attempt to avoid this logic, to impose a form of government that was irrespective of the underlying relation between government and people and depended wholly on its justice and efficiency. But its authority proved fragile, for there is an inherent logic in political authority that it must find a representative relation to the people. Political authority serves political identities, that is, the coherence and persistence of a given political community. A political community is a binding together of a determinate segment of the human race, situated in a particular local neighbourhood. Only in active relation to that neighbourhood, in consultation with it and in deliberation on its behalf, can political authority demonstrate itself as a service to humankind.

But how does it come about that a people finds its identity in submission to the sovereignty of justice exercised through representative organs? How does a people identify with itself, and so identify with the organs that uphold the sovereignty of justice over it. There have been many devices in history for reinforcing these bonds of mutual identification: royal ceremony is one such device; popular election is another. Each has had varying success at different times, and each is exposed to pitfalls. By one means or another, however, identifications of peoples with themselves and with their governments constantly arise. Christians have been more able than secular theorists to accept the element of sheer historical contingency in such arrangements, and therefore less prone to ideological absolutisms, because they believe in the sovereign action of God, who 'raises up' those who will give judgment. He brings this representative relation to exist, and he causes it to disappear again. In this governance of God over human affairs we find ourselves commanded by one another, and understanding that this is for the good of humankind, we freely and rationally obey.

3. Political authority, judgment, and the common good

Let us draw some consequences from this. First, if authority arises as God 'raises up' those who bear it, nobody has a right to bear authority. Authority is a right, the right to be obeyed; but it is not itself held by right. There is nobody who ought to have political authority, but unfortunately it is not so. Political authority is de facto. The only people who ought to have it are those who actually have it. They have it because God has raised them up to have it. 'Legitimism' is the name for the mistaken proposal that political authority is held by entitlement. There may, of course, be laws determining who should be in authority at any time in a given place—we call such laws 'constitutional laws'—and these laws, like all laws, demand our obedience. However, the constitutional law itself is part of a political regime which God has raised up and may cast down. If the regime disappears, the constitutional law disappears with it. For nearly a century the descendents of James II of England and Scotland sat on the European continent insisting that they were the rightful tenants of the throne; but their regime had come to an end. The right of succession by which they claimed to rule Great Britain was itself a human law with validity only within its context, and its context had passed away. 'The king over the water' was no king at all. We refer to their doctrine sometimes as the 'divine right of kings', but this is misleading. What they believed in was a divine right of succession; but that is something God has granted to nobody. The 'divine right' is the right of those who actually govern to claim obedience.

We could bring this point home in the contemporary setting by saying that there is no possibility of protecting a democracy by law against a successful *coup d'état*. A failed coup may indeed be prosecuted as a crime; but a successful one has swept away the democratic laws that made it criminal. Legality is not the key to defending and strengthening democratic regimes. That which we value in a democratic style of polity can only be strengthened by virtues, both on the part of rulers and on the part of citizens. But, in case this sounds like a charter to every conspiring military junta, let us stress that our point is a rather limited one. First of all, it does not imply immunity from the sanctions of the law for individuals in government, not even for heads of government or heads of state. The terms on which these individuals can be publicly charged with crimes are usually determined specifically by law. The point is simply that the law has power to include them in its scope; for those who govern, govern under the law by which they govern. Secondly, our point has validity only in terms of human law. It does not extend any moral indemnity to a *coup d'état*. Perhaps there may be instances in which revolutions are justified; that has been a proposition before Christian casuists since the middle ages, and we need not pursue the arguments here and now. But the presumption must be heavily against it because 'all authority is from God'. The point is simply that in the sight of God a successful *coup d'état* may be a sin of the greatest seriousness, to be judged before the bar of heaven—and yet at the same time the regime it installs may have political authority and rightly command the obedience of its subjects. The question of who may rule is not determined by entitlement, but by fact.

This negative point, however, does not exhaust what is to be said about the necessary connection between government and lawfulness. God gives human beings authority as an expression of his will to preserve particular communities. He preserves them through the mutual service that their members give to one another. Political authority can arise only in service of the 'common good', which is the mutual co-operation and assistance of the community's members. Communities have traditions of co-operation, and out of these are formed the laws that define their modes of co-operating. Political authority takes concrete form, then, as a state of law is preserved and maintained within a people. Without a state of law the community disintegrates, and if the community disintegrates, political authority fails in its purpose, and as it fails, disappears altogether. God allows political authority to serve the state of law by giving judgment within and for the whole community.

Lawfulness is not of itself justice. True justice is more demanding than any human state of law, which can only be a rough approximation to it. So we must not say that political authority disappears if there is a failure of justice, for that (as St Augustine observed) excludes every possible political body. But we can say that political authority depends on the giving of judgment. Particular and concrete judgments are means through which justice makes its claim on the state of law and purifies it. So while political authority has to serve the state of law that obtains within the community, even though it may have many imperfections, by giving good judgments it can purify that state of law and enable it to evolve in the direction of true justice.

Judgment is the activity of resolving disputes and controversies rightly; it vindicates offences against the common good. The validity of all political authority is, in the last resort, established by this test: does it effectively render judgment 'between a man and his neighbour'? How good its judgment is, of course, will be relative to the possibilities of enquiry, proof and discernment. It may depend on various internal constitutional arrangements, too, such as the independence of the judiciary. Not all seriously intended judgment will achieve a just result—for all kinds of reasons, some avoidable, some unavoidable. But an agency that doesn't set out to give judgment does not possess political authority; it cannot demand our obedience, for judgment is the good for which God has given political authority and for which he requires that we obey it.

In order to fulfil its service of judgment, government must be able to command the last instance, the court of final appeal, in any dispute. Its word must be final within its community. Yet since God sets all political authority before the horizon of his own coming judgment, the judgment of the Kingdom of God, the finality of political authority is only provisional. The last word is not really the last, but only a placeholder for the last. Political authorities are always bound to represent determinate peoples and states of law; they are not universal. God is bound to no determinate community, and his rule is universal, not confined to the local perspectives and practices of a given territorial neighbourhood. God is not limited in his power of investigation and knowledge and enforcement. So the kingdoms of the world will become the kingdom of our God and of his Christ. Without putting that final horizon in place, we can never understand how all authority is from God; because that which is from God must return to him.

And here we come back to the anti-authoritarian moment from which we began. For if it is possible to say that God sets all human judgment under his own judgment, it must be possible to speak of that divine judgment, and point forward to it; it must be a matter of prophecy. We have devoted this time to exploring just one aspect of the proposition 'all authority is from God', that which pertains to secular authority. There is another aspect: the authority of prophecy vested in a community, a community of the last times that crosses the borders of all political communities, not only in its universal membership but in its direct relation to the rule of God. So we do not complete what Christians have had to say about earthly government until we have said that its sphere is limited and bounded by the Spirit-filled life of the church, catholic and universal, the community of prophetic witness that points forward to the ending of all earthly kingdoms in the kingdom of God.[2]

---

2. Refer to my article 'Fellow-Citizens with the Saints' in this volume of essays, and to *The Ways of Judgment* (Grand Rapids: Eerdmans, 2005), 231–319.

7

Christian Social Responsibilities in East Asia: Lessons from the Early Church

Michael Nai-Chiu Poon

1. Two observations

This essay seeks to reflect on and elucidate the shape of Christian social responsibility in the young nation-states in East Asia today.

To place the discussion in sharper relief, I begin with two observations. Some eighty years ago, the China Continuation Committee published the Report *The Christian Occupation of China: A General Survey of the Numerical Strength and Geographical Distribution of the Christian Forces in China*.[1] It was a confident statement on the state of Protestant Christianity in China as leadership in the churches was gradually assumed by local Chinese at the turn of the twentieth century. The Report gave detailed accounts on Christian work among 'special classes' (Part IX), in 'education' (Part XI) and in 'medical work' (Part XII). Remarkably such positive assessment of Christian social engagement was reversed within a few decades. These activities are now popularly regarded in China as instruments of imperialistic aggression.[2] These contributions, initiated primarily by the missionaries and financed by foreign resources, were unable to counter the deeper malaise in the society, which perhaps required radical political changes.

---

1.   China Continuation Committee, *The Christian Occupation of China: A General Survey of the Numerical Strength and Geographical Distribution of the Christian Forces in China made by the Special Committee on Survey and Occupation, China Continuation Committee 1918–1921*, edited by Milton T Stauffer, Tsinforn C Wong, and M Gardner Tewksbury (Shanghai: China Continuation Committee, 1922).

2.   See for example Changsheng Gu, *Chuan jiao shi yu jin dai zhong guo* [Missionaries and the Modern China] (Shanghai: Shang hai ren min chu ban she, 1981), and more recently, Guanzong Luo, *Qian shi bu wang, hou shi zhi shi* [Lessons from History] (Beijing: Zong jiao wen hua chu ban she, 2003).

The other observation relates to the recent statistical compilations on the state of Christianity in the *World Christian Encyclopedia,*[3] a work that is influential in shaping evangelisation-strategies of evangelical mission agencies and churches today. I shall return to this work later on in this paper. Suffice to say here that this reference work devoted a major section on statistical analysis and projection on the development of metropolises of the world.[4] The editors observed that urban centres played a key role in the expansion of Christianity from the times of the early church by virtue of their dense population. Hence, the rise of supercities today—cities with population of four million or over— becomes a crucial consideration in mission strategies. Barrett, Kurian and Johnson then made several observations:

Firstly, in 1900, all the world's five largest cities—London, New York, Paris, Berlin and Chicago—were strongholds of Christian life, discipleship, urban evangelism, urban missions, foreign missions and global missions. By 2050, the landscape becomes drastically different. Four of the top five— Lagos, Karachi, Bombay, Dhaka and Calcutta—will be hostile to Christianity.[5] It may be of interest for our present discussion that, according to the *World Urbanization Prospects, 1996 revision,* published by the United Nations, six East Asian cities are numbered among the top twenty-five most densely populated cities in the world by 2050. They are Shanghai (29.5 million), Tokyo (28.9 million), Beijing (24.7 million), Bangkok (22.3 million), Tianjin (20.7 million), and Ho Chi Minh (18.2 million).[6]

Secondly, a major new development is that the world's dominant activity is rapidly the deepening and spreading of information and knowledge. This should be welcomed. For the real success of any city in the future will depend on its ability to pass in its knowledge base from one generation to another. They suggested:

> As for Christian patterns of urban ministry . . . Christians
> and their theologians [should] let their imaginations play
> over the fact that the major new concept describing future

---

3. *World Christian Encyclopedia: A Comparative Survey of Churches and Religions in the Modern World,* volumes 1 and 2, edited by David Barrett, George Kurian and Todd Johnson (Oxford: Oxford University Press, 2001).
4. *Ibid,* volume 2, 533–44.
5. *Ibid,* volume 2, 534.
6. Cited in *ibid,* volume 2, 537.

cities—knowledge—is also a major concept in the New Testament (*gnosis*, knowledge).[7]

Thirdly, for the world to be 'evangelised' by 2025, defined to mean that individuals have had 'adequate opportunity or opportunities to hear the gospel and to respond to it, whether positively or negatively',[8] Christians have to adopt the tactics of 'megaministries'. A megaministry is defined as one that reaches a minimum of ten thousand unevangelised persons every day.

This line of reasoning is clear. Christians should applaud the rise of cities, because the dense concentration of population allow for efficient spreading of the gospel. Christian agencies therefore should identify 'non-Christian' cities of dense populations, and invest their resources in evangelisation activities to achieve the global task of evangelisation within the next decades. Accordingly, 'to seek the welfare of the city' would simply mean a global mobilisation of Christians to bring the Christian *knowledge* to cities of dense populations that are increasingly hostile to the Christian faith.

The two compilations we just surveyed, on China about eighty years ago and of world Christianity today, were confident statements on the prospects of Christianity. However challenging the circumstances that the Christian communities find themselves—whether in turbulent years in the new Chinese nation in the early twentieth century, or the power-realignment in the twenty-first century—the compilers were confident in how the church should engage the wider world. The *nature* of the Christian activity is not under scrutiny. With hindsight of the failure of Christianity in China in the past two hundred years—in spite of considerable missionary activities—we may wish to reflect on the suppositions in Christian social engagement. To do this, we may wish to reach back to the time when the first Christians were still exploring their own identity and their relation with the present world. In the following I shall explore how the early Christians clarified their own identity in their attempts to find public expressions to their faith. Their reflections may help us to gain understanding of our Christian heritage, and help us to rediscover paradigms of understanding, and explore fresh ways in 'seeking the welfare of the city' today in East Asia.

---

7.   *Ibid*, volume 2, 536.
8.   See this definition in *ibid*, volume 1, 28.

2. Social ramifications of the church's self-understanding in the early church

The Christian community from the very start was involved in works of charity. It was 'the most potent single cause of Christian success', such was Henry Chadwick's assessment.[9] Christian charity expressed itself especially in the care for the dying. Bishop Dionysius of Alexandria contrasted how the Christian community and the pagans differed in their response to human suffering in a plague in 262:

> The vast majority of our brethren were, in their very great love and brotherly affection, unsparing of themselves and supportive of one another. Visiting the sick without thought of the danger to themselves, resolutely caring for them, tending them in Christ, they readily left this life with them, after contracting the disease from others, drawing the sickness onto themselves from their neighbours, and willingly partaking of their sufferings. Many also, in nursing the sick and helping them to recover, themselves died, transferring to themselves the death coming to others and giving real meaning to the common saying that only ever seems to be a polite cliché, 'Your humble servant bids you farewell'. The best of our brethren departed life in this way—some presbyters and deacons and some of the laity, greatly esteemed, so that, on account of the great devotion and strong faith it entails, this kind of death does not seem inferior to martyrdom. Gathering up the bodies of the saints with open hands into their laps, they closed their eyes and shut their mouths before carrying them on their shoulders and laying them out; they clasped and embraced them, washed and dressed them in grave clothes—then before long, the same would happen to them, since those left behind were continually following those who had preceded them. But the pagans (*ta ethnē*) behaved completely the opposite. They shunned those in the early stages of the illness, fled from their loved ones and abandoned them half-dead on the roads, and treated unburied corpses like garbage, in their efforts to avoid the spread and

9.   Henry Chadwick, *The Early Church* (Harmondsworth: Penguin, 1967), 56.

communication of the fatal disease—which was not easy to
deflect whatever strategy they tried.[10]

Dionysius understood that the practical expressions of Christian charity
were not simply exercises in public relation, as if Christians sought to show
that they were a responsible community and were fulfilling expected social
roles. The Christians made communal life possible in the face of social crises
where human ties were under threat of dissolution. They understood their
practical work, even at the expense of sacrificing their own lives, to be the
outworking of their faith: 'This kind of death does not seem inferior to
martyrdom.' Those who are outside the Christian community recognised the
potency of this testimony. In late fourth century, the pagan Emperor Julian
recognised that generosity to the strangers, care for the dying, and the
dignified conduct of life contributed to the growth of Christianity. He
proposed, therefore, that pagans should seek to outdo Christians in such
endeavour if there were any hope of reviving paganism in the Empire.[11]

The first exposure to the early church, for many of us, is on matters of
doctrines. Indeed, the fundamentals of Christian beliefs—on doctrines of God,
Christ, and the church, emerged during the first centuries of Christianity.
Hence, we may regard such practical expressions of Christian charity as
peripheral to understanding the life and testimony of the church. Were not
Christians simply fulfilling the social roles as prescribed by the authorities?
After all, the Tolerance Edict of Galerius in 311, which ushered the social
triumph of Christianity, stipulated that:

> Christians may exist again, and may establish their
> meetings, yet so that they do nothing contrary to good order
> . . . They will be bound to pray their gods for our good
> estate, and that of the commonwealth, and their own, that
> the commonwealth may endure on every side unharmed,
> and they may be able to live securely in their own homes.[12]

---

10. Recounted in Eusebius, *Ecclesiastical History* 7.22.7–10. Translation is from AD
    Lee, *Pagans and Christians in Late Antiquity: A Source Book* (London:
    Routledge, 2000), 38–39.

11. Julian, *Letter* 84. 429c–431b, cited in Lee, *ibid*, 97–8.

12. HM Gwatkin, *Selections from Early Christian Writers* (London: MacMillan,
    1920), 171.

The truth is otherwise. Christian doctrines, at least for the church fathers, were not simply matters to be consigned to the realm of religious feeling and private concerns of voluntary groups and individuals. Christian doctrines were deliberated with severe intensity for the reason that they were co-ordinated within an overall vision, not only of what the church should be, but what society ought to be in light of the coming of Christ the King. Far from it that the Christians were contributing to a 'society' whose terms were defined by the authorites, they were ushering a new society in their social engagement.

Jaroslav Pelikan made this point in his reflection on the social implications of the 'one, holy, catholic, and apostolic church' for the early church.[13] To summarise:

> a) 'Unity' was by no means only a part of the creed or an abstract theological concept removed from the realities of social and economic life. Christians united themselves not by ethnic ties, social class, or gender; but by common adherence to the person of Jesus Christ and to the church that he established. This became the new basis of 'unity' of the society that eventually won over the empire.
>
> b) Developing the mark of holiness was again the result of an evolution in the social teachings of the church. Initially, Christian writers had often drawn the contrast between the church and Roman society along moral lines. Yet the demand for holiness had, from the beginning, existed in tension with the offer of forgiveness. The church came to realise, through the controversies on the treatment of the lapsed, that the church is more like a hospital where the wounded would receive healing rather than a gathering for the moral elite.[14]
>
> c) The church inherited from Judaism a catholic vision. It defined its catholicity along two fronts. It refused to be absorbed into the syncretistic hodge-podge of the Roman Empire, and laid its claim for universality by being a particular faith. At the same time, it kept the whole world

---

13.   Jaroslav Pelikan, *The Excellent Empire: The Fall of Rome and the Triumph of the Church* (New York: Harper and Row, 1987), 15–28.

14.   *Ibid*, 23.

within its horizons that included the Roman Empire but was
not confined to it.[15]

d) Apostolicity again did not simply provide an acid test for
distinguishing between what is legitimate from what was
illegitimate in Christian teaching. The canons of the
Scriptures, the apostolic tradition, and apostolic continuity
provided a new infrastructure reference for the church to
reorganise and revitalise the Mediterranean world.
Henceforth, the new and Christian seat of government in
Constantinople would supersede the old and pagan Rome.

This is to say, reflections on the identity of the Christian community and
of the wider society are co-ordinated within a more fundamental reflection of
what the gospel of Jesus Christ means for human society. The manner by
which the Christian community sought to 'seek the welfare of the city' varied
according to different circumstances. Hence, the opportunities offered to the
late fourth century church would be different from that open to those in the
post-apostolic period. However, the Christian community would not regard
itself as a functional group that exists alongside others in the society, simply
tasked to fulfill specific roles as prescribed by social or state expectations. The
four notes provided the basis upon which the church developed to be a
morally and intellectually coherent society, having the necessary public
frameworks to bring forth the birth of the Western world out of the ruins of
the Roman Empire in the fifth century.[16]

3. Seeking the public space to be the church

It was not obvious that the Christian community could find the public space to
make its particular contributions to the society. I should also hasten to add that
the state's attitude to Christianity was not the determining factor in such

---

15. Thus, Cyril of Jerusalem expounded the Christian faith: 'It is called Catholic then
because it extends over all the world, from one end of the earth to the other; and
because it teaches universally and completely one and all the doctrines which
ought to come to men's knowledge.' See his *Catechetical Lectures* 18.23.
Translation is from the *Nicene and Post Nicene Fathers*, second series, volume 7,
139–50.

16. See Peter Brown, 'Christianity and Empire', in *The Rise of Western
Christendom*, edited by Peter Brown (Oxford: Blackwell, 1996), 18–33.

consideration.[17] Up to the late second century, in spite of occasions of
deliberate suppression by the Roman authorities, opposition to the tiny
Christian community came from the populace rather than from the state.[18]
The wider society considered Christians to be *odium humani generis* (hated of
the human race).[19] Because of the lack of understanding of the Christian
community, the populace accused them of refusing to offer sacrifices to the
gods, partaking of human flesh and other bizarre and immoral practices. In
particular, Christians' refusal to offer sacrifices to the gods encouraged a
popular view that Christians were disloyal to the Emperor, a charge that the
early church pointedly refuted. They emphasised that they were loyal to the
Emperor, expressed in particular in their intercessory prayer. The Christians
alone understood the true nature and destiny of the Roman Empire, and thus
were able to promote its welfare. Tertullian proposed:

> For we, on behalf of the safety of the emperors, invoke the
> eternal God, the true God, the living God, whom the
> emperors themselves prefer to have propitious to them
> beyond all other gods. They know who has given them the
> Empire; they know, as men, who has given them life; they
> feel that he is God alone, in whose power and no other's
> they are, second to whom they stand, after whom they come
> first, before all gods and above all gods. Why not? seeing
> that they are above all men, and men at any rate live and so
> are better than dead things . . . Looking up to heaven the
> Christians—with hands outspread, because innocent, with
> head bare because we do not blush, yes! and without one to
> give the form of words, for we pray from the heart—we are
> ever making intercession for all the emperors. We pray for

---

17.   See for example Trajan's reply to Pliny *c* 112 CE: 'Nothing can be laid down as a
      general ruling involving something like a set form of procedures. They are not to
      be sought out; but if they are accused or convicted, they must be punished.'
      (Pliny, *Ep* 10.97).

18.   On contemporary treatment of Christian pagan relations, see for example Robert
      L Wilken, *The Christians as the Romans Saw Them* (New Haven: Yale
      University Press, 1984) and Jeffrey W Hargis, *Against the Christians: The Rise
      of Early Anti-Christian Polemic* (New York: Peter Lang, 1999). J Stevenson and
      WHC Frend, *A New Eusebius*, New Edition (London: SPCK, 1987) and AD Lee,
      Pagans and Christians in Late Antiquity contain collections of source documents
      in pagan-Christian relationship.

19.   Tacitus, *Annals* 15.44.5.

them long life, a secure rule, a safe home, brave armies, a
faithful senate, an honest people, a quiet world—and
everything for which a man and a Caesar can pray. All this
I cannot ask of any other but only of him, from whom I
know I shall receive it, since he it is who alone gives and I
am one to whom the answer to prayer is due, his servant,
who alone worships him, who for his teaching am slain,
who offer to him that rich and better sacrifice which he
himself commanded—I mean prayer, proceeding from flesh
pure, soul innocent, spirit holy.[20]

Hargis pointed out, in a recent study of early Christian polemics, from
Celsus in the third century down to Emperor Julian in late fourth century, that
by the late second century Christianity was opposed on philosophical grounds
as Christians began to clarify their identity and work out the philosophical
basis of their belief. As Christians began 'to assert ownership of the cultural
and intellectual property of their pagan opponents', the pagans came to see
them as a formidable threat who should be marginalised at all cost.[21]

The pagans discovered however that they could not marginalise Christians
in the same way as they had successfully marginalised the Jews. After the
destruction of the Temple, Judaism assumed a Rabbinic form and did not
engage the Hellenistic cultures. It confined itself as an ethnic group. However,
Christians succeeded in penetrating into all social classes in the Empire, and
hence could not be confined within a social boundary. Among the second
century apologists, though there were those like Tatian, Hernias and
Theophilus who took a negative view of Greek philosophy, Justin was able to
affirm Greek philosophy within the framework of a logos-theology. From the
third century onwards down to late fourth century, Clement of Alexandria,
Origen and the Cappadocian Fathers took up this lead. They affirmed the
study of Greek literature as preparatory to understanding the gospel,[22] and
hence made it possible for the church to engage theologically, and transform,
the core values of the society. The discussions on personhood and identity in
trinitarian and christological debates in the early centuries did not only clarify

---

20. *Apology*, 30.1, 4–5, cited in Stevenson and Frend, *op cit*, 161–2.
21. Hargis, *op cit*, 15.
22. See for example Basil of Caesarea, *Address to Young Men on the Right Use of
     Greek Literature.*

the doctrine of God and Jesus Christ. They also offered fresh understanding of the human person.

Emperor Julian was able to see the gravity of this intellectual threat. During his brief reign in 361 to 363 he attempted to revive paganism. One strategy he employed was to proscribe Christians from the teaching profession, which in fact would debar them from public career. He argued:

> A good education is not a matter of splendid elegance in words and language, but of a healthy mental disposition and intellect, and of right judgment about good and evil, beauty and repugnance. Whoever thinks one thing and teaches another to his students seems to me to have abandoned good education as much as he has honesty. If the difference between what he thinks and what he says concerns minor matters, this is bad, but can to a certain extent be tolerated. But if a person has views on the major issues, yet teaches things at odds with those views, is this not the behaviour of petty traders, the life of men who are untrustworthy and disreputable . . .? Therefore, all who claim to teach anything should be of good character and not carry in their soul convictions at odds with the public practice of their profession. This ought above all to be the case, in my view, with those who teach the young about literature.[23]

This policy attracted strong Christian opposition, and proved to be short-lived. The proscription indicated the deep conflict between Christian intellectuals and their pagan counterparts. They attempted to exclude Christians from the public arena, and deny them the opportunity of social contribution. This is important to realise that the pagans were anti-Christian not because the latter were anti-social and anti-intellectual, but for the very opposite reasons. The fourth-century church was competing with the pagan philosophers the minds and hearts of the people, and was able to offer them a solution that was morally and philosophically more convincing. In giving social and public expressions of their faith, the Christians were raising fundamental questions about the moral and spiritual values of the Roman society and Empire. The pagan philosophers rightly saw that a society is not simply about practical arrangements. It is not a marketplace where buyers and

---

23.   Julian, *Letter* 61c, cited in Lee, *op cit*, 102–03.

sellers come to display their goods and fulfill their private needs. The pagan philosophers were perhaps not as confident as the contemporary world is in assuming that different groups can simply contribute to the welfare of the city, and that it would be obvious that 'all men of good will' would agree on what is good for the society. They were more sensitive to questions on the *nature* of the welfare (*what* welfare?) and the *destiny* of the city (*whose* city?). This is why the issues on education of the young—hence the passing on of spiritual heritage—and on public sacrifices to the ancient gods were crucial concerns for Christians and pagans in the early church, as perhaps are these issues very much alive today in East Asia as well.

For all the differences between the Latin and Greek traditions in the first five hundred years of the church, the Christian community was able to offer a comprehensive understanding of history and the world, and was able to formulate Christian doctrines with the terminologies of classical traditions, and transformed them in the very process of theological engagement. This development came to fruition especially in Augustine, who came to regard both the political structure of the Roman Empire and the classical traditions as human institutions, and therefore replaceable. This legacy provided the foundation for the ordering of a Christian society in the subsequent millennium in the West.[24]

4. The challenge to be a Christian society

How should Christians in East Asia today relate to the wider society? Social involvement certainly offers opportunity for 'evangelisation'. Christians in East Asia may find the megaministry approaches, as suggested in the World Christian Encyclopedia, attractive. Such strategies can be effective for densely populated and urbanised regions like East Asia. Furthermore, such strategies fit well with an information-technological culture. For example, the statistics on the state of Christianity in *World Christian Encyclopedia* and the *World Christian Trends* are at present updated in the World Christian Database and are made available on-line by the Centre for the Study of Global Christianity

---

24.   See for example, Peter Brown, *Augustine of Hippo: A Biography* (London: Faber, 1967), 259–69; Serge Lancel, *St Augustine* (London: SCM Press, 1999), 306–22; Oliver O'Donovan, 'The Political Thought of City of God 19', in *Bonds of Imperfection: Christian Politics, Past and Present* (Grand Rapids: Eerdmans, 2004), 48–72, and his discussion on Christendom in *The Desire of the Nations: Rediscovering the Roots of Political Theology* (Cambridge: Cambridge University Press, 1996), 193–242.

at Gordon-Conwell Theological Seminary. Mission agencies and churches can simply read off the tables and indicators and target their mission efforts accordingly to cities of exploding populations. The internet can provide the latest news on disasters around the world. Social responsibilities are then mainly matters of logistics and managerial considerations. How then could Christians seek the welfare of the cities today? They are like quick-response units on the watch, ready to be mobilised for relief and missionary operations.

Christians should neither be oblivious to the immediate concerns and opportunities that arise on the horizons, nor be dismissive of the value of practical relief work. The early church however taught us that Christian communities in East Asia need to co-ordinate their efforts within a more coherent vision of the church and the society.

Here we come to the heart of the matter. Christians in East Asia need to move out of an entrenched understanding that they are local agents of mission societies and movements. They need to recover the vision that the Christian community itself assumes a public form; its manner of life creates a social reality that contributes to the true welfare of peoples and nations. This may not be obvious. Although churches in Asia may be able to trace their roots to the first centuries of Christianity, the present forms of Christianity are more influenced by missionary initiatives in the past five hundred years. Missionaries from Portugal, the Netherlands, Spain, Scotland, England, France, Ireland, and the United States of America have bequeathed to East Asia their forms of Christian faith and church polities. How their efforts differ and overlap with colonial policies is a discussion that is outside our present scope. We simply point out that these missionaries were nurtured and guided by the legacies of Christendom in the West. They came to found along the shores in Asia—as they did in South America and Africa—new Christian empires (to replace their lost Christian empires in Europe). They came with the purpose of conversion of kings and emperors to the Christian cause. This legacy leads to a misconception that Christianity can best survive and be propagated in 'Christian' nations, with little awareness that the post-liberal values espoused by such countries may be anything but Christian today. Thus, Christians around the world could well divide the world in terms of Christian, Communist, Muslim, and post-Communist blocs. The non-Christian countries become targets for missionary operations. The manner that churches pursue the welfare of societies and nations can then be confused with post-liberal concerns, which may have little bearing on the Christian faith.

It is important to recover an understanding that Christians throughout the centuries were able to pass on their faith and contribute to the common welfare within political structures that were quite different from the Latin traditions.[25] The church fathers reminded us that under the changing fortunes of political and social conditions, the church's primary task is to insist that it is the church of Jesus Christ.

How then can we seek the welfare of the cities today? I suggest that this does not lie in scrutinising the latest databases or in advocating for political changes in our societies. Furthermore, we are not called to repeat history: to replicate what the early fathers did in their days, or to anticipate a new Constantine to emerge from our region. The central task is theological. The church today needs to recover the vision that it is the 'one, holy, catholic, and apostolic' society of Jesus Christ. This proposal may appear rather odd. Discussion on the four marks of the church seems to belong to another era and context. Here we are not revisiting the old and increasingly presumptuous ecumenical dialogues between mainline churches in the West, as if mainline churches could on their own embrace the entire Christian reality. The issue before us is more pressing and far-reaching: it is whether Christianity in the non-Western world would be expressed primarily in the form of signs and wonders, or in stable institutional forms in the coming century. We witness in this generation a gravitational shift of Christian population to the non-Western world. However, the form that Christianity assumes, in particular in East Asia, requires closer scrutiny. Statistics in the *World Christian Encyclopedia* reveal that a rapidly increasing number of Christians are becoming more fluid in their institutional ties. They are 'postdenominational', replacing 'historical denominational ties by non-centralised lifestyle and church order'.[26] They emphasise the presence of power, signs and wonders, and utilise the media, rather than physical buildings, as the main vehicle of ministry. In 2000, 386 million Christians, making up of twenty per cent of the total Christian population, are affiliated with postdenominational churches. This compares with ninety-five million (eight per cent) in 1970.[27] Liturgical traditions, ministerial order, and the systematic public reading of the Bible, may be something that is both strange and alienating to Christians today, even those in

---

25. See eg Peter Brown's discussion on Christianity in Asia in *The Rise of Western Christendom*, 167–183, and Nicolas Standaert, *Handbook of Christianity in Asia, volume 1: 635–1800* (Leiden: Brill, 2001), 1–42.

26. See *World Christian Encyclopedia*, volume 1, 29 on this definition of post-denominationalism.

27. See 'Global Diagram 5: The rise of global Christianity across the twentieth century showing the rise of global independency out of global denominationalism, AD 1900–2025', *ibid*, volume 1, 10.

leadership positions in young churches. Dependent on personal authorities of leaders rather than on orthodox traditions, coupled with the lack of established institutional framework, they can easily become spontaneous groups that come together only for ideas and sensations, and would not be able to have the theological maturity to engage with the concerns of the present world.[28]

This analysis perhaps helps us to explain a two-fold emphasis in the China Christian Council's recent efforts in theological reconstruction: that is, on the need of integration with the wider society, and on countering superstition in rural churches. The Chinese church however is not simply revisiting the fundamentalist-liberal debate of the last century. The crisis touches on whether Christianity in China is able to assume a coherent ecclesial form. Once we abandon such vision, Christianity can well survive, confined as an object of investigation in the academia (that however is unable to find practical expression in today's society), or as spontaneous spiritual phenomena (that again could not relate to the wider society). Either way, the church would remain weak and inarticulate, unable to take up a public form as the community of Jesus Christ that critically engages the present world.

This issue alerts us to the need for young churches in the non-Western world to learn again from the early church, to establish canonical frameworks that can enable them to become a confident Christian *society* for today. Only by demonstrating in its own life the welfare of the heavenly city would it be able to discern the needs of the wider society, and find fresh initiatives to seek for its true welfare. Otherwise, young churches would either cling onto the missionary and colonial past, or absolutise the present political realties. Christian social responsibilities would then either remain as part of the Christendom project in the past, or become subsumed in the nation-building projects of today.

5. Concluding remarks: building a common society

East Asia is a geographical area of young nations and young churches. We are a region bounded together by ancient cultures and empires that have been

---

28.   See the assessment of the Pentecostal/charismatic renewal in *World Christian Encyclopedia* (volume 1, 19): 'Charismatics in the nonpentecostal mainline Protestant and catholic churches experience an average intense involvement of only two or three years—after this period as active weekly attenders at prayer meetings, they become irregular or nonattending, justifying the term postcharismatics . . . This "revolving-door syndrome" results in an enormous annual turnover, a serious problem that has not yet begun to be adequately recognized or investigated.'

untouched by the Christian faith. We together have existed primarily as projections of foreign policies of the Western world. Their policies have defined our national boundaries, and in some instances, even our national identities. Peace was once guaranteed by the British Empire. English today continues to be the lingua franca in the region. We too are bound together by histories of population movements and dislocations due to war and racial conflicts in the past two hundred years. Our forebears were poor labourers and refugees, who ventured to new lands and built new cities, in which we now live, alongside fellows of different races and faiths. Today, we are still bound together by health and security concerns, and suffer together in times of natural disasters. The experiences of war, racial bitterness, and dislocation are still the reality and threat for many in our region.

To be the one, holy catholic and apostolic community of Jesus Christ is a gift and task. We have been constituted to be a new society. Once we were not a people, but now God's people (1 Peter 2:10). Human sanctity and social life are not realities that can be taken for granted. The vision simply to be the society of Jesus Christ—to re-establish this at the centre of our lives—challenges us to seek the welfare of the city beyond expected roles and familiar tasks. It challenges us to re-orientate ourselves. In brief:

a) to embody in our churches and societies the reality of the 'one' under the threats of ethnic divides and revivals;

b) to embody the reality of the 'holy' in the ministry of reconciliation with former enemies during the emergence of our nations;

c) to embody the reality of the 'catholic' in acts of sharing and hospitality with the dispossessed in a competitive society;

d) to embody the reality of the 'apostolic' by ordering our churches and societies within moral and constitutional frameworks, in a time when transitions of power often lead to instability and bloodshed in our region.

These concerns would challenge us to think through questions of legitimacy and government and the status of law; issues concerning the freedom of belief and categorisation of citizens, of relations with those who profess different faiths in our societies and in other nations; and how public life can be open to true speech. We should welcome conversations with those of other faiths on such explorations.[29] Indeed, different churches and societies would have different ways to approach these concerns. Yet, however the manner of discipleship, we would discover new ways of working for the common good along the way, and would invite peoples from all nations in the quest for peace, until the day when the Heavenly City is revealed upon the good earth that our God created and renewed in Jesus Christ.

---

29. See for example, Hamza Ates' survey of Muslim views on an ideal state in 'Towards a Distinctive Model: Reconciling the Views of Contemporary Muslim Thinkers on an Ideal State for Muslim Societies', *Religion, State and Society* 31/4 (2003): 347–66.

8

Civil Society and its Emergence in the Modern World

Hwa Yung

Present day discussions on civil society and the associated idea of liberal democracy are closely related to the increasingly prominence of political Islam in the latter half of the twentieth century as well as to end of the Marxist era in the Soviet Union and Eastern Europe. At the same time, it is also directly relevant to the on-going debate in this part of the world on the relative merits of Western values and Asian values. This paper will take as its point of departure Ernest Gellner's *Conditions of Liberty: Civil Society and its Rival*,[1] written in the context of Eastern Europe's search for civil society in the aftermath of collapse of the Iron Curtain. It will then examine some of the issues related to nation-building in the context of the values debate between Asian and Western leaders, with particular attention paid to Islam and the Chinese tradition. It will finally examine the roots of civil society in the Christian heritage of Western civilisation.

1. Ernest Gellner on civil society

Gellner begins by noting that the idea of a plurality of institutions, which both opposes and balances the state, and are in turn controlled and protected by it, is in the Marxist view 'the provision of a façade for a hidden and maleficent domination'.[2] Yet, historical developments in the Soviet Union and Eastern Europe have demonstrated that what Marxism had deemed redundant and fraudulent became that which was most sought after—which is civil society!

At its simplest, Gellner notes that civil society may be understood by some as 'that set of diverse non-governmental institutions which is strong enough to counterbalance the state and, while not preventing the state from fulfilling its

---

1. Ernest Gellner, *Conditions of Liberty: Civil Society and its Rivals* (London: Penguin Books, 1994).
2. *Ibid*, 1.

role of keeper of the peace and arbitrator between major interests, can nevertheless prevent it from dominating and atomizing the rest of society'.[3] For Gellner, however, the problem with this understanding of civil society is that it would also include segmentary communities found in most, if not all, traditional societies. Within the latter, kings rule via intermediaries who in turn control local institutions, such as kinship networks and tribal groups, and local communities. A tyrant at the centre is in turn supported by local communities or institutions, and vice versa. But within such local institutions and communities, group loyalty is fully demanded and imposed, and individual freedom in the modern sense is absent. Thus, the segmentary community:

> avoids central tyranny by firmly turning the individual into an integral part of the social sub-unit . . . It may, indeed, be pluralistic and centralization-resistant, but it does not confer on its members the kind of freedom *we* require and expect from Civil Society.[4]

What then is civil society? It excludes all forms of centralised authoritarianism, whether Marxist or otherwise, as well as the stifling communalism of segmentary societies.[5] It safeguards the individual liberties of all, even the non-vigilant or those too weak in protecting these for themselves.[6] It possesses:

> an effective central state which, while acquiring such great power, nevertheless did not pulverize the rest of society, rendering it supine and helpless. A society emerged which ceased to be segmentary—either as an alternative to the state, as a mode of efficient state-lessness, or as an internal opposition to the state or in part its ally—yet capable of providing a countervailing force to the state.[7]

Such a definition of civil society would mean that it is exemplified in what can be found in modern Western liberal democracy at its best (not at its

---

3.   *Ibid*, 5.
4.   *Ibid*, 8.
5.   *Ibid*, 12.
6.   *Ibid*, 10, 80.
7.   *Ibid*, 86.

worst). Indeed much of what of the transformation of Eastern Europe since 1985 has been described by the term 'democratisation'. However, Gellner argues that the term 'civil society' is preferable to 'democracy' because the latter is often naively understood. Underlying the democratic model is the idea that a society is shaped by the will of the people or its members, based on the equality of all, with each having a vote. What is considered good for a society is when it reflects or implements the will of the people, otherwise it becomes pathological. Two things at least are overlooked. First, many of the communities in which we find ourselves are not egalitarian, and these, therefore, do not generally give equal weight to all members of the community in decision-making. Furthermore, our choices are usually shaped by our cultural pre-conditioning, which may not lead us to the right choices for our communities.[8] Certainly civil society includes the idea of democracy, but as a concept it is preferable to the latter because it is 'a more realistic notion, which specifies and includes its own conditions . . . Without these institutional preconditions, "democracy" has very little clear meaning or feasibility'.[9]

Gellner also tries to address the question of how is civil society possible at all? In his words, 'how is it possible to have atomization, individualism, without a political emasculation of the atomized man . . . and to have politically countervailing associations without these being stifling'.[10] Gellner's answer is found in his concept of the 'modular man', who despite his particular culture and value systems is able to blend effectively and cohesively with others whose cultures and values may be very different. Modern modular man is both individualistic and egalitarian. At the same time he is capable of associations which are effective without being rigid. What makes civil society is:

> the forging of links which are effective even though they are flexible, specific and instrumental . . . [Men] honour contracts even when they are not linked to ritualized status and group membership. Society is still a structure, it is not atomized, helpless and supine, and yet the structure is readily adjustable and responds to rational criteria of improvement.[11]

---

8.   *Ibid*, 184–9.
9.   *Ibid*, 189.
10. *Ibid*, 99.
11. *Ibid*, 100.

The modularity of modern man is thus a pre-condition for civil society, which is made up of institutions and associations strong enough to prevent oppression by the centre, and yet can be entered and left freely at will.

How did modular man emerge? Gellner recognises that according to the most influential sociological theory, modular man is a product of Protestantism. But he himself remains agnostic about modular man's ultimate origins.[12] Yet surely this is *the* question to which we must eventually return.

2. Asian values versus Western values

While the quest for civil society has been ongoing in Eastern Europe, a heated debate has been taking place largely in the context of East Asia about the relative merits of Asian values versus Western values. Much of the debate has centred around the issues of democracy, human rights, press freedom and the like, all of which are directly related to the discussion on civil society.[13] The debate however inevitably spilled over into the question of the relative superiority of the two sets of values as measured by the comparative successes of the respective economies in Asia and the West. In the aftermath of the Asian economic crisis in 1997, many Western commentators had a field day crowing over the apparent end of the challenge posed by Asian values to the West, as if the debate was settled by one crisis! However, today the picture is clearly very different.

Nevertheless, framed in competitive economic terms, the debate is in danger of taking on nasty ethnocentric and negative overtones. The key issue is a much more positive one. Asian leaders clearly recognise the strengths of the West. They certainly wish to emulate these societies in their scientific, technological and economic successes, as well as many of their cultural achievements—not least the civil liberties found in many Western societies. But they also wish to avoid the pitfalls of the West. Greg Sheridan points out that, from Asia's perspective, the values debate is really about Asian leaders asking:

> How can we become fully modern and affluent economies while avoiding some of the obvious social problems which have beset Western societies in recent decades? Or . . . how can we retain something (especially the feeling of community and the coherence of family structures) of our

12.   *Ibid,* 100f, 109.
13.   Kishore Mahbubani, *Can Asians Think?* (Kuala Lumpur: Times Books International, 1998), 57–80.

indigenous traditions as we experience the full effects of
rapid modernisation and Western consumerism?[14]

One clear expression of this central concern can be found in the 1994
National Day speech of the previous Singapore Prime Minister, Goh Chok
Tong:

> Singaporeans today enjoy full employment and high
> economic growth, and low divorce, illegitimacy and crime
> rates. You may think decline is unimaginable. But societies
> can go wrong quickly. US and British societies have
> changed profoundly in the last 30 years. Up to the early 60s
> they were disciplined, conservative, with the family very
> much the pillar of their societies. Since then both the US
> and Britain have seen a sharp rise in broken families,
> teenage mothers, illegitimate children, juvenile
> delinquency, vandalism and violent crime . . . Western
> liberals, foreign media and human rights groups also want
> Singapore to be like their societies and some Singaporeans
> mindlessly dance to their tune. See what happened to
> President Gorbachev because he was beguiled by their
> praise. Deng Xiaoping received their condemnation. But
> look at China today and see what has happened to the
> Soviet Union. Imploded! We must think for ourselves and
> decide what is good for Singapore. Above all we must stay
> away from policies which have brought a plague of social
> and economic problems to the US and Britain.[15]

Or, as Kishore Mahbubani puts it, good government is not necessarily
defined merely by Western perceptions of democracy and human rights.
Rather in Third World societies facing huge development demands, good
government must include '(1) political stability, (2) sound bureaucracies based
on meritocracy, (3) economic growth with equity, (4) fiscal prudence and (5)

---

14. Greg Sheridian, *Asian Values, Western Dreams: Understanding the New Asia*
     (St. Leonards, NSW: Allen and Unwin, 1999), 75.

15. Cited in Sheridian, *ibid*, 72f.

relative lack of corruption'.[16] These concerns also lie at the heart of the values debate today.

In the course of this debate, Asian leaders have urged the need to draw on indigenous cultural and religious values to provide the necessary underpinnings for nation-building. Lee Kuan Yew, the founding Prime Minister of Singapore, over the years has argued brilliantly on the interrelationship between values, culture, economic growth and social development.[17] His concern can be summed in part by the statement he once famously made, when he urged his fellow citizens to go back to Confucian values to prevent Singapore from becoming 'a nation of thieves and robbers'. Similarly, Mahathir Mohamad, the previous Prime Minister of Malaysia, has sought 'to harness the traditional moral virtues of Islam—thrift, honesty, family, fidelity, obedience, abstemiousness, communal solidarity—with the traditional Chinese and Japanese ingredients of East Asian economic success'.[18] Anwar Ibrahim further notes that the primary role given to religions in Asian societies will increasingly distinguish them from Western nations, because the Enlightenment has robbed religion of its power to effect cultural rejuvenation in the West.[19]

All these bring us back to the question of civil society, and what it is that makes it possible in the first place. As Gellner notes, the most influential theory credits Protestantism with its genesis. But in light of the values debate, the question must be asked whether Asian values by themselves also can provide the moral and cultural foundations upon which to build civil society? This is the question which we will now briefly explore.

3. Asian values and civil society

For the purpose of this essay, it would not be possible to cover the whole range of Asian religions and cultures, nor even any one religion or culture in detail. We will therefore look briefly at Islam and Chinese culture. But before we proceed it may be helpful for us to delineate for ourselves some of the key elements in what we call civil society here. These include the following:

---

16. Mahbubani, *op cit*, 49.
17. Sheridian, *op cit*, 9f, 67–72.
18. Sheridian, *op cit*, 92.
19. Anwar Ibrahim, *The Asian Renaissance* (Kuala Lumpur: Times Books International, 1996).

a) *Democratic Election of Government*: The government is elected by the people through the one-person, one-vote principle.

b) *Civil Liberties*: The fundamental rights and the equality of all members which are carefully safeguarded through unambiguous constitutional and legal guarantees, which challenges all forms of stifling communalism and wrongful restrictions on human freedom. Ideally, it will provide for individual freedoms without destroying family and community, and cultural and religious pluralism without fragmenting society.

c) *Separation of Powers*: An effective and stable central government which authority is balanced by countervailing institutions (for example, the constitution, law courts, and the press) and communities (for example, political parties and NGOs), that are not working in opposition to but, rather, in the interest of the state. This will prevent the central government becoming authoritarian and thereby reduce the rest of the society to helpless subservience.

d) *Economic Pluralism*: There is economic freedom, with state oversight and regulation to optimize efficiency and productivity, check unfair practices, and ensure a level playing field for all.

Given the above, can Islam or the Chinese tradition provide the necessary basis for civil society? We will look at them in turn.

3.1 Islam
In his discussion of Islam, Gellner notes that long before the West formulated the modern ideals of the separation of power and an entrenched constitution, Islam possessed both. The *Sharia* (formulated from the *Qu'ran* and the *Hadiths* via the Islamic rules of jurisprudence) occupied the role of the Constitution, and separation of powers was practiced because the ruler can and has been challenged in the name of the *Sharia*. Nevertheless, even today, Gellner argues that in practice:

> Muslim politics are pervaded by clientelism. There is a government-by-network. The formal institutional arrangements matter far less than do the informal

connections of mutual trust based on past personal services,
on exchange of protection from above for support from
below. Law governs the details of daily life, but not the
institutions of power . . . So, instead, society is ruled by
networks, quasi-tribes, alliances forged on the basis of kin,
services exchanged, common regional origin, common institutional experience, but still, in general, based on personal
trust . . . rather than on formal relations in a defined
bureaucratic structure.[20]

He goes on to comment that in Muslim societies, what is interesting is that
'this system is not much resented and is widely accepted as normal. What
strikes observers is the curious combination of religious moralism and cynical
clientelism'.[21] He sums up by suggesting that Islam 'exemplifies a social
order which seems to lack much capacity to provide political countervailing
institutions or associations, which is atomized without much individualism,
and operates effectively without intellectual pluralism'.[22]

Whether or not Gellner's observations are correct, what is clear is that
Islam has traditionally struggled with the issues of civil liberties and the
equality of minorities, especially of non-Muslims in particular. For example,
according to the *Sharia*, women do not have the same rights as men in family
and inheritance matters. Moreover in a court of law, a woman's testimony is
equal only to half that of a man. The treatment of non-Muslims in history as
dhimmis, that is, as 'protected peoples', without full civil rights has been fully
documented by different scholars.[23] This remains a serious problem today in
many parts of the Muslim world.

Islamic thought is clearly in ferment today. Whereas many Muslim leaders
are seeking a restatement of the *Sharia* in its original forms in Islamic states
today, others are wrestling with an understanding of Islam that is compatible
of modern conditions. The latter are calling for a new *ijtihad*, a reinter-
pretation of the classical sources of Islamic law as a means of revitalising

20.   Gellner, *op cit*, 26f.

21.   *Ibid*, 27.

22.   *Ibid*, 29.

23.   See especially Bat Ye'or, *The Dhimmi: Jews and Christians under Islam*, with
       preface by Jacques Ellul, translated from French by David Maisel, Paul Fenton
       and David Littman (London: Associated University Press, 1985), *Islam and
       Dhimmitude: Where Civilizations Collide*, translated from French by Miriam
       Kochan and David Littman (Madison, NJ: Fairleigh Dickinson University Press,
       2002) and other publications by the same author.

Islam in the world of today. The problem, however, is that the process of *ijtihad* is strictly forbidden within classical Islam, which had essentially fossilised the *Sharia* in the context of the early centuries of the Islamic era. The resulting tension is played out in different forms in the modern world.

Thus among Muslim thinkers, fundamental disagreements exist. For example, Ayatollah Ruhollah Khomeini, the first Shi'ite leader of post-revolution Iran, spent years crafting a philosophy of theocracy whereby clerics would create a perfect Muslim state and thereby turn their followers into perfect Muslims. But Grand Ayatollah Ali Sistani, the religious leader of a majority of today's Iraq's Shi'ite community rejects any role for clerics in the government of a country.[24] And although Sistani insists to his followers that no laws in the new Iraq should contradict Islam, he also says that 'there is nothing written in the *Qu'ran* about elections'.[25] For that he turns to textbooks on democracy. Again, like many Islamic intellectuals, Rachid Ghannoushi, a Tunisian exile, will agree that the rule of law, freedom and human rights are essential for modern societies, and that all are equal regardless of race, religion or creed. Yet he wants to maintain the traditional Islamic notion of non-Muslims as 'protected' people, and to provide for two classes of citizenship.[26] But there are others, like the leading Iranian scholar Abdolkarim Soroush, who insist that all citizens must have equal rights, irrespective of whether they are Muslims or not.[27] Indeed, Soroush has gone on to argue that the rule of law, human rights, civil society, increased freedom, political parties and democracy are essential for Iran's future.[28]

To sum up, whilst it must be noted that there may be many strengths and achievements in classical Islam on issues of justice, rule of law, human rights, and so forth, in and of itself it did not and could not produce civil society as defined here. Indeed for Islam to come to terms fully with civil society, people like Soroush must be taken seriously. But it is far from certain that this is where the majority of Muslims wish to go at the present.

---

24. 'What Sistani Wants', in *Newsweek* (14 February 2005): 13–17; here 15 and 17.
25. Cited in 'What Sistani Wants', *Newsweek* (14 February 2005): 17.
26. John L Esposito and John O Voll, *Makers of Contemporary Islam* (Oxford: Oxford University Press, 2001), 114f.
27. Valla Vakili, 'Abdolkarim Sorousch and Critical Discourse in Iran', in Esposito and Voll, *ibid*, 150–76; here 162f.
28. Vakili, *ibid*, 174f.

3.2 The Chinese tradition

One thinker who has wrestled rather more specifically with the relationship between the Chinese tradition and democracy (rather than civil society *per se*) is Hu Shih, a scholar of an earlier generation. In a paper first written in 1941, 'Historical Foundations for a Democratic China',[29] he lists three philosophical ideas and three historical institutions, which together can help provide a proper foundation for democracy. The most important philosophical idea is the Confucian concept of the essential goodness of human nature, which means that it is completely mouldable through education. This has help produced an almost classless society in China. The second democratic idea is that the right to rebel against tyrannical governments is warranted by the ancient classics. The third is that the subordinate has a sacred duty to criticise and oppose the wrong doings of one's superior.[30]

Building on the above, historically China developed three institutional practices which are important to democracy. First, through the abolishment of feudalism, the equal division of hereditary property (which especially limited the size of land holdings by any one person), an anti-mercantile tradition (which discouraged the emergence of a rich merchant class) and the ease with which the poor could rise to power, Chinese society developed a thoroughly democratised social structure. Second, the two thousand year old tradition of imperial examinations for the civil service meant that even the most humble village boy, with very limited means, could reach the highest echelons of social and political life. Third, the office of the Imperial Censor and the implementation of similar practices at various levels of state administration provided the government with its own 'opposition' to check malpractice.[31] For Hu Shih, these are the foundations upon which China can build a democratic future.

Here again, as with Islam, we see clearly cultural values which can be drawn upon for the building of civil society. Whether in themselves they provide a sufficient foundation for civil society cannot be answered in this short space. A much more detailed study of the Chinese tradition would need to be undertaken. Certainly there were many negative factors in traditional Chinese society that militate against civil society, such as the subjugation of women and the tendency towards authoritarian totalitarianism by the central government, to name but two. But what can be said with certainty is that civil

---

29.   Hu Shih, *The Chinese Renaissance,* bilingual edition (Beijing: Foreign Language Teaching and Research Press, 2001), 295–314 (English) and 315–26 (Chinese).

30.   *Ibid,* 296–8.

31.   *Ibid,* 299–314.

society did not emerge in China throughout its long history, despite its great cultural achievements in many other spheres. Where it is now seen in some form or other in places like Taiwan, it can be argued that it is more the result of Western impact than an indigenous development of its own based on Confucian values.

Earlier we noted Lee Kuan Yew's appeal to the Confucian tradition. I think it would be fair to say that Lee's concern is not primarily about building civil society but rather about good government. He thus uses the Confucian tradition of a wise and benevolent patriarch ruling over the family as the ideal and model for the government's relation to the citizen. Moreover, he sees in the Confucian values of respect for authority, filial piety, thrift, education, and harmony in home and society as crucial to national development.[32] This is not to say that Lee is not interested in civil society. For him, it is a matter of which has priority: national development and economic growth or issues like human rights, unbridled press freedom, and the like. Based on a comparison between China and Russia over the last fifteen years, one is tempted to say that Lee and others like him may well be right. Even Gellner seems to agree:

> The cold Chinese calculation that economic improve-ments must come first and that political changes . . . must wait, is not something which warms one's heart. The sad thing is that, alas, it may well be the correct strategy: a prosperous and visibly growing country can eventually liberalize with impunity, whereas liberalization in a period of economic deterioration and crisis . . . may well lead to some new kind of dictatorship.[33]

But herein also lies a danger. As Goh Chok Tong noted in his quoted speech above, societies can change very fast. In US and Britain, family and social breakdowns of all kinds have greatly accelerated in the decades after the 1960s. Or, take the example of Pakistan. At its independence in 1947, Pakistan had a national constitution, which is similar to Malaysia's on civil liberties and religious freedom. Yet things within a few years in the 1970s, under a military dictatorship which introduced an Islamic constitution, religious minorities became severely oppressed. History has demonstrated again and again that the slide towards either centralised authoritarianism or

---

32. Sheridian, *op cit*, 9.
33. Gellner, *op cit*, 181.

anarchy can take place almost overnight. The one sufficient safeguard against such occurrences is when a nation matures into one that is characterised by civil society. Thus even if we prioritise national development and economic growth for the moment, the goal of attaining civil society should always be clearly set before us and sought after conscientiously.

It is at this point that we need to come back to the question that Gellner posed: What made civil society possible? His answer is found in modular man. But what led to his emergence in Western civilisation? Gellner's answer is that 'it does not matter for our present purposes: what matters for us is that modular man has emerged and helped bring about Civil Society'.[34] But surely this is inadequate. For after all, modular man is not found everywhere in the modern world. Nevertheless, he is essential to the development of civil society. By refusing to address the question of how modular man—as he defines it—came into existence, Gellner provides no help to those who are seeking to bring about the emergence of civil society within our own cultures and nations. After all, man does not become 'modular' within a moral and cultural vacuum!

Thus, despite Gellner's professed indifference to the fact that Protestantism may be the possible answer for the emergence of civil society, we need to pursue this matter. After all, as we have seen, despite the elements that can contribute to civil society found in Islamic and the Chinese traditions, civil society did not emerge from within these or any other culture apart from the West, shaped as it is in large measure by its Christian heritage. For if we are serious in wanting our own nations to become civil societies, it would be wise for us to ask how that came about in the only one place where we meet it in human history.

4. Christianity and the emergence of civil society

Without going into details, what appears almost certain is that the foundational ideas, upon which the modern Western liberal vision of society or civil society is based, had gradually emerged over the past two thousand years in Western civilisation, largely as a result of its Christian experience. Many of these ideas are theologically rooted in the Christian understanding of God and humanity, and were brought together at the time of or soon after the Reformation. For example, democracy and universal franchise reflect the Christian concept of humans as each having a dignity premised on our being

---

34.   *Ibid*, 101.

created in God's image. Or, as one writer in *The Economist* puts it in another way:

> Democracy is the child of the Reformation . . . The Reformation declared that every individual was responsible before God for the way he lived his life. Priests might say what they thought God wanted, but in the end it was the individual who decided.
> It took almost three centuries for that proposition to work its way through into the realm of politics, but when it did the result was, literally, revolutionary . . . It was the people themselves who would decide. Each man and woman would have an equal voice in making the people's decision. That is democracy.[35]

Similarly, the idea of having checks and balances in government is rooted in the Christian doctrine of sin which recognises that no person, however good, should be trusted with absolute powers. The importance of the need for countervailing institutions to check the power of the government is so firmly held in John Calvin's Switzerland, for example, that to this day, although the administrative capital is in Berne, the Supreme Court is located elsewhere in Lausanne!

Again, Harold Berman, the doyen of American scholars on the relationship between religion and law, has argued that it was people like the Calvinistic Puritans of the seventeenth century, who carried forward the Lutheran concept of the sanctity of the individual conscience and thereby helped lay the foundations of the English and American laws of civil rights and liberties.[36] In the history of the evolution and life of Western society, law and religion were simply inseparable. As Berman notes, the great principles of the Western legal tradition were largely created by the impact of Western civilisation's Christian history. These include:

> The principle of civil disobedience, the principle of law reform in the direction of greater humanity, the principle of the coexistence of diverse legal systems, the principle of

---

35. 'Islam and the West: A Survey', *The Economist* (6 August 1994): 1–18; here 13.
36. Harold Berman, *The Interaction of Law and Religion* (London: SCM Press, 1974), 66f.

the conformity of law to a system of morals, the principle
of the sanctity of property and contract rights based on
intent, the principle of freedom of conscience, the principle
of legal limitations on the power of rulers, the principle of
the responsibility of the legislature to public opinion, the
principle of predictability of the legal consequences of
social and economic actions, as well as newer socialist
principles of the priority of state interests and of public
welfare.[37]

He goes on to argue that:

These principles may appear to some to be self-evident
truths, and to others they may appear to be utilitarian
policies, but for Western man as a whole they are, above
all, *historical achievements created mainly out of the
experience of the Christian church in the various stages of
its life . . . These successive ages of the church have
created the psychological basis, and many of the values,
upon which the legal systems of democracy and socialism
rest* [my emphasis].[38]

Finally, Max Weber's thesis on the contribution of Protestant ethics to the
rise of capitalism and economic growth in the modern world, though still
questioned in some circles, has found strong support in many others.[39] This is
yet another of the foundational ideas upon which civil society is founded—
maximum economic freedom, coupled with proper state regulation, to protect
the weak as well as to provide a level playing field.

Admittedly, some of these ideas have also emerged in fragmented forms
throughout history in various societies, not all of which were Christian.
Further, within Western civilisation itself, after the Reformation, these ideas
were further shaped by secular and other forces. But what is beyond doubt is

---

37. *Ibid*, 72.

38. *Ibid*, 72f.

39. See Alister E McGrath, *Reformation Thought: An Inroduction*, second edition
     (Oxford: Blackwell, 1993), 220–7, for an Oxford historical theologian's
     comments; and David S Landes, *The Wealth and Poverty of Nations: Why Some
     are So Rich and Some So Poor* (New York: WW Norton, 1998), 174–9, for a
     Harvard economist's historical analysis.

that no other culture or society, in Asia and elsewhere, built upon a non-Christian basis has ever evolved the same comprehensive vision in and of itself. Its emergence in the modern world, underpinned by a strong legal framework which was developed to protect it from being compromised, presupposes the whole experience of the history of Western civilisation, which was strongly impacted by and undeniably shaped by Christianity.

Despite Gellner's agnosticism, it is difficult to deny that herein is found the roots of civil society. As he himself notes, the democratic ideal is not natural to the human condition.[40] Civil society can only emerge in the context of a certain set of preconditions. That set of preconditions is defined by the finely-tuned social balance that came about through the coming together of specific laws and a particular moral vision, undergirded, in Western history, by a certain set of religious beliefs. Indeed, today in the West this balance is in serious danger of falling apart, with militant secularists bent on ejecting religion from public life, with its accompanying dire consequences. This is precisely what people like Richard J Neuhaus are seeking to draw Western society's attention to. Writing out of late twentieth century American context, he pleads with cogent urgency:

> This, then, is the burden of our historical moment—to be facing moral dilemmas of unprecedented complexity at a time when we are inclined to throw away compass and map and to scuttle the ship. In our public life we are feverishly engaged in moral disarmament when the battle for what it means to be human, for the *humanum*, has not yet reached its peak. We cannot rely upon law alone. The great atrocities of our century were all perpetrated with the color of law, from Hitler to Stalin . . . The law is a friendly fellow, amenable to our wishes, plastic in the hands of the powerful. Nor can we rely upon moral sentiment alone, for as it can in rare instances move from vice to virtue it does more frequently move from abhorrence to the embrace of wickedness . . .What is required is law combined with moral sentiments that is rooted in a tradition of belief. Moral sentiment that is not grounded, institutionalized, and transmitted in a living tradition is always subjected to becoming mere sentimentality. Such living traditions

---

40.   Gellner, *op cit*, 186f.

cannot be created *ex nihilo* . . . When in our public life no
legal prohibition can be articulated with the force of
transcendental authority, then there are no rules rooted in
ultimacies that can protect the poor, the powerless, and the
marginal . . .Our problems, then, stem in large part from the
philosophical and legal efforts to isolate and exclude the
religious dimension of our culture.[41]

If the above is correct, then two conclusions follow. First, with respect to
the present values debate, it would clearly mean that a resolution can only be
found if we are willing to look beyond what is merely Asian or Western to that
which is properly transcendental! Second, many of us in the non-Western
world have taken for granted that civil society with its accompanying
democratic practices, which we have inherited in various forms through our
national constitutions drawn up at the time of national independence, will
somehow remain with us always. In this we may be badly mistaken. The high
incidence of nations, which began with such constitutions, sliding backwards
into some form or other of dictatorship, authoritarianism or 'guided
democracy' in the world today should warn us that we cannot take our present
liberties and blessings for granted. We need to be reminded that civil society
has to be rooted in certain moral values and religious beliefs, and adequately
protected by appropriate laws and institutions. These are the fundamental
preconditions for its emergence. Those of us who are concerned with building
civil society must ask how we may labour incessantly to help bring about
these preconditions within our communities, and to maintain a vigilant watch
at ensuring that these are strengthened, protected and preserved. What
implications all this has for us in Asia as we 'Seek the Welfare of the City' in
our respective nations is something that we must wisely ponder together!

---

41.   Richard John Neuhaus, *The Naked Public Square: Religion and Democracy in
       America*, second edition (Grand Rapids: Eerdmans, 1986), 151–5.

9

Resident Aliens and Alienated Residents

Daniel KS Koh

1. Introduction

Is there a place for Christian social engagement in the public square? This has been a question occupying the minds of not just Christian social ethicists and political philosophers, but also politicians and informed laypersons in Singapore.[1] It is a pertinent question to ask, especially in the context of a society that claims to be both plural and secular, and where the Christians are in the minority, and therefore theoretically, may be easier to silence by, say, a coercive state or agents of the state. In some ways, without having an affirmative answer to the question which I have posed, it might seem like a waste of time for anyone to consider secondary questions of how Christians should go about being socially engaged.

I write as one who is convinced that Christians should be aware of the affairs of the world, not as detached observers, but as participative people who are interested in the welfare of fellow human beings. That means that those who name Jesus as Saviour and Lord ought to be engaged in debates, both in the church as well as in the public square, as an extension and an expression of who we are, that is, our identity as responsible and faithful disciples of

---

1. See a sample of letters and articles in *The Straits Times*, the main English language newspaper in Singapore: Aletheia Woon Cheng Chan, 'Why Govt should listen to religious opinions', *The Straits Times* (Singapore), 22 February 2005; Li-Ann Thio, 'In a democracy, all have a right to be heard', *The Straits Times* (Singapore), 22 February 2005; *idem,* 'The responsibility imposed by free speech', *The Straits Times* (Singapore), 28 April 2005. See also, 'Politics, religion must be kept separate: Balakrishnan', *TODAY* (Singapore), 4 May 2005. The comment was attributed to Dr Vivian Balakrishnan, the Minister for Community Development, Youth and Sports, who spoke at a conference organised by the Institute of Defence and Strategic Studies, Singapore.

Jesus Christ.[2] This is also to say that social engagement of the participative people is another dimension of Christian witness in a world tarnished by sin and sometimes mired in religion-inflicted violence, though it is still God's world and a world loved by him.

2. Hauerwas and 'resident aliens'

In the main, when Christians, as students of the Bible, read about 'aliens' and 'strangers', they would not pay excessive or particular attention to those two terms. There is nothing in the Bible or in the Christian tradition to suggest that these are the only two groups of people—both in the actual descriptive sense and in the theological-metaphorical sense—to whom we have to give preferential attention. In fact, the metaphor, 'resident aliens', catchy though it is, like any faddish term might have been easily forgotten or consigned to some inaccessible pages of certain obscure journals or books of interest only to limited number of students, had it been used or uttered by some lesser known authors. Who among the uninitiated would have heard, for example, of the one who wrote the Epistle to Diognetus, a second century document? This anonymous writer, probably influenced by Petrine teaching, offers a piece of pastoral comment, which has now become a favoured reference among some contemporary theologians.[3] Christians, the anonymous writer tells us, 'reside in their respective countries, but only as aliens. They take part in everything as citizens and put up with everything as foreigners. Every foreign land is their home, and every home a foreign land'.[4]

If the Epistle to Diognetus, that develops the Petrine idea of Christians as aliens, has regained favour among scholars doing research in ecclesiology, theological and social ethics, we may attribute this interest in Diognetus to the popularity of Stanley Hauerwas. He and William Willimon, his one-time colleague at Duke University, co-authored the readable book, *Resident Aliens:*

---

2. For example, Daniel KS Koh, 'The State of Morality and the Morality of the State', in *A Graced Horizon,* edited by Roland Chia and Mark Chan (Singapore: Genesis Books, 2005), 221–32.

3. For example, Richard John Neuhaus, 'Foreword', in *Building the Free Society,* edited by George Weigel and Robert Royal (Grand Rapids: Eerdmans, 1993), xviii; Roland Chia, 'Resident Aliens: Some Reflections on Church and Society', *Transformation,* 17/3 (2000): 92–8; and Alan Kreider, 'Initiation: Becoming Resident Aliens', Bethel College, http://www.bethelks.mennonitelife/2002june/kreider.php (accessed 8 August 2005).

4. *The Epistle to Diognetus* 5.5, in *Ancient Christian Writers,* edited by James A Kleist, volume 6, (New York: Paulist Press, 1948), 139.

Life in the Christian Colony, which re-introduced us to the idea of Christians as 'resident aliens'. Interestingly, there is an intriguing and longish sub-title which asserts that the book is 'a provocative Christian assessment of culture and ministry for people who know that something is wrong'.[5] The interest and provocation generated by the book and its clever title has contributed, in no small measure, to the association of the idea of 'resident aliens' with Hauerwas' theological ethics, which is highly critical of, principally, post-enlightenment American Christian social ethical engagement, and especially the social ethics said to be influenced by Reinhold Niebuhr.[6]

There is however a downside to Hauerwas' close association with the idea of 'resident aliens' which, as far as I am aware, no one from outside the Euro-North American world has addressed. The downside which I am referring to is that the emphasis on 'resident aliens', as a sheltered people living 'in a Christian colony',[7] as Willimon and Hauerwas have presented, has given support, perhaps unintentionally, to those who take an explicit stand that Christians should not be socially engaged. They may be right in reminding us of our special identity as Christians, or, to use their popularised term, resident aliens. But Christians, as resident aliens (in the sense that we have been invited by God and initiated into his tradition-forming faith community called the church), while obviously different from 'others,' should not be so insulated and isolated by our own search for an unblemished peculiar narrative, that we give reasons for others to view us not so much as resident aliens but as alienated residents—ones who have deliberately distanced ourselves from a wider participative role of fostering the common good.[8] This would not have been an issue if, in fact, it is Hauerwas' view that Christians should not be socially engaged, as he has sometimes been accused of holding such a view. But he has asserted that that is not his stand,[9] although what he

---

5.   Stanley Hauerwas and William H Willimon, *Resident Aliens: Life in the Christian Colony: A Provocative Christian Assessment of Culture and Ministry for People Who Know that Something is Wrong* (Nashville: Abingdon Press, 1989). They later co-authored a sequel, *Where Resident Aliens Live* (Nashville: Abingdon, 1996).

6.   Stanley Hauerwas, *With the Grain of the Universe* (Grand Rapids: Brazos, 2001).

7.   Hauerwas and Willimon, *op cit*, 69ff.

8.   Kah Soon Daniel Koh, 'Genetic Science, the Person and the Common Good', in *Beyond Determinism and Reductionism,* edited by Mark Chan and Roland Chia (Adelaide: ATF Press, 2003), 128f.

9.   In an interview with the Institute for Global Engagement on 15 February 2002, when it was pointed out to him that he has been labelled as a 'pacifist', a

has written and his sometimes combative and provocative style may have, unfortunately, given rise to that impression, or raised doubt about his assertions.[10]

3. Purpose of this essay

The purpose of this paper is to examine the metaphor, 'resident aliens,' briefly in the context of 1 Peter and to a lesser extent in the context of the Epistle to Diognetus. More critically, however, this metaphor will be placed and discussed in the context of an Asian plural society where the Christian faith is still relatively young and often viewed by many people with suspicion. If anything, because of the baggage which a metaphor like 'resident aliens' unwittingly carries, there is a need to scrutinise the metaphor and critique its usage by theologians in our contemporary world. It is also my aim to show how such an idea may or may not be helpful for social engagement as faithful Christian witness in a plural society, and at the same time, we shall point to other metaphors from the Bible which may be more appropriate for Christian participation in a modern multi-faith Asian society like Singapore.

'sectarian', and a 'fideistic tribalist', Hauerwas declared, 'I am a Christian. I get those kind of labels because I am trying to remind Christians that what it means to be a Christian and what it means to be an American are not the same thing. Many people interpret that as a kind of withdrawal strategy, but I'm not withdrawing. I have no difficulty with Christians being involved with politics. I just want them to be there as Christians.' See Stanley Hauerwas, 'Faithfulness First', Institute for Global Engagement, http://www.globalengagement.org/issues/2002/02 /hauerwas-p.htm (accessed 8 August 2005).

10.   We can agree that our 'first task is not to make the world better or more just', as he reminds us in *A Community of Character* (Notre Dame: University of Notre Dame Press, 1981), 74. But issues like doing good, helping to make the world 'better' and 'just' are not foreign to Christians. There may be conflicting ideas as to what constitute 'good', 'better', and 'just'. Some of those ideas may be articulated by outstanding minds whose presupposition and *telos* are completely different from Hauerwas' view, for example, the Rawlsian theory of justice. But the Bible speaks about justice, quite forcefully as well, even if it is not considered as our first task. And if justice in the Rawlsian perspective is a bad idea, as he suggests that it is (in his chapter, 'The Politics of Justice: Why Justice is a Bad Idea', in *After Christendom?* (Nashville: Abingdon, 1991), 45–68) what about justice implied in James and spoken by Amos and Micah? Or 'justice' as discussed in Duncan B Forrester, *Christian Justice and Public Policy* (Cambridge: Cambridge University Press, 1997)?

4. 'Resident aliens' in 1 Peter

The verse with the phrase *paroikous kai parepidēmous*, translated in the New International Version as 'aliens and strangers',[11] in 1 Peter 2:11 reads: 'Dear friends, I urge you, as aliens and strangers in the world, to abstain from sinful desires, which war against your soul'. These 'aliens and strangers' were the Christian diaspora (1:1) who were probably discriminated[12] against by adherents of established religious groups and the political authorities of the time. The discrimination that marginalised early Christians came about, because of and, after their conversion to the Christian faith.[13] Clearly, the author was aware of the challenge posed by widespread discrimination against Christians. He was perturbed enough to write this pastoral letter reminding

---

11. Translated as 'strangers and pilgrims' (King James Version), and 'aliens and exiles' (Revised Standard Version). However, another helpful way of translating the two words is to render the first as 'resident aliens' and the second as 'visiting aliens'. See Troy W Martin, *Metaphor and Composition in 1 Peter* (Atlanta: Scholar Press, 1992), 191. Oddly, in the New International Version, while the translator(s) retains 'strangers' for *parepidemoi* (1:1), *paroikoi* was translated, not as 'aliens' but as 'strangers' in 1:17.

12. L Goppelt, *Theology of the New Testament*, volume 2, translated by John Alsup (Grand Rapids: Eerdmans, 1982), 161ff. Though it should be clear, however to avoid confusion, when 'discrimination' or its verb form is used here, we mean negative discrimination.

13. John H Elliot, *A Home for the Homeless* (London: SCM Press, 1982) puts forward the idea that the early Christians, mentioned in 1 Peter, were marginalised people—the real 'aliens' and 'strangers'—before they became Christians. These people found in Christianity a 'home' to which they could belong. In other words, in Elliot's sociological construct, discrimination was not the result of conversion, but a continuation of discrimination of people who were literally regarded as 'aliens' and 'strangers'. See also his *1 Peter* (New York: Doubleday, 2000), 101. Elliot's assumption is not widely followed. Most scholars, however, see discrimination as targeted against the followers of Jesus Christ who came from different social backgrounds. It is granted that included among them were people who were poor and socially disadvantaged, the literal 'aliens' and 'strangers'. See I Howard Marshall, *1 Peter* (Downers Grove: IVP, 1991), 24; Paul J Achtemeier, *1 Peter* (Minneapolis: Fortress Press, 1996), 55ff; and Eileen Poh, 'The Conflicting Demands of Gospel and Culture: Another Look at 1 Peter 2:13–17', in *A Graced Horizon*, edited by Roland Chia and Mark Chan (Singapore: Genesis Books, 2005), 11f.

Christians under his care of their true identity *vis-à-vis* the competing claims and counter-claims of the world.

As 'aliens and strangers' Christians were different from the rest of the people because they were born into 'the living hope through the resurrection of Jesus Christ from the dead (1:3)'. However, it is clear that although Christians were to see themselves as 'aliens and strangers,' a new status acquired after their journey from darkness to light (2:9), these were not the only metaphors, nor were they the crucial metaphors describing their identity and new status as followers of Jesus Christ. Other metaphors were also used by the author to illustrate this newly acquired difference and identity for Christians. Elsewhere the writer had informed the original recipients of his letter that they were 'God's elect' and the 'scattered,' or the 'diaspora' (1:1). With regard to their status, they were still considered as infants in faith or 'newborn babies' (2:2). And they were, as a new community of faith, God's 'chosen people,' a 'holy priesthood,' a 'holy nation' and a 'people belonging to God (2:9)'.[14]

How then are Christians to understand this difference and identity, informed by various Petrine metaphors? Perhaps we should turn to Miroslav Volf for a helpful explanation. Volf captures it well when he says:

> I suggest that the crucial question is not to what degree one stresses difference, but rather on what basis Christian identity is established. Identity can be forged through two related but clearly distinct processes: either through a negative process of rejecting beliefs and practices of others, or through a positive process of giving allegiance to something distinctive. It is significant that 1 Peter consistently establishes the difference positively, not negatively. There are no direct injunctions not to behave as non-Christians do. Rather, the exhortation to be different centers primarily on the positive example of a holy God (1:15f) and of the suffering Christ (2:21ff). This is surprising, especially given the situation of social conflict in which the Petrine community was engaged. We expect injunctions to reject the ways of the world; instead we find admonitions to follow the path of Christ.[15]

---

14. See Poh, *ibid*, 11.

15. Mirslav (sic) Volf, 'Soft Difference: Theological Reflections on the Relation Between Church and Culture in 1 Peter', North Park Theological Seminary,

Christians are different not so much as a reaction against others or a rejection of what others believe and advocate, but because of who we are, as followers of Jesus Christ. That is the positive explication of our difference as people called by God who still hold membership in this world, though this membership, reflected in the idea of 'resident aliens' may sometimes be ambivalent and disconcerting. On the other hand, a negative reactionary approach to understanding the Christian difference may lead to violence. Volf is insightful here. He shares an observation for his preference for the positive approach of how Christians should understand their difference and identity. According to him:

> The faith of the Petrine community is nourished more on its own intrinsic vision than on the deprecatory stories of others . . . When identity is forged primarily through the negative process of the rejection of the beliefs and practices of others, violence seems unavoidable, especially in situations of conflict. We have to push others away from ourselves and keep them at a distance, and we have to close ourselves off from others to keep ourselves pure of their taint.[16]

The positive view of Christian difference and identity is what Volf has in mind when he talks about 'soft difference'. It is a difference of a confident people that openly allows for social engagement without having to press for a stark choice of either accepting or rejecting, prematurely, the presuppositions of others or the perimeter in which Christians have to interact with others. Volf got it right when he says that such a stance may be 'soft' but it is not 'weak'. Instead it is reflective of a people 'who are secure in themselves— more accurately, who are secure in their God—(and) are able to live the soft difference without fear'.[17]

What we have done, so far in this section, is to show that the variety of metaphors used by the author of 1 Peter to help discriminated Christians during his time have a deeper and broader understanding of who they were, not so much to cut them off from their interaction and relationship with people

---

http://campus.northpark.edu/sem/exauditu/papers/volf.html (accessed 8 August 2005).

16. *Ibid.*
17. *Ibid.*

of other faiths and those with no religious affiliation, but in the hope that with this self-understanding, they might at least be able to cope with suffering, when it befalls them, as a shared suffering with Christ (4:13), and to do so without ceasing 'to do good' (4:19).

On the matter of 'doing good' there is a sagacious resemblance, a contextual paraphrase of sort, between this Petrine advice, 'Live such good lives among the pagans that, though they accuse you of doing wrong, they may see your good deeds and glorify God on the day he visits us' (2:12), and the call of Jesus Christ in Matthew 5:16, 'Let your light shine before men, that they may see your good deeds and praise your Father in heaven'. It seems obvious that 'doing good deeds' for the sake of wider societal benefit is not an option for Christians. If anything, in advising the Christians to continue to do good, in spite of being discriminated against, 1 Peter does not allow for Christians to take leave from the world in which they reside nor should Christians be overly concerned about drawing their boundaries to demarcate their spheres of interest in the public square.

5. 'Resident aliens' in the contemporary world

If Christians as 'aliens,' whether 'resident aliens' or 'visiting aliens', are understood to be people who have been discriminated by others, as the original recipients of 1 Peter were discriminated against, then being able to hold on to that Petrine identity as 'resident aliens' and 'visiting aliens' can be reassuring. Christians, in a sense, were unreasonably pushed to a corner. In such a discriminatory situation, knowing that they were not exactly citizens of this world must have given them the spiritual resources and eschatological reserve to persevere and to remain faithful. That identity as 'aliens' provides strength and solace in the face of unfair discrimination against Christians for no other reasons than because they are Christians who seek to be faithful followers of Christ and the teachings of his church.

It is possible that just as Christians in ancient 'Pontus, Galatia, Cappadocia, Asia and Bithynia' (1:1) were discriminated against, there will be countries where Christians are discriminated and persecuted because they believe in Jesus Christ. In such countries—for example in the former Union of the Soviet Socialist Republics or in a non-Christian theocratic country that favours only one dominant religion—where Christians are not granted the freedom to share the Gospel or to worship openly, and where churches are not allowed to be built, it makes sense, under those circumstances, for Christians to see themselves as 'resident aliens' and be comforted by that self-identity.

Bear in mind that when Christians as 'resident aliens' are discriminated against in an oppressive society, it is discrimination that is imposed on them by others usually for no justifiable reason other than because they are Christians. When that happens, civil privileges of Christians are usually curtailed and basic freedom of worship restricted. In extreme situations, force may be used against Christians to coerce them to denounce their faith or to stop them from practising their faith.

But what seems odd for an observer in Asia, however, is the use of 'resident aliens' coming out of the Euro-North American world where the church is allowed to thrive almost unimpeded, in situation where freedom is available for people to decide what they want to believe and where to build their places of worship. Compared with the world of 1 Peter, or even the time when the Epistle to Diognetus was written, Christians in Euro-North America 'have had it good' in the sense that they can practise and propagate their faith without blatant or subtle discrimination. If anything, Christians in Euro-North America are privileged people. In the main, they enjoy greater favour than followers of other faiths in Euro-North America and Christians in many countries in the Two-Thirds World, though such favours may sometimes be considered, or perhaps ridiculed, as residues of a church which has lost her nerve, her cutting edge and her unique identity as a church redeemed by Christ. 'Resident aliens' in the context used by Hauerwas and Willimon is therefore not, in a significant sense, a reference to the kind of 'resident aliens' who were openly discriminated against.[18] There is a twist to the understanding of 'resident aliens' emanating from Hauerwas and Willimon. For them, 'resident aliens' seem to be a badge that differentiates those Christians who reject the influence and infiltration of the dominant ideology of a post-enlightenment West. Specifically, to be a 'Resident Alien' in the Hauerwasian term is to reject the philosophical liberal ideology which has seduced a Constantinised church. For them to be a faithful Christian is not the same as being a protector of American interest or to champion the pervasive political liberal ideology that has shaped the American life, so favoured by the academia.

The often strident criticism—a hard stand, we may call it—against a Constantinised church may be seen as attempts to draw clear lines between

---

18. The 'resident aliens' of Euro-North America are materially and socio-politically different from the 'resident aliens' mentioned in 1 Peter. This point is understood by Howard Marshall who said, 'There are many places in the world where contemporary readers of 1 Peter live in circumstances much more like that of the original readers (of 1 Peter) than is the case for Christians in North America and Europe', in Marshall, *op cit*, 25.

those who are faithful Christians; the 'resident aliens,' and those who have strayed away from what the faithful church ought to be. These are efforts to reclaim the peculiar character of the church as church and not as the mirror-image or mouthpiece of political interest and nihilistic vision drawn from outside the church. The church has a peculiar identity and difference[19] which we ought to retrieve from the absorbing power of post-enlightenment false promise. This peculiarity is a difference which we should reclaim and celebrate—a *vive la différence*.

Interestingly, in the Euro-North American world, such a harsh criticism of the Constantinisation of the church is facilitated by a political liberal society still in many important ways sympathetic to and informed by Christian values, even if those values are residues of a more influential Christian past. The irony which should not escape us is that it is the liberal society, undergirded by a hybrid of liberal political philosophies, that allows for, and in some ways underwrites, the kind of project which we see coming out of the Euro-North American world. For without such a society that offers certain democratic rights and freedom of expression, important voices like Willimon, Hauerwas and those associated with the Radical Orthodoxy movement[20] would not have been given the ecclesial and academic platform to speak their minds, even in languages which may seem impolite. That is not a privilege and luxury which the 'resident aliens' of 1 Peter and Diognetus' time and those 'resident aliens' living in oppressive societies of our time have enjoyed. It still has to be remembered that the Petrine 'resident aliens' and those mentioned in the Epistle to Diognetus were Christians who were socially and politically disadvantaged and discriminated by others. However, in the contemporary setting of Euro-North America, the 'resident aliens' are ordinarily privileged people who, if they were disadvantaged or discriminated, can still openly exercise their civil and legal rights to address those wrongs without fear of added threats to their general well-being and freedom of worship. Christianity is still widely recognised and accepted as part of what shaped Europe and North America. Even if it has been Constantinised, it is not a religious faith that is foreign to Europeans or Americans.

---

19. For those who find the Hauerwasian emphasis on peculiarity and difference too hard, if not harsh, we have already indicated that Mirslav Volf offers an alternative perspective, using 1 Peter, that stresses what he calls a 'soft difference'. See Mirslav Volf, *op cit.*

20. *Radical Orthodoxy*, edited by John Milbank, Catherine Pickstock and Graham Ward (London: Routledge, 1999), 3f.

6. 'Resident aliens' in a plural Asian context

Except for the Philippines and Timor-Leste, which are predominantly, though some may argue nominally, Roman Catholic, Christians are in the minority in most Asian countries. In Singapore, the majority of the population is of Chinese origin. Fifty-one per cent of resident Singaporeans above fifteen year-old consider themselves Buddhists or Taoists, while most if not all Malays are Muslims (14.9% of the total population), and the Indians are largely Hindus (4%). Christians—sixteen per cent of the Chinese population and twelve per cent of the Indian population—constitute about fifteen per cent of the total population.[21] A population census taken in 2000 showed that though the Christian population is relatively small in Singapore, compared with adherents of other faiths, Christians are, nevertheless, people who are better educated, holding better paid jobs and staying in more expensive houses. In other words, while in the minority, Christians do enjoy a disproportionately bigger share of the socio-economic cake. For example, one out of three university graduates in 2000 was a Christian,[22] and thirty-four per cent of the more expensive apartments and houses are owned by Christians.[23] Though Christians in Singapore are in the minority, many of them have enjoyed wide material benefits and favourable career development which make them, in the main, members of a privileged minority.

As a country Singapore is extremely small and yet, relatively speaking, it is an economically vibrant island republic, located in a politically sensitive and sometimes volatile region surrounded by countries much larger in geographical size and population. Indonesia to the south has the largest population of Muslims in the world. Malaysia in the immediate north has a strong Islamic presence. Thailand, Myanmar, Cambodia and Vietnam further north, are mainly Buddhists. Further afield, China and India, two countries with the world's largest populations, are homes to some of the world's oldest and richest cultures with long-held religious traditions which continue to attract strong followings and provide the social ideology and belief system that shape and sustain the lives of Indians and Chinese. India is basically Hindu, while China, Japan and Korea still have deep Confucian-Buddhist influence. Confucian teachings, Buddhism and Hinduism, for example, have

---

21. Bee Geok Leow, *Census of Population 2000: Advanced Data Release* (Singapore: Singapore Department of Statistics, 2001), 33ff.

22. *Ibid*, 37.

23. *Ibid*, 39.

had a longer continuous presence and larger number of adherents in South and East Asia than Christianity. That is the kind of formidable plural world surrounding Singapore which Christians should be aware of, and interact with.

It is true that the Christian faith originated from West Asia, and made early attempts to reach other regions of Asia, evidenced, for instance, by the presence of the Mar Thoma Church in India and the Nestorian foray into China, but significant missionary works and wider church presence in Asia started relatively late. It took more than 1,800 years before the faith returned and began to expand in countries, in the continent of its birth, via Europe and North America, this time clothed with additional layers of Euro-North American cultural garbs and prejudices.

One negative memory of the missionary arrivals in the eighteenth and nineteenth century Asia that coincided with European expansionist strategies, unfortunately, is the association of Christianity with colonial gunboat diplomacy. This association, no doubt sometimes exaggerated,[24] has unwittingly contributed to the making of an entrenched myth in the popular folklore and political narratives of post-colonial Asia that insinuates Christian faith as a Western religion. The sub-texts of such a myth and their subtle variance, raise questions about the true identity of Asians who adopted a 'foreign' and therefore, an 'alien' religion; a religion of their past colonial masters and what some see as the present arrogant decadent West, represented by the United States of America.

To complicate matters, Christians in Singapore have not been helpful in debunking the myth of the faith being a foreign religion that propagates Western values.[25] From observations as a theologian-pastor for some twenty-five years, most Christians in Singapore tend to be indifferent to or uncritical in embracing teachings, primarily imported from the West.[26] This problem

---

24. For example, see comment in Titus Presler, *Horizons of Mission* (Cambridge: Cowley Publications, 2001), 140.

25. References to 'Western values' have in the past been used as a 'straw-man' by nationalist ideologues or people who hold the view that some form of 'Asian values'; Confucian values, for example, are more desirable than the more liberal 'Western values'. We are not using this term here in any derogative or ethnocentric way—see Roland Chia, 'Resident Aliens', *op cit*, 97—but to point to the existence of serious competing ideological and cultural claims, and the need to be critical, and contextually sensitive when doing theological reflection and Christian social engagement.

26. When, for example, missionaries in the post-second world war period were still exerting influence in Singapore, especially in the mainline churches, liberal theology was in vogue, reflective of theological development in the English-

has also been identified by Singapore's former Foreign Minister, Mr S Dhanabalan, a well-respected Christian layperson, who told a gathering of Christian graduates that 'apart from the Evangelical doctrine which is the basis of our Faith and which we derive from the Bible, almost everything about us portrays us as a Western institution'.[27] 'The core of our faith is Biblical,' he reminded the members of the Graduates Christian Fellowship in 2003, 'but we present it in an elaborate wrapping or packaging which is European or American in culture and tradition.' He went on to caution:

> If we do not make conscious attempt to discard this wrapping, the people to whom we want to present the gospel, may never get past their antipathy to the wrapping and may never get to the point of answering the question that Jesus poses to all of us: 'Who do you say I am?'[28]

The warning from Dhanabalan should not be ignored or brushed aside too quickly especially so when he speaks as a person who had been at the centre of political power in Singapore. As a former banker who had held senior position in the world of finance and also having served as a Foreign Minister, he would have had close contacts and interaction with important leaders in politics and commerce, not just in Singapore, but also in the international scene. His call for the Christians to discard Euro-North American wrappings and trappings would have been informed by conclusion drawn from his reading of a sufficiently widespread negative perception others have of the church and Christians.

Even if we know that the perception of Christianity as a religion of the Euro-North American world is nothing more than a myth, albeit deeply

---

speaking West of that time. The churches are no longer under the influence of liberal theology. But now when one were to visit a Christian book shop in Singapore, one cannot fail to notice the overwhelming display of popular books of questionable quality and dubious teachings, plus a full array of music and "holy hardware" mainly from America, and also from Britain and Australia. Some of the more popular books are written by authors who take strong pro-Israel stand and those who promote a superficial faith that glorifies American consumeristic culture and lifestyle. The pendulum has swung, but it is still in many ways under Euro-North American captivity.

27. S Dhanabalan, 'The Church in Singapore: Time to Distance from the West?', *GCF Bulletin* (November 2003): 1.

28. *Ibid*, 1.

ingrained in the narrative of a post-colonial Asia, controversial but important
voices have continued to express their criticism of the West and by association
of Christians, particularly of what they see as the Asian Christians' uncritical
relationship with the Western world and Western interest. Former Prime
Minister of Malaysia, Mahathir Mohamad, not known for diplomatic nicety,
has been strident in his criticism. Here is a selection:

> Modern Europe eclipsed Asia, in terms of industrial
> strength, and the booty of imperialism gave it great
> economic and political power. Europeans felt they were
> superior people with a superior culture and had a duty to
> civilize the world, which meant, first of all, converting
> people to Christianity.[29]

> 'Justice' is often thrown up as a smoke screen by the West.
> In the Gulf War, it was clearly a pretext for the Western
> powers, led by the United States, to use their massive might
> to ensure a supply of oil.[30]

> Although predominantly Christian, in recent times Western
> societies have witnessed an almost complete separation of
> religion from the secular life and the gradual replacement
> of the religious with hedonistic values. Materialism, sens-
> ual gratification, and selfishness are rife. The community
> has given way to the individual and his desires.[31]

To be fair to Mahathir, he concedes that the sins of the West should not be
attributed to Christianity as such, but more so to what he sees as the white
supremacist attitude of the Western world.[32] But that is not a concession
allowed by Shintaro Ishihara, the outspoken but popular Governor of Tokyo.
His negative views of the West and Christianity are captured in his vitriolic
remarks made in the same book he co-authored with Mahathir:

---

29.   Mahathir Mohamad and Shintaro Ishihara, *The Voice of Asia* (Tokyo: Kodansha
       International, 1995), 74–5.
30.   *Ibid*, 79.
31.   *Ibid*, 80.
32.   *Ibid*, 76.

Racism is one of Christianity's sins because monotheism has encouraged discrimination. If Buddhism had spread across Europe, I doubt Caucasians would harbor such racist sentiments. As far as I know, Christianity never tried to liberate the colonial peoples who were being cruelly mistreated. Nor have I heard Europeans or Americans acknowledge that the way they ruled Malaya or the Philippines violated their religious principles. On the contrary, Westerners endlessly brag that the conversion of Africans and Asians to Christianity was a great blessing, a mark of progress. The link between the propagation of Christianity and colonialism deserves further study.[33]

In the name of spreading the faith, Europeans seized parts of Africa, settled the North American continent, and moved into the periphery of Asian civilization. The flowering of European modernism saw the Spanish, Portuguese, British, French, and Dutch turn Asian lands, once the center of civilization, into colonies. The conquerors were accompanied by priests and ministers who brought the word to the subject peoples; Christianity was the hand-maiden of aggression.[34]

Both Mahathir and Ishihara are not academics and their book is not an academic treatise. They are populist politicians and nationalists more than political philosophers. In that sense, the strong and negative views against Christians and the Euro-North American world expressed by these two eminent Asian leaders will not stand the test of academic rigour. In fact, for all their protestations, we do not have to dig deep to detect a degree of ethnocentric undercurrent and prejudices in their remarks. Ishihara, for instance, was conspicuously selective and trenchant in his criticism of Christians and their monotheistic faith which, according to him, gave rise to racism. If monotheistic faith breeds or encourages racism, what has he to say about Judaism and Islam, the other monotheistic faith? Perhaps for expedient reasons, since Mahathir was his co-author, he chose to be silent on this matter.

---

33. *Ibid*, 94–5.
34. *Ibid*, 99.

Selectivity and superficiality aside, both Mahathir and Ishihara's views still represent a widely accepted perception of Christians and their association with Euro-North American interest and agenda. As we have said, the prejudice is made worse by the Asian churches uncritical import and embrace of not just the Christian gospel but also the cultural values and biases that gift-wrapped the gospel. This is a serious indictment on the church in a place like Singapore for not being able to or if they are able to, for refusing to differentiate the gift from the wrapper, no matter how attractive or expensive the wrapper might be. In that sense, it is no wonder then that Christians in a place like Singapore, who lack an incarnational theology, has sometimes been accused of being ungrateful people who despise their own culture by adopting a foreign culture.

A church that does not understand the requirement of an incarnational presence and engagement in our complex and at times hostile world, informed by Jesus Christ's intentional entrance into and active participation in human culture and history—no doubt tarnished by sins and complicated by claims and counter-claims—has an impoverished view of Christian social engagement in the world where we currently reside and belong. An incarnational presence and participation in any society is not a free licence to endorse the way of the world or to support the status quo. It would be foolish for the church to think that the Gospel of Christ and the claims of God's kingdom can find full expression in any human culture or in any political system adopted by a state. History has taught us how disastrous it can be when Christians identify themselves and their faith with the ideology of the state, for example, Nazism and Apartheid. We do not have to think hard to conclude that no one human culture or political system is favoured by God. Nevertheless, any responsive and responsible Christian social engagement should be both critical and contextual, especially in an Asian plural society that is still suspicious of Christians and their close association with Euro-North American interest.

7. 'Resident aliens' reconsidered

Christians in Singapore are not living in conditions like Christians during the time when 1 Peter and the Epistle to Diognetus were written. The Singaporean followers of Christ are not persecuted, nor are they targeted for discrimination in this plural Asian society, the way Christians in early church history were discriminated. While it is true that all Christians are 'resident aliens' in the theological sense that we are citizens of God's Kingdom, and therefore our ultimate loyalty should be to God and the demands of his Kingdom, we are also citizens of the world which is God's creation and his gift to humanity. Needless to say, the theological understanding of our identity as 'resident aliens' should remind us not to place too much trust in the principalities and powers of this world, or the status quo, yet it does not require of us to denounce the world or to be preoccupied with a 'hard difference' that emphasises on the peculiarity of our identity. Even in time of undeserved discrimination, Christians were advised to 'do good,' not within the confines of the Christian community, but also for the sake of others who are not Christians. Properly understood, one cannot 'do good' without intentional participation and active engagement in fostering societal well-being, as faithful disciples of Jesus Christ.

When we take into consideration our contextual concerns, it would appear that the Petrine understanding of 'resident aliens' that describes Christians as people being unfairly discriminated, may not be an appropriate metaphor to use for Asian Christians who are not discriminated against, but who are in fact misunderstood as followers of an 'alien' religion. To take an explicit stand as 'resident aliens' will only give further credence to the already suspicious Asians that the faith we hold and our belief in Jesus Christ is an adoption of a foreign faith that supports the political and commercial agenda of the Euro-North American powers. In other words, even if Christians understand themselves as 'resident aliens' in its fullest theological sense, there is no need to concentrate too much on this metaphor. To do so might make us, even unwittingly, self-inflicted 'alienated residents'. Christians in a plural Asian society like Singapore should not give more reasons to further consolidate the popular myth of others who think that we disparage all things Asian and mindlessly worship only a Western God with all its cultural wrappings and trappings.

How about the Hauerwasian retrieval of 'resident aliens' as a critical response to the Constantinisation of the church in America and Europe?

Obviously, it is a clever and effective move and we would be unjustly dismissive if we say that it is not a valid response to the particular challenges of that part of the world, where a Constantinised church is judged to have lost her self-identity and confidence as a community which is supposed to be shaped and nurtured by the tradition-forming narrative provided by and centred on Jesus Christ. Christians outside that materially privileged world would do no disservice to observe and learn from the on-going debate, led by Hauerwas and others, and hopefully benefit from their theological reflection and their critical engagement with the competing ideas and philosophies of our time. But, as we have shown, those who argue against the seductive power and infiltration of Constantinian ideology in the contemporary Western world, could do so safe in the knowledge that their freedom to argue and rebut openly and robustly, is underwritten by a hybrid of political liberalism which they criticise and wish to jettison. This is not a luxury available to the majority of Christians living outside the Euro-North American world. There is no need for contextually sensitive public theologians outside the Euro-North American world, concerned about Christian social engagement that is both responsive and responsible, to adopt the Hauerwasian agenda or carry the Hauerwasian banner of 'resident aliens' in an Asian context.

8. Conclusion

'Resident aliens?' Maybe.

There is no denying that Christians are citizens of two cities, but we do not have to overemphasise that identity by displaying the 'resident aliens' membership card. Our ultimate loyalty, we know, must be to the City of God although as citizens of the earthly city we are also expected to do good and to seek after its welfare. The contextual challenge for Christians, in an Asian plural society with a rich cultural heritage, is not to align themselves too uncritically with Euro-North American political agenda or to take in wholesale some of the popular but spurious Christian teachings coming from that region, and in the process end up been self-inflicted 'alienated residents'. Taking such a stance, we must add, is not being anti-West.[35] What we are asking for is that in as much as we should be critical in our social engagement in the local public arena, we ought also to be critical in our engagement with the Euro-North American world. This is not endorsing the status quo or glorifying all things Asian.

Our concern, we may say, is missiological. By that we mean we are interested in providing faithful witness in an Asian plural society. That is why the need to cultivate contextual sensitivity in Christian social engagement cannot be overemphasised. If we recall the observation which we made earlier regarding the close resemblance between the teaching of 1 Peter 2:12 and Matthew 5:16, where Christians, even as 'resident aliens' were encouraged to engage in doing good deeds, even in a hostile environment, so that God will be glorified, then perhaps a more appropriate metaphor which should take greater prominence for Christians in a country like Singapore, who desire to be faithful witnesses, is that of being the 'salt and light' of the world rather

---

35.   Many, if not most, Asian theologians have benefited from the opportunity to pursue post-graduate studies with reputable teachers in the best universities in Europe and United States. The need for Asian Christians to journey West for higher learning will continue in the foreseeable future and this is not something we should mindlessly unlink.

than 'resident aliens'. 'Salt and light' associated with food and energy, something Asians can easily identity with, might be better understood and appreciated than a metaphor that may add unnecessary confusion to an Asian society that does not deliberately discriminate against Christians but is nevertheless still suspicious of the commitment of Christians to the Asian plural society. As 'salt and light', Christians are to be participative people who are socially engaged in the wider community as faithful disciples of Jesus Christ (Matthew 5:13–15).[36]

It is the vocation of the church to 'do good' and to address issues of justice both within and outside of herself, and not to be sheltered in the safe confine of the community of believers, if the church is to be the church.

---

36. One contextual approach to Christian social engagement is Critical-Reciprocal Solidarity. See my 'The State of Morality and the Morality of the State', in *A Graced Horizon*, 231f.

Contemporary Engagements

10

The Role of Chinese Christians in the Development of China

Cao Shengjie

In the introduction to his book *Seek the Welfare of the City*, Dr Bruce Winter mentioned that contrary to popular perception that the early Christians withdrew from society, they had positive commitments in the Gentile regions of the Roman Empire. He further noted that 'in some areas of *politeia*, the Asian scene has more in common with the Graeco-Roman world than the present Western world'.[1] I appreciate his aspiration to understand life in its Asian context. When I was reading the book, I found, astonishingly, that what he studied and quoted from the Bible (Romans 13:1–7, 1 Peter 1:1–2:17, Philippians 1:27 and such like) has also often been cited within our Chinese churches during the past half a century. A recent example would be our discussions for the Theological Thinking Reconstruction Ministry.[2] What follows is a sharing of our experience in 'seeking the welfare of the city'.

1. Lessons from history

After the Opium War in 1840, China gradually became semi-colonised under the invasion and oppression of Western powers. The Chinese people suffered large land losses and reparations on the one hand,[3] and lived in bitter and hard social conditions on the other. At that unfortunate time, Western missionaries

---

1. Bruce W. Winter, *Seek the Welfare of the City: Christians as Benefactors and Citizens* (Grand Rapids: Eerdmans, 1994), 6.
2. In November 1998, China Christian Council and the Three-Self Patriotic Movement held its second meeting of the Sixth National Christian Conference in Jinan, Shandong Province. 'Resolution on Strengthening Theological Thinking Reconstruction' was discussed and adopted at the conference.
3. The Treaty of Nanjing required China to make reparation of twenty-one million silver dollars, and ceded Hong Kong Island. The British government enjoyed Consular Jurisdiction, and the 'Most-Favoured-Nation Clause'.

came to propagate the gospel in China, guided by the Gunship Policy and protected by the Unequal Treaties Policy. Many church cases occurred, leading to more humiliation for the Chinese. [4]

At the same time, the 'tolerant provisions' in the Unequal Treaties extended protection even to the Chinese believers, isolating them from the rest of the Chinese.[5] There used to be a saying: 'One more Christian, one less Chinese'. During the invasion by Eight-Power-Allies in 1900, some Chinese believers helped Western missionaries fight against Chinese people; those who were killed were even honoured as 'martyrs' by Western missionaries. Obviously they were just victims of the 'mission' which was manipulated by the colonialists.

These missionaries taught that the poverty of Chinese people came from their unbelief. Believers only needed to pursue the 'heavenly kingdom' but not about anything on earth. What is more, they need not to care about the welfare of their fellow people.

Evidence shows that Christians, as a part of all Chinese people, could not escape from the miserable fate when the whole nation was suffering. During the anti-Japanese War, many church buildings were left in ruins; many Christians were killed. When the Japanese army occupied Shanghai, a pastor and his family members (except for a small girl) were murdered together.

In April 1948, Dr YT Wu, pioneer of the Three-Self Patriotic Movement later, pointed out that if the religion that we are propagating keeps itself far away from reality and even stands opposite to people's basic interests, we are doomed to be judged and mercilessly punished by history, which would be a tragedy for Christianity in China.[6]

Undoubtedly some missionaries were sincere in their beliefs and made some contribution in East-West cultural exchanges. However their missiological outlook was not in accordance with the truth of the gospel. They harmed the interests of the nation to which the Chinese believers belong, and

---

4.   For example, the Qingpu Case in 1848: WH Medhurst, W Lockhart and W Muirhead, three London Missionary Society missionaries, broke local regulation, went to Qingpu to distribute evangelical tracts, and caused conflict with sailors. The British Consulate in Shanghai exploited the situation to send their fleets to threaten the Chinese official. The matter was resolved only after the local officer was dismissed, ten sailors were punished in the public square and three hundred silver dollars were given to the missionaries.

5.   In the Treaty of Tianjin promulgated in 1858, American missionaries Samuel Wells Williams and William Alexander Parsons Martin drafted the provision: all those who learn and spread the Christian doctrine should be protected.

6.   YT Wu, 'Ji du jiao de shi dai bei ju', *Tianfeng* 5, Number 14 (April, 1948): 1–4.

separated them from their own compatriots. Their presentation of the 'gospel' made the majority of Chinese people reject Christianity and regard it as 'an alien religion'. Before 1949, even with great input of personnel and material, there were only 700,000 Protestant believers after over one hundred years of Western missionary initiatives in China.

2. Three-Self Patriotic Movement

After the founding of New China, the People's Republic of China (in 1949), the Chinese Church faced a serious choice: either to continue to rely on Western missionaries, or to be independent and stand together with the Chinese people. In 1950, Dr YT Wu with forty other church leaders initiated the Three-Self Patriotic Movement and published a manifesto, in which they clearly expressed: 'to struggle for an independent, democratic, peaceful, united and prosperous new China', 'to establish a Chinese church that is managed by our own Chinese people', and to execute the principle of 'self-administration, self-support and self-propagation of the gospel'. The statement received wide support on a large scale. On 23 September 1950, names of the first signatories were published in an editorial of the largest newspaper in China (*The People's Daily*) with an editorial indicating that our government warmly welcomed Chinese Christians' solidarity with the people. Within four years, 410,000 Christians openly subscribed to it. This indicated that it was well accepted within the churches. Ever since then, Chinese Christians decidedly 'stand and breathe together' with their fellow Chinese.

The Three-Self Patriotic Movement encourages believers to love the country and the church, which means that they should keep two identities at the same time, as Christian and as citizen. As citizens, they have the responsibility to bear good witness to other people and make contributions to their country's development, as St Paul taught: to 'conduct yourselves in a manner worthy of the gospel of Christ (Philippians 1:27)'. Our motto today is: 'Live as light and salt; glorify God and benefit people (Matthew 5:13–16)'. We put serving God and people together.

We encourage doing good deeds for the people around us as part of our Christian witness, as taught by St Peter, to 'support mutual affection with love (2 Peter 1:7)'. Many Chinese academics researching religion today have recognised the wonderful witness of Christians in social ethics, vocational virtues and family moralities. These witnesses rectify the popular misunderstanding toward Christianity, that it is an anesthetic, backward and unreasonable idea. Now it is commonly recognised that Christianity is a respectable religion which encourages people to be kind. A small Christian community started in Inner Mongolia with less than one hundred people and has since grown to a congregation of 5,000. That is a very cold and snowy place. For the recent seven years, each year after each snow, the church organised Christians to sweep out the snow in public place voluntarily. This ministry involved hundreds of Christians, and it is widely welcomed by the society. Many people who were moved by good Christian witness started to appreciate Christianity and came finally to join the churches. In Grace Church, the church where I worshipped in Shanghai, each year some two to three hundred people were baptised. They were all brought to the church through their family members, relatives, friends and workplace colleagues. Most of them are inspired by Christian integrity and kindness.

Turning to the political sphere in China, while the ideology of our leading Communist Party is atheism, it does not persecute Christianity. It now upholds a policy of religious freedom to keep the unity of the whole country (as opposed to the time of the Cultural Revolution Upheaval, when the political authority was usurped by the Gang-of-Four). According to Romans 13:1–5, we Christians should obey the authority that rewards the good deed but punishes the wrongdoing, and to respect each other's belief and co-operate for the common good. In God's eyes, no human institution is perfect. What we can do is to support the good and resist the evil. We respect each other's different beliefs, and can still co-operate for common good. There is a cordial relationship between church and society in China today. It is underpinned by consultation through constitutional channels. For example, hundreds of representatives in the Christian Church participate at varying levels within the Chinese People's Political Consultative Conference. Indeed, Bishop KH Ting is one of the national vice presidents of the conference.

Our efforts in the Reconstruction of Theological Thinking in Chinese Churches today helps believers overcome the barriers that may separate or even alienate them from those who hold different beliefs. Thus, Bishop KH Ting stresses: 'love is the supreme attribute of God'; 'the cosmic Christ bestows his grace to all people in the world'; 'there also exists truth, kindness and beauty outside of the church'; and 'Chinese Christians shall combine two 'Cs' together, namely, Christ and China'.[7]

The Chinese Church emphasises self-independence. Its purpose is to build up the churches on the Rock of Christ, and at the same time to bring peace and blessings for Chinese people. We are developing church models and ministries

---

7.   KH Ting, *Love Never Ends: Papers by KH Ting*, edited by Janice Wikeri (Nanjing: Yilin, 2000).

for our own situation. It does not mean that we separate ourselves from churches around the world. However, only when we root our lives and ministries within the Chinese people can we contribute to the ecumenical ministry.

While carrying on the Three-Self Principle, through our efforts in promoting unity and good works, we have won the recognition of our society. There are now over sixteen million Protestant Christians in China. That is over twenty times more than in 1949. There are more than 55,000 church buildings and meeting points, eighteen theological seminaries and Bible schools in China. By the end of 2004, we have published and distributed 3,600 million copies of Bible. We are, however, not satisfied merely with the increase in numbers but are trying to improve our believers' understanding of the faith.

3. New opportunities in constructing harmonious society

In recent years, our government advocates the building up of a 'harmonious socialist society'. The content of a harmonious society includes 'democracy and legal system, fairness and justice, credibility and friendliness, vitality, stability and order, and concord between human and nature'. These aspirations are in line with Christian social ethical concerns. In 2001 the Central Government convened the National Religious Work Meeting, which has contributed to a better understanding of the nature of religion. It importantly emphasised 'the development of the positive content of religious doctrines'. This really gives encouragement to Christianity. As a religion that promotes peace, concord and reconciliation, we find that present-day policies offer a great opportunity for churches in China to contribute to building up a harmonious society.

I mentioned earlier in this paper that the Chinese church is engaging in Reconstruction of Theological Thinking. We are reflecting on issues which impact on the minds of Chinese Christians. Our discussion is biblical centred, but is also informed by useful elements from various historical traditions of the church and the experience of churches in other parts of the world. We hope we can gradually formulate a series of Chinese theological ideas that are adaptable to our social context.

Currently, our focus is on how the Bible reveals God's will which may enable us to keep a harmonious relation with God, with other people and with nature. The opening chapters in the book of Genesis described how God created the heaven and earth from a formless void and darkness, leading to the beautiful set up of the garden of Eden. All these disclosed that God wills his people to live an orderly life (Genesis 1–2). Though our ancestors sinned against him and spoiled the original harmonious relationships (Genesis 3:1–4:15), God has never forsaken human being. Through Moses' Law, he confirmed his covenant with the Israelites. Through many prophets he reminded his people to return to him.

The New Testament proclaims the fulfilment of the salvation that God has prepared for us. Jesus, God's only Son, humbled himself in human form and died on the cross to accomplish salvation, to reconcile us with God, and to break down the wall among people (Philippians 2:6–11, Ephesians 2:14–18).

With regard to our relation to nature, the problem of ecology has not been widely discussed in Chinese churches before. We are now studying the Scriptures (Romans 8:22, Colossians 1:20, Revelation 5:15), and learn that we should not do things harmful to nature. We hope for the new heaven and earth when all creatures would come together to praise God.

Chinese Christians used to pay much attention to personal devotion, wishing to be 'spiritual', to keep a proper relation with God. They stressed the need to having concord and forgiveness among Christians, (though in reality we have been far from this goal). The primary need today is to emphasise the necessity of a harmonious relation between Christians/churches and the wider society. Some Christians are still influenced by conservative theological ideas: that a Christian lives only for his own benefit in order to go to heaven after this world and that too much care about this world will weaken commitment to God. These ideas are obstacles for Christians trying to respond positively to what the society expects from the church.

We are resolving this problem by stressing two points. First, that God loves the world. All human being, believers and non-believers, are all created by God, and lived in him. We are all loved by God. We should not confine our love to Christians only, but to understand God's universal love. Bishop KH Ting said:

> Because God is love and God is an eternal God, love never ends. Thus we do not lose hope, even for the extremely selfish, even for the cynical. We hope they will finally be drawn by love, surrender to it, repent and come to the Lord.[8]

---

8.   *Ibid*, 110.

Second, that Christians have the responsibility to manifest God's love through social concern. Some Christians think that love toward other people could only be expressed by caring for the salvation of their souls. Nowadays, some Christian organisations outside of China, under the banner of realising the 'great commission', are advocating that the primary task of Chinese churches is evangelism. Churches in China do emphasise evangelism. We use all opportunities to tell people the gospel, not only in evangelistic meetings, but also in the occasions of Christian weddings and funeral ceremonies when many non-Christians are present. For example, in my church, almost every sermon at Sunday worship includes some words of welcome to new converts. Yet some so-called Christian groups from outside China sneak into our country without the invitation of our churches, and engage in secret activities. They even encourage such illegal practices. When they are discovered and punished, they raise the loud voice 'Persecution!'.

Through studying the Bible, we discover that we are created whole. God cares for all aspect of our lives (Micah 6:8). Jesus healed and also showed compassion to people with physical needs. He asked us to do the same (Matthew 25:31–46). We find such concern expressed in many traditions (for example, the monastic rule, and the Reformers, and Charles Wesley). We gradually understand that social concern is also part of the church's mission, and is a good way to reach people. We should not see it as simply an instrument to win people to Christ. Of more importance, Jesus said: 'Just as the Son of Man came, and not to be served, but to serve, and to give his life a ransom for many (Matthew 20:28).'

Based on the above theological thinking, we are strengthening the following aspect of our ministries:

a) In pastoral ministries, we help our believers understand that reconciliation between God and human beings should lead to reconciliation among peoples and between humans and nature. There should be concord not only within the church but also in the church's relation to the wider society. We work together to prosper the gospel in the church, and at the same time, to be actively involved in promoting social development and stability in the nation. Our country is undergoing economic reform in this age of globalisation, and is increasingly open to the outside world. Great economic progress is taking place. However, this also results in social and economic destabilisation of some

people. For example, the reconstitution of work-units leads
to lay-offs. Our government is organising various training
projects to provide new job opportunities. We encourage all
believers to face the issues with a positive and co-operative
attitude. For example, some jobless people in Shanghai
would not accept certain menial jobs because of the loss of
face. Our churches teach Christians that all labour is
valuable, without distinction in dignity or inferiority; and
they can then accept their new job happily. Such ministry is
recognised as helpful for both the believers and society.

b) We attach importance to social ethics. As Christians we
believe that all are created equally by God and that all
should therefore enjoy equality and democracy. Yet in
China, a country with relatively poor education and a large
population, democracy could only be realised by upholding
law and order and moral values. The Cultural Revolution
has shown us the disasters that anarchy can bring. We
cherish law and order in our country. During this time of
social and economic transformation, there is some injustice
in the distribution of wealth and sometimes corruption
appears. Christians should uphold justice and condemn
crimes through proper channels, rather than to promote
conflict in society. We believe 'fairness and justice,
credibility and friendliness, vitality, stability and order' are
God's will; and we as Christians should set examples in
society through living out the image of Christ. Through this
we will enable our people to realise that Christian moral
values can play a positive role in society.

c) We will strengthen our more social service programmes.
Christianity has a long tradition of social service. The
YWCA and YMCA (which were established on Christian
principles) and the Amity Foundation (initiated by Chinese
Christian leaders) are all playing active roles in China.
According to incomplete statistics for 2004, there are
twenty-three senior citizen's houses, twenty kindergartens,
and twenty-three clinics run directly by our churches in
different parts of China. The National Three-Self Patriotic
Movement and the China Christian Council have set up a
Social Service Department. We are extending care to those
suffering from HIV and AIDS, training personnel to help

autistic children and all those in our society who have been neglected. Some training projects will be sponsored by our churches in Qingdao, Shanghai and Dalian.

d) We shall further enhance the harmonious relation with other religions. Since the establishment of New China, Christianity has given up the elitist way of thinking, of relying on Western powers and looking down other religions. In the past, for example, some preached at the temple fairs of Buddhists and Taoists that they would go to hell. Nowadays, religious leaders in China have good relations with each other. There is also an organisation called the Religion and Peace Committee in China. However, in some grass-root churches, some believers are still influenced by conservative theological thinking and exclusivist thoughts. It is hard for them to respect believers of other faiths. We shall foster mutual understanding, mutual respect and even co-operation with people who have different beliefs. There is a need, therefore, for further inter-faith dialogues.

e) As we 'seek the welfare of our city', we shall also pray for the welfare of the whole world and seek together to contribute towards world peace and security. This year is the sixtieth anniversary of the end of the Second World War, the anti-Japanese War. On 14–20 August 2005, all Chinese churches will heed the appeal of the Religion and Peace Committee of China, to pray for peace. We wish that all nations in the world will prosper together following the principles of peace and justice. Only when peace is achieved everywhere, could world peace be guaranteed.

Our experience in China confirms those of the early Christians: Christians are not escapists. The apostles taught the believers to attach importance to the responsibility of present citizenship. Discharging our duty to our country and serving our people do not contradict our faith. Our context today is different from that of Prophet Jeremiah (when people were in exile) or in the early church (when Christians were persecuted). Christians should work for peace and fulfil their social responsibilities. This is an unchanging truth. That is what we Chinese Christians should always remember.

I believe that in the process of the construction of a harmonious socialist society, Chinese Christians will not only make a contribution to our country and society but will also progress in theological thinking, church life and social service practice. Please pray for us.

11

The Christian Contribution to China in History

Zhuo Xinping

1. Introduction

The first introduction of Christianity to China can be traced back to 635 CE. This first Nestorian mission was accepted as a 'Luminous Religion' (*jing jiao*) from Persia by the Tang Chinese. Though its assimilation of Buddhism at that time was an important cause for its extinction after a short period of its mission in China, there was already an interesting cultural dialogue between Christianity and Chinese Buddhism, which set up an example for the possible way or method of its future mission, exchange and acceptance in China. The revival of the Nestorian mission and the arrival of the Catholic missionaries in the Yuan Dynasty under the Mongols marked the actual connection of the Western and Chinese societies through the famous 'Silk Road'. The Franciscan mission stimulated the curiosity for knowing other cultures from afar, both for Europeans and Chinese. People in the West and in China began to form a preliminary impression of each other and the Chinese were exposed to the different expressions of Christianity for the first time. The Christian mission in these two periods were carried out mainly in Chinese cities, which laid the foundation for Christianity to 'seek the welfare of the city' in China.

The Jesuit mission in the late Ming and Qing was the heyday of cultural exchanges between Christianity and China. The strategy of inculturation by Matteo Ricci and other missionaries built a bridge between two worlds. Subsequently, sinology became an internationally established academic discipline and, in parallel, many Chinese were attracted to Western forms of knowledge. Beijing recently held a World Chinese Language Conference with hundreds of participants from all over the world.[1] This enthusiasm for learning the Chinese language, initiated mainly by early Christian

---

1. The Conference, held on 20–22 July 2005, was on the development of the Chinese language in the multi-cultural settings of today.

missionaries, actually came out of a process of 'Western learning dawning upon the East, whereas Eastern learning was brought to the West'. When we talk about the contribution to the cultural exchanges between the West and China today, we should not forget the pioneering works of those Christian missionaries.

We can discern an interesting pattern in the history of the Christian mission in China since the time of the Qing Dynasty. Namely, that the missionary's empathetic understanding towards other cultures would create a congenial political atmosphere for understanding and dialogue. Cultural misunderstandings would however result in political controversies and conflicts. The fundamental and sharp turn-around in Emperor Kangxi's attitudes towards Christianity before and after the Rites Controversy was a case in point. The policy change eventually destroyed the possibility of Christian mission in China as a peaceful and friendly cultural exchange. Earlier, through his contact with the Jesuit missionaries, Kangxi was friendly to Christianity. His following poem showed his grasp of the Christian faith as well:

> With his task done on the cross,
> His blood forms itself into a streamlet.
> Grace flows from West Heaven in long patience:
> Trials in four courts,
> Long walks at midnight,
> Thrice denied by friend before the cock crew twice,
> Six-footer hanging at the same height as two thieves.
> It is a suffering that moves the whole world and all ranks.
> Hearing his seven words makes all souls cry.[2]

Bob Whyte quoted this poem in his book and made the following comments:

> The attitude of the Emperor towards Christianity was more complex than has been generally allowed. There is no doubt that he was deeply interested in the science taught by the Jesuits, and he developed an active knowledge of mathematics and astronomy under instruction from Verbiest and other Fathers. He also developed a close friendship

---

2.   Quoted in Bob Whyte, *Unfinished Encounter: China and Christianity* (London: Collins, 1988), 49.

with them, and showed himself to be sympathetically interested in their religious beliefs, as his poem cited at the head of this chapter reveals. There seems no reason why the friendly relationships and toleration should not have continued throughout his reign, if the Roman Catholic Church had maintained its previous support for Ricci's original policies.[3]

As a result of the Rites Controversy, China and the Catholic Church both suffered heavy losses. The Christian church lost its normal existence and potential development in China. China lost the possible chance of a rapid development in its period of social transition. For without the worldview brought by missionaries, China remained conservative and insular. When China met the West again, more than one hundred years later, China was already so weak that it was easily defeated by the Western powers.

After the Rites Controversy the Christians complained that they were persecuted. But the Qing authority was also suspicious about the Christian connection with the Western powers. Ever since the Opium Wars, most Chinese have considered Christianity, at least partly, as an inseparable part of imperialist aggression in China; many contemporary Chinese Christians still hold this view. This means that Christianity was henceforth closely connected with Western politics in the eyes of many Chinese, and that Christianity was consequently understood mainly as a political religion, harmful and unsuitable to Chinese society. Many feared that the propagation of Christianity in China might be an 'occupation of China', both spiritually and politically. This attitude casts a heavy shadow over the relationship between China and Christianity. As early as the time of Emperor Yongzheng, the son and successor of Kangxi, there was such a political evaluation or understanding of Christianity. Yongzheng explained, at the imperial court, the reason why he forbade a Christian mission in China to the Jesuits by saying:

> You want that we Chinese people all become Christians. I know that this is the demand of your religion. But if so, you can imagine, what would we become, namely should we all be subjects of your emperor? The Christians would only recognize you. If there is any border incident, the common people would only obey you. Though we needn't worry

---

3.   *Ibid*, 69–70.

about it at present, but if there are thousands of warship coming to our coast, then it could be a great disaster to us.[4]

Even today, Christianity is still described as a possible political infiltration or interference against China because of this historical background. Chinese Christianity faces an existential embarrassment: its religious connection is with the Western Christian tradition and yet it has political opposition against any Christian connection with Western politics. The Chinese church seeks to maintain its faith-identity; at the same time, it is anxious to dissociate itself from its missionary past, for fear of being implicated with the missionaries and being regarded as 'imperialistic tools' against China.

In order to avoid further misunderstanding and conflict in the contemporary encounter between Christianity and China, it is necessary for us to create an atmosphere of mutual trust and sincere dialogue. In the past decades we have emphasised the negative aspects of the history of the Christian mission in China because we were experiencing the continuation of controversy and conflict with the Western powers during the period of the Cold War. But now we are in the age of globalisation. China has opened its door and is committed to coexist with the whole world. In this new situation we should encourage improving political relations through cultural understanding, and vice versa. If we can find some positive elements in the Christian mission to China and give a positive evaluation of Christian efforts in the progress and development of Chinese culture in history, we will surely have a more solid base in fostering mutual understanding and cultural exchange between Christianity and China in the future. Hopefully this historical reflection will give us certain insights in our understanding and evaluation of religion, faith, culture and politics, and help us to find the wisdom for our peaceful coexistence and harmonious development in the new era. This is the purpose of my paper.

2. The Christian contribution to spiritual cultivation in China

Christianity, as a system of faith and culture, has its own identity and characteristics which form the basic elements or principles of its world outlook and conscience. The most important, and yet also challenging, aspects of the cultural encounter are in the exchange of ideas and spiritualities. Each culture has its own strengths and weaknesses, so cultural exchange should

---

4.   Zongze Xu, *Zhong guo tian zhu jiao chuan jiao shi gai lun* [*An Outline of the History of the Catholic Mission in China*] (Shanghai: Shang hai shu dian, 1990), 256.

bring mutual acceptance and improvement. The Christian mission to China brought about certain changes in the personal mentality and spiritual cultivation in the Chinese converts. We can discern roughly the following aspects as Chrisian influences in the spiritual cultivation of the Chinese.

Firstly, the Christian concept of original sin has improved the Chinese estimation and evaluation of the possibility and ability in the human self. Superficially, the concept of original sin should be unacceptable to the Chinese tradition which believes in the good nature and unlimited possibility of the human being. But this concept of Christian faith helped the Chinese to understand the limitation and weakness in their existence and their striving for perfection. The awareness of self-limitation is the basis and prerequisite for self-transcendence. So, the understanding of original sin in this way improved the mental cultivation and meditation on the significance of human life by many Chinese Christians. For example, a Chinese Catholic scholar, Li Jiugong from Fuzhou in the seventeenth century, emphasised in his 'Meditations' (*shen si lu*) that 'Christians should only note down their transgressions, as a basis for repentance, for entering their positive acts could easily lead to complacency and laxity'.[5] In connection to this self-consciousness of human limitation, the humble spirit of Christianity has given the Chinese another orientation in understanding the universe and humanity.

Secondly, the Christian concept of transcendence has brought a new dimension to the Chinese understanding of transcendence in the Confucian and Taoist traditions. Generally speaking, the Confucian spirit is understood as a kind of 'inner transcendence' which cannot easily be dissociated from its dependence upon politics and social environment. So, it is no more than self-cultivation and self-improvement within the given realities of a situation. The Taoist spirit is sometimes interpreted as a kind of 'outer transcendence'; it focusses on 'nature' and is in reality a 'naturalist transcendentalism' which advocates a return to, or unification with, nature. In comparison, the Christian concept of transcendence has introduced to China a new horizon in its understanding. It points out a transcendence based outside oneself, and even outside of natural bounds of human beings, and aims at the unification with the Absolute Being. Though it is directed to the other-worldly, this transcendence, as a means of ultimate concern or ultimate transformation, is

---

5.   Erik Zürcher, 'Li Jiugong and His Meditations (*Shensi Lu*)' in *Encounters and Dialogues, Changing Perspectives on Chinese-Western Exchanges from the Sixteenth to Eighteenth Centuries*, edited by Xiaoxin Wu (Nettetal: Steyler Verlag, 2005), 88.

still an important guiding principle for the human pursuit of truth, goodness and beauty in this world. In this 'Transcendence' or 'Transcendental Oneness' we can understand the basis of 'harmony' as interpreted by Confucius or others. We do not seek uniformity in the understanding of God. John Hick has explained that the ideas of God should be the various interpretations or acceptances of this 'Transcendental One', and these ideas of God form the multi-dimensions, the colourful pictures of the world religions.

Thirdly, the Christian concept of *agape* (or 'universal love') has sublim-ated the human love or benevolence in Chinese tradition. The understanding of love in common sense is based on the social relationships and so conditional. But the Christian love is unconditional. By emphasising this love, Christianity is regarded as a 'religion of love'. This love includes the spirit of salvation which shows itself typically in the self-sacrifice of Jesus Christ. So 'love' is interpreted in terms of self-sacrifice and service to the people. With this spirit of love, Christians have promoted social service, and shared also their social concern and social responsibility in China. Many Christian missionaries in the past served the Chinese in heart and soul, especially in rural or mountain areas. Some even died in China during their time of service. These Christians are remembered as close friends by the local Chinese. Today the construction of Chinese theology is also based on the Chinese Christians' understanding of this 'universal love', namely 'God is love'.

3. The Christian contribution to China in public education

From the Sui Dynasty, there was mainly one system of imperial examination by which Chinese feudal dynasties selected candidates for civil and military posts. This educational system was composed of classic scripture reading and an eight-episode written essay, which allowed almost no space at all for other knowledge in the natural and social sciences. In the nineteenth century Christian missionaries introduced the modern educational system to China. With the introduction of 'Western schools' run by missionaries with 'Western knowledge' taught by these schools, a fundamental change took place in the traditional Chinese educational system, which became the catalyst in the process of modernisation of the school system and curriculum in China, and led to the final abolishment of its traditional system of imperial examination.

The first Western school in China was Morrison Education Society School, established in Macao in 1839 by the Protestant missionaries. It systematically introduced the modern curriculum which included arithmetic, geometry, physics, chemistry, physiology and hygienics, geography, history and music. It had both Chinese and English courses. This school was the cradle of many Chinese reform-thinkers in modern times. The first group of Chinese students studying abroad came from this school.

In 1843, the Anglo-Chinese College (*ying hua shu yuan*) moved to Hong Kong from Malacca and became a well-known Protestant school at that time. In 1844, the first school for women was established in Ningbo by British missionary, Miss Mary Ann Aldersey. That was also an important step in raising the status of women in China. In 1850, College St Ignatius (renamed as Xuhui Public School shortly after) was established in Shanghai by Jesuit missionaries. This was the earliest middle school in Shanghai. By 1860 there were fifty church schools throughout China with more than one thousand students. Though these church schools were small in scale and most had a level of primary school only at the very beginning, they constituted the embryonic form of the modern educational system in China. After 1860, the government of the Qing Dynasty began to run schools according to the Western models; its purpose was mainly to train translators or interpreters.

By the end of the nineteenth century there were more than 2,000 church schools with 40,000 students. In 1920, China had then 13,000 church schools with 350,000 students. This Christian education reached its height in 1937, when there were one million students in church schools, including 8,000 university or college students and 90,000 middle school students.

In 1901, the Protestant churches established Soochow (in Chinese, *Dongwu*) University. It was the first Chinese university based on the modern educational system and symbolised the beginning of Christian higher education. By the 1920s there were approximately fourteen Protestant universities including three women universities and three Catholic universities in 1920s in China. In comparison there were only three national universities sponsored by the Chinese government and five private universities during that period. Besides the church schools, Christian organisations in China also developed a kind of 'mass education' (*ping min jiao yu*) to help the common people, especially the poor, to receive the basic education. This was initiated by the YMCA in China, which established the Mass Education Movement Society in Beijing in 1923.[6]

. In fact, church schools played a decisive role in the modern history of China's educational development. Not only did they lay the foundation of the Chinese modern education but they also promoted the transition of Chinese

---

6.   Yan Yangchu was its first secretary-general. See Changsheng Gu, *Chuan jiao shi yu jin dai zhong guo* [Missionaries and Modern China] (Shanghai: Shang hai ren min chu ban she, 1981), 307.

educational system from the old traditional model to a new and modern model. Church schools cultivated many new talents in natural and social sciences in modern China. Outstanding figures in various fields of contemporary Chinese society are graduates of church schools or universities. Though there are different evaluations of the function of church schools in China, their contribution to China in public education and its development is undeniable. As a matter of fact, the reforms in education made preparations for other reforms in modern Chinese society.

4. The Christian contribution to China in the development of news and publications

The systematic translation of Chinese and Western classics was started during the Ming and Qing Dynasties by the Catholic missionaries. The publication of those translations was a great event in the history of cultural exchanges between China and the West. In 1584, the Jesuit Michaele Ruggieri published his book *The True Record of the Holy Religion* (*sheng jiao shi lu*), which was the first work on Christian doctrine written in Chinese. Matteo Ricci studied Chinese alongside Ruggieri, and within a few years he translated into Latin the 'Four Books' (*The Confucian Analects, The Book of Mencius, The Great Learning and The Doctrine of the Mean*). In 1595, Ricci published his book *The True Meaning of the Heavenly Studies* (*tian xue shi yi*) in Chinese in its first form, which was reprinted with the title *The True Meaning of the Lord of Heaven* (*tian zhu shi yi*) in its final form in 1604. Together with Xu Guangqi, Ricci also translated Euclid's *Elements of Geometry* (*ji he yuan ben*) and other Western monographs into Chinese. Through these cross-cultural translations, the Europeans were exposed to the classic Chinese culture systematically for the first time, and the Chinese received not only the Christian knowledge, but also the discoveries and new achievements from the European Renaissance. During this time more than a thousand books were translated and published by Catholic scholars in China.[7] This tradition of cross-cultural translation was continued by missionaries from both Catholic and Protestant churches in the nineteenth and twentieth centuries. The Chinese Christian scholars also took an active part in it.

The introduction of newspapers, journals and other modern publications was another contribution of Christianity to China. In 1815, two British Protestant missionaries—Robert Morrison and William Milne—and a Chinese

---

7. See Nicolas Standaert, *Handbook of Christianity in Asia, volume 1: 635–1800* (Leiden: Brill, 2001), 138–143, 592–906 for comprehensive bibliographies of this literature.

Christian—Liang Fa—started the first Chinese magazine, *Chinese Monthly Magazine* (*cha shi su mei yue tong ji zhuan*), in Malacca. In 1832, an American Protestant missionary Elijah C Bridgman produced and edited an English monthly magazine *Chinese Repository* in Canton. This was the first journal started by Protestant missionaries in China. It reported the situation of Chinese social politics, economy and culture in details to the outside world before and after the Opium War, and for this reason was 'the first outlet in China for serious Western sinological scholarship'.[8] In 1833, the Prussian Protestant missionary, Karl Gützlaff, edited the first Chinese journal, *Eastern Western Monthly Magazine* (*dong xi yang kao mei yue tong ji zhuan*). After the Opium War there were more journals and newspapers run by Christian missionaries and Shanghai became the centre for Chinese modern publications. From the 1840s to the 1890s, there were 170 journals in Chinese and foreign languages, run by Christians, which constituted ninety-five per cent of the total publications of journals and newspapers in the whole of China at that time. The most influential journals included the English journal *The Chinese Recorder* (*jiao wu za zhi*) started in 1867 and the Chinese weekly *Church News* (*jiao hui xin bao*) in 1868, which was re-entitled *The Globe Magazine* (*wan kuo kung pao*) in 1874.

The Protestant missionaries founded a Society for the Diffusion of Useful Knowledge in China (*zai hua shi yong zhi shi chuan bo hui*) in Canton in 1834, and the Christian Literature Society for China (*guang xue hui*) in Shanghai in 1887. Young John Allen explained the reason for naming it *guang xue hui* as 'introducing broadly the knowledge from Western countries to China'.[9] Their motivation for these publications was 'the peaceful opening of China through information about the West'.[10]

Up to 1936, there were in China 238 Protestant journals, including 211 journals in Chinese and twenty-seven journals in English, and one hundred and fifteen Catholic journals including sixty-six religious journals and forty-nine journals for social problems and sciences. During this period there were also sixty-nine Protestant publishing houses or institutions with 4,000 various publications and about twenty-six Catholic publication institutions. These Christian publication activities were instrumental in the rapid improvement and development in Chinese news media and academic publications.

---

8. Whyte, *op cit*, 102.
9. Changsheng Gu, *Cong ma li xun dao si tu lei dun* [*From Robert Morrison to John Leighton Stuart* (Shanghai: Shang hai ren min chu ban she, 1985), 273.
10. Whyte, *op cit*, 102.

5. The Christian contribution to China in social welfare and philanthropy

Christian philanthropies in China included medical works, orphanages, relief works and other activities. In 1834, Peter Parker, a missionary doctor from American Protestant church arrived in China. He combined evangelistic outreach with medical care. Missionaries then began to develop church hospitals and published many medical books and journals. These activities were the important beginnings of the introduction of Western medicine to China. In 1838 Thomas Richardson College headed the China Medical Missionary Society in Canton. In 1886, the China Medical Association was founded with John Glasgow Kerr as the first chairman. In 1932, this missionary association was merged into the Chinese Medical Association which was responsible for the medical development in China.

Before 1900, there were about forty Protestant hospitals and clinics and also some Catholic hospitals in China. According to the statistics in 1933, there were already 266 Catholic hospitals and 744 pharmacies. In 1937, there were 271 Protestant hospitals and clinics, including 297 foreign doctors and 561 Chinese doctors, 256 foreign nurses and 340 Chinese nurses, 278 medical technicians and 197 probationers. There were 18,266 sickbeds in church hospitals and 1,034 sickbeds in church clinics.[11] In this time seventy per cent of the total Chinese hospitals were church hospitals and ninety per cent of nurses were Christians.

Orphanages among the Chinese were started by missionaries in 1820s. In 1855, the Jesuits began to run orphanages in Shanghai. Up to 1935, their Mary Orphanage had taken in 17,000 orphans. In 1914, the Protestants in China had thirty-seven orphanages. In 1928, Christians established the Chinese Orphanage Helping Association in Shanghai with five separate divisions for children protection, cultivation, sanitation, research and social education. In 1874, the first school for blind children was set up in Beijing by the Scottish missionary W Murray. Since then many church schools were opened for blind children. In 1926, there were thirty-eight such schools with a total enrolment of over a thousand blind children. In 1887, an American Presbyterian missionary, JL Nevius and his wife, established in Shanghai the first school for deaf and dumb children in China. These Christian schools laid the foundation for special education in China.[12]

---

11.   See Senfu Yang, *Zhong guo ji du jiao shi* [A History of Christianity in China] (Taibei: Tai wan shang wu yin shu guan, 1968), 275–6.

12.   See Xinping Zhuo, *Ji du jiao you tai jiao zhi* [A History of Christianity and Judaism in China] (Shanghai: Shang hai ren min chu ban she, 1998), 276–8.

Relief works included the establishment of such institutions as homes for the old people and for the handicapped, relief agencies for those in disaster-stricken areas and care for smoking, alcohol and drug addicts.

These forms of social work reflected how Christians applied their social teaching in Chinese contexts.

6. Conclusion

What is our assessment of Christianity in China before 1949? Often there is a strong sentiment of mistrust towards Christianity. Christianity was regarded as historically involved in the process of imperialist aggression and the colonisation of China by Western powers. This cast a shadow over the Christian image in China. But Christianity should or could not be interpreted or represented by political images, which are at best partial. As I have observed, Christianity essentially is a true religion that seeks for transcendence and ultimate transformation. So, we can still discern or discover its light behind the political shadows. Christianity has made a significant contribution to China in social service, spiritual enlightenment and cultural exchanges. These efforts can be understood as the realisation of the Christian ideal in 'seeking the welfare of the city'. Recognition of this contribution may offer a way towards the re-establishing of a friendly and trustful relationship between Christianity and China today. This would enable Christians in China to make further contributions in building up a harmonious society in China, and at the same time sustain its development in the future.

12

The Christian Role in a Pluralistic Society, with Specific Reference to Singapore

Richard Magnus

1. National context and environment

Singapore is a pluralistic secular society. Christian truth and reality are not however in themselves pluralistic, post-modernism notwithstanding. (That itself calls for a separate discussion which is not the ambit of this discourse). Truth and reality do not adapt to us. On the surface this can create a tension; and it has in a couple of instances in the past by misconceived persons. By and large however we see a generally constructive and evolving respectful interchange of the secular and Christian realities in our nation. The revelation, history and traditions of Christianity were invariably unfolded in the arena of pluralistic societies. The Bible and secular history evidence this. The out-working of Christianity and the language used by Christians in other societies elsewhere in the world may not necessarily be helpful to us. We are a multi-racial, multi-cultural and multi-religious society. As the Deputy Prime Minister reiterated recently, on the 18 July 2005, we have in Singapore a unique pluralistic and progressive society and a globalised and secular state. We express our respective identities in different languages which carry, among others, different social, ideological and theological nuances.

In fact, broadly, the Asian Church has developed differently from the Western Church. For one, the Asian Church is far more experienced with challenges presented by competing truth claims and the need to live in a multi-religious society with tolerance and mutual respect. Though a minority religion, Singapore's church history and involvement is very much part of Singapore's history and Singapore's efforts in nation-building, contributing significantly to the development of the rule of law, community policies, education, the sciences, social and welfare programmes. If one digs deep, one can palpably see Christian or Christian-like values and norms underpinning several practices in our public and private sector governance.

Singapore separates religion from politics. This is a deliberate national policy of secularisation. This does not mean that Singapore is anti-religion. The Government recognises the reality, significance and meaningfulness of religious beliefs in the lives of its citizens and residents. Indeed, religious freedom is guaranteed by the Singapore Constitution. In many ways the Singaporean Government encourages the orderly practice of religion through legislative and administrative and community means. The 'Maintenance of Religious Harmony' Act is one such major legislation. The 'Religious Harmony Code' and the 'Inter-Religious Harmony Circles' are consensual mechanisms. With this secular policy, the Government is aware that Singaporeans have different views on matters of conscience and faith; and that it cannot enforce the choices of one group on others, or make private choices the basis of national policy.

Pluralism in Singapore secures a social context in which full and free interchange of different views on life and reality can be conducted to the greatest advantage of all. There are great benefits to all with this open and free interchange of information and ideas. The Singaporean Christian has reason to favour such interchange and be confident about its outcome. 'Openness' does not necessarily require relativism in truth. The Singaporean Christian appreciates the challenges and indeed welcomes pluralism in our society. Pluralism simply means that social or political force is not to be used to oppress the freedom of thought and expression of any citizen, or even the practice that flows from it, insofar as that practice is not morally wrong. He should therefore regard pluralism as a social principle, dictated by trust in God and love for one's neighbour, which respects and cares for the individual member of our society.

2. Social involvement

The Singaporean Christian faces two material options as a citizen of Singapore. One is escape and the other is engagement.

'Escape' is to turn our backs on our Government and our fellow neighbours in rejection, washing our hands of it and determining to harden our hearts against it. This is *laissez-faire*, the defeatist decision to leave people alone in their non-Christian ways and not interfere or try to influence them in any way. History does not support this. The gravest modern example of Christian *laissez-faire* is the failure of the German Church to speak out against the Nazi's treatment of the Jews.

In contrast 'engagement' is to turn our faces towards our nation, our leaders and our neighbours in respect and in compassion, getting our hands dirty, sore and worn out in service, to change the views or practices of others, by all appropriate means of persuasion, where we believe them to be mistaken; and feeling deep within us the stirring of the love of God for our nation and our people which cannot be contained.

The Christian chooses engagement. This is his social responsibility. This social concern is his human response to the divine commission, the voice of God who calls his people in every age to go out into the lost and lonely world, as he did in Christ Jesus, in order to live and love, to witness and serve, like him and eventually for him. The Singaporean Christian is obedient to this conviction that Christ sends us out into the world to live and work.

This engagement is through persuasion and not by way of imposition. Again, history does not support imposition. 'Imposition' is the crusading attempt to coerce people to accept the Christian way. This is the Crusades of the Roman Catholic Church in 1252 and the fifteenth century Spanish Inquisition. Christians of all traditions are deeply ashamed that such methods could ever have been used in the name of Jesus Christ. All Christians affirm that such totalitarianism and torture are both wholly incompatible with the mind and spirit of Jesus.

3. Thought framework

In his engagement role, the Singaporean who is a Christian is equipped with a unique and a full revelatory doctrine. Of this rich doctrine, five doctrinal pillars will be my framework on this subject. These motivate the Singaporean Christian's social concern and responsibility and his involvement in nation building. These pillars are:

a) of God: that he is the creator, lawgiver, lord and judge;
b) of human beings: our unique worth because we are made in God's image;
c) of Christ Jesus: who identified with us and calls us to identify with others;
d) of salvation: a radical transformation;
e) of the church: distinct from the world as its salt and light, yet enhancing it.

I will use this framework to discuss further the role and specific contributions of the Singaporean Christian.

3★

3.1 Loyalty to the nation

The living God is the God of nature as well as of religion and of nations, of the secular as well as the sacred. God made the physical universe, sustains it, and still pronounces it good (Genesis 1:31). It is stated quite clearly that 'everything God created is good, and nothing is to be rejected if it is to be received with thanksgiving' (1 Timothy 4:4).

The Singaporean Christian citizen's loyalty to this nation is unquestioned. He stands prepared, shoulder-to-shoulder with his other citizens, to defend this country against her enemies, to guard our public and private institutions and to bear arms to defend this country with his life. That is why the Jehovah's Witness Church, which teaches its members not to carry arms in the Singapore Armed Forces, has been banned, and rightly so.

3.2 Enhancing the social sector

The Singaporean Christian's work is also to preserve the good gifts of a good creator: marriages, families, work and leisure, friendships, the inter-racial and inter-cultural community, the arts and our environment which enhance our quality of human life. There are several Christian faith based private and voluntary infrastructures to facilitate these. The Anglican, Methodist and the Presbyterian Churches have established a wide reaching network of community, counselling, and welfare services. For example, the Singapore Anglican Community Services (SACS) runs the St Andrew's Community Hospital which teams up with a public hospital to provide secondary medical care and provides specialised care in mental psychiatric treatment. As I speak, plans are being finalised for an integrated Autism Centre, the first of its kind in this part of the world. It provides not only educational and developmental needs for the autistic child but teaching them social behaviour and environmental awareness and critically moral values. This Centre is open to all, irrespective of race or religious beliefs. The SACS also has under its umbrella charitable institutions, some of which work closely with our public grassroots groups—for example, the Community Development Councils which are run by our mayors who are appointed by the Government—to reach out to the elderly, the sick and the poor.

3.3 Supporting the nation's leaders

In Christian churches across the nation, the community of Christians fervently prays, weekly at least, for Godly wisdom for our leaders that they will govern Singapore well. You will be able to hear the public prayer in all our churches and see this prayer for the nation and our leaders—from the President, to the Cabinet Ministers, all our policy makers and all our judges—in our prayer books. The Singaporean Christians believe and know that God answers prayers for his will to be done.

This attitude is translated in the daily prayer of the Singaporean Christian to do so also in his daily prayer time.

Indeed Christians in the marketplace of commerce, financial and service and trade institutions meet monthly to pray and uphold our leaders and all those who run our public and private institutions. This group is under the auspices of the National Council of Churches of Singapore (NCCS), currently led by Archbishop John Chew. NCCS assembled Christians in Singapore on 15 August to pray for the prosperity, peace, security of the nation, families, and good relationships with neighbouring countries.

I recall vividly during the SARS period, the Singaporean Christians, believing and knowing that God answers prayers, made a rallying call to meet in the center of our city, in St Andrew's Cathedral, to pray to God in Christ Jesus to give his wisdom to our policy leaders, doctors and citizens as they tackle and manage this crisis.

3.4 Promoting justice

The living God is also the God of justice as well as of justification. He is the saviour of sinners. He is also concerned that our community life is characterised by justice. He is concerned with the truth of his moral law that underpins our law and our society. Where the law of the land is so underpinned, there is high moral ground universally for its acceptance. So to use an example you are familiar with, the sentence of the young American, Michael Fay, was universally accepted when it became a public issue between Singapore and the USA. He was found guilty of vandalising public properties; and was imprisoned and caned. He had breached the law of the land underpinned by the moral law of respect of authority and your neighbour's properties. In our corporate and stock exchange governance, with the disclosure based regime, honesty of dealings, transparency of disclosures, due diligence in corporate affairs, and giving priority to shareholders' interests have all their originating values in the corresponding Christian moral values. Again, you will also know the Nick Leeson's case, the English man who brought down the very well established Baring's Bank. The long arm of the Singapore law reached out to him for offences he has committed against the law of this nation even when he was in Germany seeking refuge. Justice must be done. The Bible says that justice, righteousness and truth are the pillars of the kingdom of God. This wisdom has found expression in this case.

Moreover, God's righteousness is an essential expression of his love. He loves justice and hates oppression.

3.5 Encouraging reconciliation and peace

The Christian value of seeking peace among neighbours and in society sees mediation in civil, business and relationship disputes as a norm in this nation. The living God of the biblical revelation, who created and sustains the universe, intended the human beings he made to live in loving community. The Singaporean Christian involves himself in work through various social and community mechanisms that promote such reconciliation and peace.

3.6 Helping dysfunctional individuals

In addition, the Singaporean Christian has a sound basis for serving his fellow citizens with a fuller doctrine of human beings. Our citizens are made in God's likeness, and possess unique capacities which distinguish us from the animal creation. True, human beings are fallen, and the divine image is defaced, but despite all contrary appearances it has not been destroyed (Genesis 9:6; James 3:9). It is this which accounts for their unique worth and which has always inspired Christian philanthropy to seek their welfare.

Therefore, as he truly loves our neighbours, and because of their worth, he desires to serve them; he shall be concerned for their total welfare, the well-being of their soul, body, and their community. And it is this concern which has led the Singaporean Christians to relief, development and evangelistic programmes. As a group, they have established top schools, much needed hospitals, sensitive community and social services, expert family service centres, unique halfway houses, common tuition centres, special prison rehab-ilitation programmes, downstream care centres for the mentally handicapped and the elderly and the destitute, felt-need refuge centres for the estranged families, leprosy centers and care for the blind and the deaf, the orphaned and the widow, the sick, the distressed, the suffering, the lonely and the dying. They get alongside drug takers and stay alongside them during their recovery. They get involved in the heartlands of our housing estates. There are too many such institutions for me to identify them in full.

3.7 Promoting the sciences

They have done this because people matter. Because every man, woman, and child has an intrinsic, inalienable value as a human being. This value is again so abundantly clear in the field of biomedical sciences which Singapore is now developing as the third pillar of our economic growth. For responsible work and research to be done in this area, the Government has established the

Bioethics Advisory Committee (BAC) to examine ethical, legal and social issues arising from research on human biology and behaviour and its applications, and to develop and recommend policies to the Ministerial Committee for Life Sciences on these issues. The aim is to protect the rights and welfare of individuals, while allowing the development of the biomedical sciences for the benefit of mankind. This is a very difficult area. It is also a new area, not only in Singapore but also internationally.

The first concern was with human stem cell research. Given our pluralistic society, the BAC conducted a thorough public consultation process to obtain input and views from our Singaporean community on these issues. The BAC received written submissions from religious, patient, professional, research and medical groups and had dialogues with them. There were fourteen submissions from the religious groups: the Hindus, the Taoists, the Sikhs, the Jewish, Buddhists, Catholics, Protestant Christians and the Muslims. The BAC's fundamental approach was to balance two ethical commitments: to protect human life and the right and welfare of the individual and to advance human life by curing disease. One of the critical recommendations of the BAC, which was accepted by Government, was that reproductive cloning was absolutely not allowed. The reasons for this recommendation are significant, setting out to reflect the intrinsic value of the human being:

> The BAC is of the view that the implantation of a human embryo created by any cloning technology into a womb, known as reproductive cloning, or any other treatment of a human embryo intended to result in its development into a viable infant, should be prohibited. There are strong public policy reasons for this position. These include: (a) the view that human reproductive cloning goes against the moral ideas that holds that a human being is not to be treated as a means to an end, but only as an end. This translates into the fear that a whole human being may be brought into existence for a utilitarian purpose; (b) that the social and legal implications of reproductive cloning are very serious, including issues of identity and responsibility; and (c) the fear that it will result in a reduction in biodiversity.[1]

---

1.   Bioethics Advisory Committee, *Ethical, Legal and Social Issues in Human Stem Cell Research, Reproductive and Therapeutic Cloning: A Report from the*

In the event, the Human Cloning and Other Prohibited Practices Act 2004 was passed into law. This is also Singapore's position at the 59th United Nations General Assembly Cloning Debate in October 2004. On the 5 November 2004, Singapore's position was presented at the Fifth International Meeting of National Bioethics Advisory Bodies. The participating countries were impressed with our position; some countries will review their positions, some had asked for assistance in this area. The International Advisory Council to the Singaporean Government in the area of biomedical sciences, comprising Nobel Laureates and world-renowned experts, also agrees with our recommendations. Many nations, the international media and responsible and established research scientists have applauded Singapore for having in place what they term a responsible ethical framework.

The other seminal work in progress of the BAC is concerned with genetic testing and genetic research. Again, views from all religious and faith based groups were sought. The submissions from Singaporean Christian groups contained a fully principled response.

3.8 Helping societies in other countries

Next we are called to identify with our neighbours whatever their race or culture or religion. 'As the Father has sent me, I am sending you (John 20:21)'. The Singaporean Christian takes this seriously. It involves him in entering into other people's worlds. It will mean entering their thought world to understand them, and the world of their tragedy and lostness, in order to share his compassion as he has learnt from Jesus Christ. It also means his willingness to renounce comfort and security of his cultural background in order to give himself in service to people of another culture, whose needs he may have never before known or experienced. As a philosophy, these values of compassion and care beyond our comfort levels find expression in the Singapore International Foundation, a public body, and not a religious body. Its mission is expressed in these terms:

> We help Singaporeans integrate their aspirations and
> achievements at home and abroad into the global society
> and the global economy while preserving the Singaporean
> identity and the sense of national belonging. We support
> Singaporeans in building on their achievements as they
> search for fresh experiences and perspectives to prosper in

---

Bioethics Advisory Committee Singapore (Singapore: The Bioethics Advisory Committee Singapore, 2002), 31.

the new millennium. We promote active citizenry at home and abroad, help Singaporeans appreciate their place in the world community, while spontaneously and enthusiastically reaching out to the world with a hand of warm friendship.[2]

Singaporean Christians, individually and as a group, realise that they are part of the 'world community' and are involved in educational and welfare and medical programmes in many countries: including Indonesia, Thailand, Cambodia, Myanmar, Vietnam, Laos, India, Africa, and South America. These are conducted openly in these societies with local participation to benefit the local populace.

3.9 Contributing to society in love

I now refer to the remaining two other aspects of the Singaporean Christian's doctrinal pillars—of salvation and of the church. The Singaporean Christian realises that his experience extends beyond being religious and embraces the whole of his experience, public or private, home and work, church member-ship and civic duty, evangelistic and social duties. Above all, he is motivated by love for his neighbour.

It is this motivation that moved the NCCS to make a submission to the Singaporean Government as to whether we should, as a society, encourage homosexuality as a life style. The then Prime Minister, Mr Goh Chok Tong, in his National Day Rally speech in 2003, acknowledged this contribution and announced that we should not encourage homosexuality as a lifestyle. This again found expression in the Government's policy to curb AIDS. NCCS had also made submissions to the Government on the building of integrated entertainment and gambling resorts. The Government had decided to proceed to establish these resorts. The Prime Minister recently (on the 26 April 2005) said that he was heartened that the NCCS would cooperate with the Government in dealing with the social fallout and offer counselling for people with gambling problems. He acknowledged that religious groups can propagate good values, support and help families in need of assistance; and he looks forward to our contributions.

---

2. Singapore International Foundation, 'Vision and Mission', Singapore International Foundation, http://www.sif.org.sg/ca/ca_cp_visionmission. html (accessed 6 August 2005).

4. Conclusion

It is a reasonable conclusion from what has been discussed that the Singaporean Christian's role in Singapore is well supported by the biblical claim that there is a meta-narrative which is descriptive of all, and normative of all. Therefore, although Christianity is a minority religion in Singapore, Christian values and thought, as practiced by the Singaporean Christian, find expression in major fields in Singapore. This meta-narrative affects his social behaviour and institutions and benefits the whole of Singapore. He neither imposes Christian standards by force on an unwilling public, nor remains silent and inactive before the contemporary issues. He does not rely exclusively on the dogmatic assertion of biblical values but rather reasons with people about the benefits of Christian morality, commending God's laws to them by rational arguments. He believes that God's laws are both good in themselves and universal in their application because they fit the human beings God has made.

13

Roman Catholic Perspectives on Seeking the Welfare of the City

Kenson Koh

1. Introduction

Tracing through the development of the city through the centuries, we begin to understand the importance of its health and welfare. From ancient times, people have moved from the agrarian lifestyle in the rural regions to urban life in cities. Cities gradually became larger with time. However, dramatic changes have occurred since the mid-nineteenth centuries. The industrial revolution brought about a great displacement of peoples from the rural areas to the cities. Scientific and technological advances have brought cities into a new age: the era of globalisation. With the process of globalisation, cities are now 'centres of business, education, research, travel, communication and religion, having networks and organisations that reach around the world'.[1]

The Catholic Church has, since the end of the nineteenth century, considered its mission within the human community. With the Second Vatican Council, the Church reflected anew the relationship between the Church and the world. These teachings often refer to whole societies and states, but could also be applied to cities.

This paper will present recent Catholic teachings in response to the contemporary city in the age of globalisation.

2. Cities and globalisation

Cities have existed since ancient times. With the formation of cities, there is a distinction between the rural agrarian populace and the urban city-dwellers. Living in the city usually meant a different lifestyle. Whilst people from the

---

1.   PG Hiebert and EH Meneses, *Incarnational Ministry: Planting Churches in Band, Tribal, Peasant and Urban Societies* (Grand Rapids: Baker Book House, 1995), 265.

rural areas toiled on the land, city dwellers were more involved with commerce. Recreation was also different as the cities offered interaction with more people. From antiquity, people from the rural areas migrated to the cities in search of a better life. As cities were centres of communication, industry and commerce, it was natural that globalisation, a process that is accelerated by modern communication technologies, would find itself at home in cities.

In simple terms, globalisation is a social process by which barriers between different communities in the world are broken down, creating inter-relationships and interdependence between these communities.[2]

Globalisation, so defined, seems to be a good process. The divide between rich and poor, the barriers between different cultures and religions, and the walls that separate the free and the oppressed would slowly be broken down. The dissemination of information is almost instantaneous; so can be our responses. A good example is the speed in which nations all over the world responded to the plight of the victims of the tsunami which occurred at the end of 2004. New technologies are being adopted by developing nations more quickly to aid their economy. Yet barriers are being put up as quickly as they are being torn down. Is globalisation really beneficial?

The free market economy flourishes with globalisation. However, the ideal of globalisation had not taken into account human greed, which actually reverses the good that globalisation can ideally bring.[3] JL Touadi lists seven principles governing globalisation which has moved in the economic direction:

a) The global market is absolute and nothing else exists outside it.

b) Deregulation achieves maximum profit with minimum costs

c) The market is self-regulatory. This is an internal process.

d) Be competitive.

e) Everything is to be privatised.

---

2.   See J Arjun, 'Taming the Global Demagogue I: A Spirituality for Globalization', *Vidyajyoti Journal of Theological Reflection*, 66 (2000): 421; S Bharracharji, 'Challenges to Mission in the Context of Globalization', *International Review of Mission*, 86 (1997): 399; YH Jo, 'Globalization as a Challenge to Churches in Asia Today', *Asia Journal of Theology*, 15 (2001): 349–50; J Joblin, 'Chiesa e Mondializzazione', *La Civiltà Cattolica*, 1 (1998): 130.

3.   See PF O'Donoghue, 'Globalization and the Church', *The Japan Mission Journal*, 54 (2000): 149.

f)   There is no limit to growth.

g)   Politics is subordinated.[4]

The above reveals that greed-motivated globalisation of the free market is a ruthless process. Cities today need globalisation to survive economically but at the same time can be devastated by it.

This devastation comes in two forms: cultural homogenisation and social polarisation. The reasons are not difficult to see. The mass media, aided by the advances in information technology, accelerates cultural homogenisation. The internet and wireless communications have broken down traditional barriers to information. Combined with the fact that cities are actually highly compressed spaces with large population densities, interaction between people is no longer affected by space and time. A person's sense of belonging does not depend on physical space and historical roots, but on economic factors; leading to the erosion of communal responsibility. The huge advertising industry influences the outlook of young people all over the world. Young people are particularly susceptible to messages that suggest gratification of their desires and self-image.[5]

Globalisation breaks down barriers to emphasise the universal. The 'connectedness' between communities, however, is important to reap its benefits. To be connected, one must have access to technology. The poor may not be able to afford the technology and thus not get connected. The old may not be familiar with a technological mode of communication. As a result, the poor and the old may be excluded from the benefits of globalisation, though they are still exposed to a global culture through less sophisticated forms of media, like advertisement billboards.[6] Globalisation is strongest in the city where social services adopt information technological communication networks for the sake of efficiency. Hence city-dwellers who are unable to access these

---

4.   JL Touadi, Untitled paper presented at the *Globalizzazione e Missione Conference*, Brescia, 23 April 2002, 19.

5.   See A Araujo, 'Globalization and World Evangelism', in *Global Missiology for the 21st Century: The Iguassu Dialogue*, edited by W Taylor (Grand Rapids: Baker Academic, 2000), 59. Araujo here refers to TL Friedman, *The Lexus and the Olive Tree* (New York: Farrar, Straus and Giroux, 1999), 373. See also È. Perrot, 'The Ambiguities of Globalization', *Concilium*, 5 (2001): 17–18.

6.   See RJ Schreiter, 'Globalization and Reconciliation', in *Mission in the Third Millennium*, edited by RJ Schreiter (Maryknoll: Orbis Books, 2001), 125–8.

networks would be excluded from these services and may find themselves excluded from the ordinary necessities in city life.[7]

Social polarisation is increasingly prevalent in the culturally and religiously plural societies today. The 'globalised' city is a converging point for various cultures and religions. However, the homogenising effect on culture, which in turn affects religion, can produce strong reactions from those who want to hold onto one's individual religion and culture.[8] The fundamentalists may perhaps only delay what is inevitable in globalisation,[9] yet this is too heavy a social cost. This polarisation does not happen only in the non-Western world, but also in the United States of America and Europe, whose culture was once based on the Christian faith. The new cultural outlook brought about by economic globalisation now opposes the traditional interpretation of the Christian faith, creating a crisis in society.[10] The city can thus be polarised into those who accept and even embrace a more liberal way of thinking and those who remain stubbornly attached to a fundamentalist interpretation of the faith.

3. The Church's social teaching

The phenomena we pointed out above have only been evident within the last few decades. However, the theological principles from which the Catholic Church develops her pastoral activity have already been in place since the beginning of the twentieth century.

The body of Catholic social teaching is substantial. I wish to focus on three points: the common good, subsidiarity and solidarity.

One constant within Catholic social teaching is that any social decision or action must be for the common good. The phrase 'common good', which means 'for the good of everyone', does not imply a consensus. The object of this good is the human person rather than the entity we call 'the city'. Although his predecessors had alluded to or explained what the common good demanded, it was Pope John XXIII who expressed that the common good

---

7.   See AP Davey, 'Globalization as Challenge and Opportunity in Urban Mission: An Outlook from London', *International Review of Mission*, 88 (1999): 383.

8.   See M Zago, 'The New Millennium and the Emerging Religious Encounters', *Missiology*, 28 (2000): 6–7.

9.   See TH Sanks, 'Globalization and the Church's Social Mission', *Theological Studies*, 60 (1999): 637–41.

10. See F George, 'The Laity and the Contemporary Cultural Milieu', *Cultures and Faith*, 12 (2004): 22; and A Sodano, 'Verso Quale Civiltà?', *Cultures and Faith*, 12 (2004): 192.

concerned the whole human person in his encyclical *Pacem in terris* in 1963. He stressed that the civil authorities' existence was solely for the attainment of the common good and that this common good concerned the whole person, body and soul. He also noted that the universal common good presents us with problems of worldwide dimension, which can only be solved by the establishing of public authorities.[11] This teaching would pervade the Second Vatican Council and is seen most clearly in the Pastoral Constitution of the Church in the Contemporary World, *Gaudium et Spes*. A good definition of 'common good' that is based on Christian anthropology can be found in a document from the Catholic Bishops' Conference of England and Wales:

> That common good is the whole network of social conditions which enables individuals and groups to flourish and live a fully, genuinely human life, otherwise described as 'integral human development'. All are responsible for all, collectively, at the level of the society or nation, not only as individuals.[12]

Pope John XXIII had also highlighted the principle of subsidiarity,[13] which was concretely stated by Pope Pius XI about two decades before.

> Just as it is gravely wrong to take from individuals what they can accomplish by their own initiative and industry and give it to the community, so also it is an injustice and at the same time a grave evil and disturbance of right order to assign to a greater and higher association what lesser and subordinate organizations can do.[14]

---

11. John XXIII, *Pacem in terris* (11 April 1963), 53–9, 136–7.
12. Catholic Bishops' Conference Of England And Wales, 'The Common Good and the Catholic Social Teaching (October 1996)', in *The Christian Faith in the Doctrinal Documents of the Catholic Church,* seventh edition, edited by J Neuer and J Dupuis (Bangalore: Theological Publications in India, 2001), 967.
13. See John XXIII, *Mater et magistra* (15 May 1961), 117.
14. Pius XI, *Quadragesimo anno* (15 May 1931), 79. Translation is from *The Papal Encyclicals 1903–1939*, edited by C Carlen (Raleigh: The Pieran Press, 1990), 428.

Pope John Paul II stated that the praxis of totalitarianism opposes the principle of subsidiarity.[15] He then puts forward the concept of solidarity:

> On the path towards desired conversion, towards the overcoming of the moral obstacles to development, it is already possible to point to the *positive* and *moral value* of the growing awareness of *interdependence* among individuals and nations . . . It is above all a question of *interdependence*, sensed as a *system determining* relationships in the contemporary world, in its economic, cultural, political and religious elements, and accepted as a *moral category*. When interdependence becomes recognized in this way, the correlative response as a moral and social attitude, as a 'virtue', is *solidarity*.[16]

With respect to globalisation itself, Pope John Paul II, in 1991, affirmed that it has the capacity for good:

> Today, we are facing the so-called 'globalization' of the economy, a phenomenon which is not to be dismissed, since it can create unusual opportunities for greater prosperity.[17]

However, ten years later, in an address to the Pontifical Academy of Social Sciences, he commented:

> The globalization of commerce is a complex and rapidly evolving phenomenon. Its prime characteristic is the increasing elimination of barriers to the movement of people, capital and goods. It enshrines a kind of triumph of the market and its logic, which in turn is bringing rapid changes in social systems and cultures. Many people, especially the disadvantaged, experience this as something that has been forced upon them rather than as a process in

---

15. See John Paul II, *Centesimus annus* (1 May 1991), 44 and 46, from *L'Osservatore Romano*, English Weekly Edition, 6 May 1991, 13.

16. John Paul II, *Sollicitudo rei socialis* (30 December 1987), 38, from *L'Osservatore Romano*, English Weekly Edition, 29 February 1988, 10.

17. John Paul II, *Centesimus annus*, 58, *op cit*, 15.

which they can actively participate . . . One of the Church's
concerns about globalization is that it has quickly become a
cultural phenomenon. The market as an exchange mechanism has become the medium of a new culture. Many
observers have noted the intrusive, even invasive, character
of the logic of the market, which reduces more and more
the area available to the human community for voluntary
and public action at every level. The market imposes its
way of thinking and acting, and stamps its scale of values
upon behavior. Those who are subjected to it often see
globalization as a destructive flood threatening the social
norms which had protected them and the cultural points of
reference which had given them direction in life.[18]

The Church in Asia also viewed globalisation with suspicion. In 1995,
when the Federation of Asian Bishops' Conferences met for its Sixth Plenary
Session on the theme 'Christian Discipleship in Asia Today: Service to Life',
it considered the global economy as one of the death-dealing forces in the
world today:

We identified some of these forces of death at work in Asia.
And we concluded that as promoters of life, we could only
denounce them. We are alarmed at how the global economy
is ruled by market forces to the detriment of peoples' real
needs. We considered the insecurity and vulnerability of
migrants, refugees, the displaced ethnic and indigenous
peoples, and the pain and agonies of exploited workers,
especially the child laborers in our countries.[19]

Yet, globalisation itself is not at fault. Pope John Paul II makes this clear:

Globalization, a priori, is neither good nor bad. It will be
what people make of it. No system is an end in itself, and it
is necessary to insist that globalization, like any other

---

18.   John Paul II, *Address to the Pontifical Academy of Social Sciences* (27 April
      2001), 2–3, from *Origins* 31(2001): 44–5.
19.   *The Final Statement of the Sixth FABC Plenary Assembly* (10–19 January 1995),
      7, from *FABC Papers*, 74 (1995): 83.

system, must be at the service of the human person; it must
serve solidarity and the common good.[20]

Pope John Paul II recognises the importance of solidarity in the world
affected by globalisation. He urged international organisations to 'promote a
sense of responsibility for the common good' and to 'ensure a globalization in
solidarity, a globalization *without marginalization*'. [21]

Solidarity and interdependence implies that there is distinctness. This is
opposite to homogeneity. A city affected by economic globalisation would not
only breakdown barriers in culture but also dissolving the distinctiveness in
each culture and group, the pope's proposal of solidarity is an important
understanding of a proper use of globalisation. A Christian is called to
promote distinc.iveness and interdependence in a global process that tends to
homogenise lifestyle according to economic lines.

A person who has no sense of belonging and who is bombarded with a
consumer culture in the media will surely be indifferent to the needs of the
city. A Christian is called to take stock of his roots, both in the material realm
and that of faith. It is against the principle of subsidiarity to relinquish one's
culture to the dictates of organisations whose chief purpose is profit and have
no interest in the formation of one's identity and culture.

Thus, when considering the common good, the Christian must have in
mind the integrity and dignity of the human person. The Christian must
recognise the image of God found in every person. As globalisation can result
in the exclusion of certain groups of people within the city, a Christian is
called to find ways to truly break the barriers that economic globalisation can
erect. A divided city cannot be a healthy city. Thus, to seek the welfare of the
city, the common good must be sought at all times.

The economic well being of a city today depends on globalisation. While
the city can reap the benefits of globalisation, it is inevitable that the city will
inherit the ills and problems that accompany globalisation. Thus, from the
Catholic perspective, a Christian living in the city has first to consider
whether the actions he or she makes is really for the common good, respects
the principle of subsidiarity and strengthens the solidarity of the human
family.

---

20.   John Paul II, *Address to the Pontifical Academy of Social Sciences* (27 April
      2001), 2, in *Origins*, 31 (2001): 44.
21.   John Paul II, *Message for 1998 World Day of Peace*, ' *From justice to each
      comes peace for all*', 3, from *L'Osservatore Romano*, English Weekly Edition,
      17–24 December 1998, 3.

4. A pastoral proposal: inculturation

Simona Beretta remarks that there are three distinctive features in Catholic social teaching. First, Catholic social teaching is based on a 'solid' understanding of the human person. This can be seen in the fact that the common good i; based on 'integral human development' rather than on mere consensus. The second feature is that it does not simply provide static laws or regulations, but offers a foundation on which human beings can be assisted and motivated towards salvation. Thirdly, it offers a formidable proposal for innovation in thought and deed. Catholic social teaching demands critical thinking and reflection enlightened by faith, and hence it affirms the place of reason in the shaping of social life.[22]

The scriptural basis for the understanding of Christ as the first of a new humanity can be found in Paul's epistle to the Romans.[23] As the common good involves the whole person towards the true humanity in Christ, it follows that the gospel values and the Christian principles of subsidiarity and solidarity, as outlined above, serve the common good. Therefore, seeking the welfare of the city involves insisting these concerns in every context. This is described as the evangelisation of culture, an idea that was put forth by Pope Paul VI in the document produced after the Synod on Evangelisation, *Evangelii nuntic ndi.*

> The gospel must impregnate the culture and the whole life of man . . . The gospel, and therefore, evangelization cannot be put in the same category with any culture. They are above all cultures . . . Accordingly, we must devote all our resources and all our efforts to the sedulous evangelization of human culture, or rather of the various human cultures. They must be regenerated through contact with the gospel.[24]

One process that would be an asset to this end is inculturation. The term 'inculturation' has been linked to several other terms and was not fully

---

22. See S Beretta, 'Wealth Creation and Distribution in the Global Economy: Human Labor, Development and Subsidiarity', *Communio*, 27 (2000): 475.

23. Romans 5:12–21; see 1 Corinthians 15:45–9.

24. Paul VI, Apostolic Exhortation *Evangelii nuntiandi* (8 December 1975), 20, in *Vatican Council II: More Postconciliar Documents*, edited by A Flannery (Dublin: Domincan Publications, 1982), 719.

understood and explained until the last decade or so. Inculturation is a dialogical process between the cultures and the ecclesial community for the growth and enrichment of persons. It involves the incarnation of the gospel and its values into a specific culture, and the introduction of various cultural values, practice: and mentalities into the ecclesial community so that a more universal and faithful expression of the gospel can be achieved.[25] Pope John Paul II describes it as 'the intimate transformation of authentic cultural values through their integration in Christianity and the insertion of Christianity in the various human cultures'.[26]

In plain words, JM Waliggo describes inculturation thus:

> Inculturation means the honest and serious attempt to make
> Christ and his message of salvation evermore understood
> by peoples of every culture, locality and time. It means the
> reformulation of Christian life and doctrine into the very
> thought patterns of each people. It is the conviction that
> Christ and his Good News are even dynamic and
> challenging to all times and cultures as they become better
> undersoood and lived by each people. It is the continuous
> endeavour to make Christianity truly 'feel at home' in the
> cultures of each people.[27]

Inculturation is a process that involves two major stages. The first stage is the Church's contact with a culture. It is the stage where the Church expresses her faith to a culture and accepting what is positive within that culture. In a practical sense, this stage is delicate as the initial dialogue between the Church and the culture occurs. At one end, arrogance on the part of the Church or the culture might bring up barriers of prejudice. At the other end, a syncretic situation might result. Only when the first stage is firmly established can the second stage begin. The second stage is the transformation of the culture. It must be noted that the culture is not changed or rejected, but is

---

25.   See P Giglioni, *Inculturazione: teoria e prassi* (Vatican City: Libreria Editrice
      Vaticana, 1999), 29; and H Carrier, *Evangelizing the Culture of Modernity*
      (Maryknoll: Orbis Books, 1993), 67–8.
26.   John Paul II, *Redemptoris Missio* (7 December 1990), 52, in *L'Osservatore
      Romano*, English Weekly Edition, 28 January 1991, 13, which is a quote from
      Extraordinary Synod of 1985, *Final Report*, II, D, 4.
27.   JM Waliggo, 'Making a Church that is Truly African', in *Inculturation: Its
      Meaning and Urgency* (Kampala: St Paul Publications, 1986), 12.

transformed or renewed from within because the gospel has taken root within that culture.[28]

The Church's description of inculturation has the role of faith as the starting point for the process of inculturation. Aware that there is no pure 'culture-less' form of the gospel, another approach to inculturation takes the dynamics of culture as the starting point whilst not denying the transcending character of the gospel and of faith. The danger here is that the gospel message itself might be changed in identifying with culture. According to Robert Schreiter, both approaches are part of the inculturation process and the understanding of faith and culture is important to determine the nature and level of inculturation taking place.[29]

The Church is firmly committed to the process of inculturation. In his message to the people of Asia, Pope John Paul II reiterated that '*the process must show forth the faith which is proclaimed and appropriated*'.[30]

Thus, in practical terms, the inculturation process should take place at all levels, especially at the grassroots. The witness of the Christian community would be the most effective way of renewing the culture of the city that has been affected by a greed-motivated globalisation. In the cities, where there are large population densities, the fundamental Christian community is usually the parish. To complement the usual weekly activities of the parish, I propose that special forms of basic ecclesial communities (BEC) complement the larger parish community. Participation in BEC would be a way of being a Christian at the grassroot level in heavily populated cities. BEC can be initiated at the workplace, where a city dweller spends most of his or her time, or at the neighbourhood level, for those who are homemakers. In a city

---

28. See A Roest Crollius, 'Inculturation: Newness and Ongoing Process', in *Inculturation: Its Meaning and Urgency* (Kampala: St Paul Publications, 1986), 36–42; idem, 'Inculturation and the First Evangelization: Some Remarks from the Point of View of Social Linguistics' in *La missione senza confinia—Ambiti della missione ad gentes*, edited by M Rostkowski (Rome: Missionari Oblati di Maria Immacolata, 2000), 369. See C Dotolo, 'La dimensione culturale nella evangelizzazione', *Redemptoris Missio*, NS 17/1 (2001): 21; and M P Gallagher, *Clashing Symbols: An Introduction to Faith and Culture* (London: Darton Longman and Todd, 1997), 103.

29. See RJ Schreiter, 'Inculturation of Faith or Identification with Culture?' in *New Directions in Mission and Evangelization*, volume 3: *Faith and Culture*, edited by JA Scherer and SB Bevans (Maryknoll: Orbis Books, 1999), 68–75.

30. John Paul II, *Ecclesia in Asia* (6 November 1999), 21, in *L'Osservatore Romano*, English Edition (10 November 1999), Special Insert, vii.

environment, these communities must be existential. That means that communities are initiated from within and not an imposition from without. Only when Christians are convinced of their identities and their mission can they decide to be communities. Christians must be convinced of the relevance or necessity of BEC as part of their ecclesial consciousness, or else there is no true sustenance within the BEC. People organised into groups, which take the guise of BEC, c₁n end up as special interest groups.

Thus, Christian formation is vital. In a certain sense, Christians must first be inculturated before becoming agents of inculturation for the welfare of the city. The manner in which individual Christians and Christian families interact and live their lives will serve to plant the seeds of the gospel into the living culture of the city, transforming the greed-driven globalisation-affected culture in cities into communities of people moulded in the humanity of Christ. The Caḥolic Church in Asia already has a task force in place for Christian formation directed towards BEC.[31]

---

31. See John Paul II, *Ecclesia in Asia*, 25; Federation Of Asian Bishops' Conferences Office of The Laity, 'Report of the Consultation on Integral Formation: *Asian Integral Pastoral Approach towards a New Way of Being Church in Asia (AsIPA)* (Malaysia, 3 November 1993)', in *For All the Peoples of Asia: Federation Asian Bishops' Conferences Documents from 1992–1996*, Volume 2, edited by FJ Eilers (Quezon City: Claretian Publications, 1997), 107–111; and *idem*, 'Report of the First AsIPA General Assembly: *Asian Integral Pastoral Approach (AsIPA) Message to the Churches of Asia* (Thailand 5–15 November 1996)', in *For All the Peoples of Asia*, 137–9.

Concluding Reflections: Ways Forward in Seeking the Welfare of the City

14

Fellow-Citizens with the Saints

Oliver O'Donovan

There is another side to the New Testament's teaching about 'the welfare of the city', and that is, that the church *is* a city. 'You are no longer strangers (*xenoi*) and aliens (*paroikoi*)', says the letter to the Ephesians, 'but fellow-citizens with the saints (2:19)'. The contrast with 1 Peter 2:11 is very marked. There we were 'aliens and exiles' (*paroikoi, parepidemoi*). And the contrast is not unintended: both texts look back to the famous letter of Jeremiah to the exiles in Babylon (Jeremiah 29), which warned them that their stay would be a long one and that they must make a common life with the community around them. That letter also looked to an eventual return. And of these two New Testament texts the one takes up the note of *waiting,* the other the note of *fulfilment.* Both are characteristic of the New Testament picture of the church's existence—awaiting the coming of the city of God, while yet experiencing its social reality in the life of the church already. And the irony of the Ephesians text is that it is *Gentiles* who are assured that their time of alienation is over. It is not a Jewish return to a Jewish metropolis that forms the horizon now, but a return of all the nations into the Kingdom of God.

How does the Ephesians picture fit into the context of the 1 Peter picture that has been before us throughout the conference? First we must say that there are *two overlapping public realms,* each with its proper integrity, not separate or remote but co-involved. So, in the passage we have heard referred to from the *Letter to Diognetus,* the author speaks of Christians as 'following the local customs both in clothing and food and in the rest of life, they show forth the wonderful and confessedly strange character of their own citizenship'.[1] This was the conception of Augustine, in writing his great work entitled *The City of God,* which was, however, about *two* cities, not one:

> This heavenly city, then, on its earthly pilgrimage calls out
> its citizens from each nation, and in each linguistic

---

1.   *Ep Diogn* 5.6

community gathers a society of pilgrims. It is not
concerned what differences there may be in the morals,
laws or institutions by which earthly peace is achieved and
preserved. These do not have to be abolished or destroyed;
no, though different traditions prevail in different peoples,
they may be protected and observed insofar as they serve
the one end of earthly peace, provided they do not impede
the religion which teaches the worship of the one supreme
and true God.[2]

In the second place, we have to say that the heavenly citizenship *lends life
and strength to the first.* 'What the soul is to the body, the Christians are to
the world', the *Letter to Diognetus* continues.[3] The soul preserves the body
from decay, fights against purely 'physical' instincts that depart from
rationality and wisdom. Wherever the church makes its home, the local
community and its political relations can only be purified and strengthened by
having the church in their midst.

What are these political relations? 'Community' is *communication.* Not
only verbal or informational communication, but the 'holding in common' of
material and spiritual goods that give the community its identity. Yet words
have a peculiar importance in communication, for it is they that communicate
an *understanding* of the sphere of communication itself. It takes a word to
make a community conscious of itself, to help it understand itself as a
community, and so to make it 'political'. 'The word of God', as the apostle
wrote, 'is not bound'. It is available for every political community. And its
presence tests, purifies, supplements, and confirms the words that organise
and govern communication in that community. To put it simply: the word of
God holds a political community to account for its truthfulness, and to the
extent that the community is ready to meet the challenge, it guarantees the
stability of the way the community conceives itself. The church, then, to fulfil
its calling in the political community, must be a community *of the word,* a
biblical and discursive community, a community of scriptural study and herm-
eneutics.

In the course of this conference we have heard about the Chinese church's
programme of 'theological reconstruction'; and to avoid misunderstanding Dr
Cao has helpfully warned us against over-emphasising the prefix 're-' in this
common English translation of the Chinese term. To the extent that 'theo-

---

2.   *De Civ Dei* 19.17.
3.   *Ep Diogn* 6.1.

logical re-construction' is to be understood as the *continual* task of theological *construction*, never completed once and for all but always demanded afresh, always seeking out its principles from the reading, study and interpretation of Scripture to provide a conceptual framework for the tasks that face the community, it can serve as a summary of the role of the church everywhere, not least in Singapore and China. This may seem to underplay the role of the church in *spiritual resistance* to false trends and in the correction of grave errors. But if we look at what is perhaps the greatest church-resistance document of the twentieth century, the *Barmen Declaration* of 1934, in which the German churches attempted to define their position against the corruptions of Nazism, we can only be struck by its wholly *constructive* approach to the role of the state in principle, and its determination to warn the state against the errors that had the power to destroy it from within. The independence of the church which it asserts is *not separateness*, but *independence in the service of the protection of the political community.*

In connection with the initiative of theological reconstruction we may recall the words of John Paul II of which we were reminded by Father Koh: 'the process must involve the whole people of God'. The discourse of the church in response to the word of God cannot be 'managed' or 'prearranged'. It can only occur as the Spirit of God gives to each member of the community the contribution which will serve the health of the whole. But it can be *facilitated.* It can be well initiated and well guided by the preachers and teachers of the church. Theological resources can be put at its disposal through education, publishing and research. It can be commented on and mistakes corrected by reference to the authority of Scripture and the testimony of the worldwide church. In a successful 'theological reconstruction' I would expect to find all these things happening, as well as a good deal of initiative and innovation, marked by a spirit of freedom (for 'where the Spirit of the Lord is, there is liberty', 2 Corinthians 3:17), yet without degenerating into a spirit of anarchy (for 'our God is not a God of disorder, but of peace', 1 Corinthians 14:33). The initiative will have succeeded to the extent that it elicits an answer. Sometimes there may be trends within the discourse of the church that cause genuine alarm—as some trends in the Western church discourse do at present. But the church responds to these not by suppression or silencing, but by a tireless *testing of the spirits,* to prove which voices truly come from God. This process, though it may be wearying, is the one that lays foundations that endure, since it allows the true word to emerge authentically, in clear distinction from the false, proving itself and establishing its authority over subsequent generations.

To such a discourse, with its testing, questioning and examining, the Seek the Welfare conference at Trinity Theological College has, in the grace of God, contributed among the churches of Asia; and for this we are all grateful.

15

The Role of Christianity in the Construction of a Harmonious Society Today

Zhuo Xinping

This book offers a good opportunity to trace back the original foundation of Christianity, as a faith and outlook; to rethink the role of Christianity in the development of human history; and to strengthen confidence in finding the possible Christian contribution in building up a harmonious society in the contemporary world.

Many papers in this volume bring us back to the milieu of early Christianity. However, the most fruitful outcome lies in the reflection on guidelines and practical wisdoms in dealing with the present relation between church, state and society. 'Seeking the Welfare' is an important biblical theme, both in the Old Testament and the New Testament. The welfare of the city means more than individual peace, benefit and salvation. The focus is on the harmonious coexistence of human beings; namely on an ideal relation between individuals and their collective life, between religious believers and their wider societies, and between human spiritual pursuit and political orientation. There is no simplistic solution in establishing such an ideal relation, both in history and in the present.

Because of the tension between faith and politics, the first Christians suffered a lot under the Roman Empire. It was remarkable that after repeated persecutions by the Roman authorities, Christianity became finally the state religion of the Roman Empire. This was due to the patience and perseverance of the early Christians in 'seeking the welfare of the city' in their day. They committed no violence in realising this aim. They showed only good will to others on the one hand and trusted in God on the other. With a spirit of *sursum corda* (of lifting their hearts to God), those Christians changed not only their own destiny, but also of the Roman 'city' in which they lived, and turned it into a Christian empire. So the early Christians paved the way for the future 'Christendom' in Europe and introduced Christian characteristics into

Western civilisation. They regarded this as part of a journey from an earthly kingdom to the 'heavenly kingdom', from 'the secular city' to 'the city of God'. This decisive victory by early Christians reminds me also the Chinese saying of 'returning good for evil' and 'conquering hardness with softness'.

The situation in East Asia for Christianity is totally different compared with the Western world. Philip Jenkins points out optimistically the so-called 'transformation' of Christianity from the North to the South, from the West to the East in his sensational book *The Next Christendom*.[1] However, in the real situation, Christians in Asia still exist as a minority and are dispersed in multicultural contexts. This is certainly true in China. Chinese Christians are striving to 'sinicise' their faith. They seek to become real Chinese Christians by adopting Chinese cultural elements and engaging the wider Chinese society, in order to correct the traditional negative impression of 'one more Christian, one less Chinese'.

Since Asian Christians are still living in a climate that is suspicious of the Christian faith, they should follow the early Christians' example in how they sought 'the welfare of the city'. To realise the real welfare of the 'city' in East Asia, the Christians must learn from the early Christians the spirit of patience, perseverance, tolerance and confidence. They should overcome any sign of impatience or arrogance, enter into their societies with kindness and modesty, even if they may face misunderstanding or suspicion for the moment. It is necessary for Asian Christians to engage in various cross-cultural dialogues, learn from local cultures and religions and keep a proper attitude towards the political structures (and their development) in which they live. These are useful preparations, or even necessary conditions, for Christians to 'seek the welfare of the city'.

In China today we talk frequently about two essential expressions or forms of Christian spirit or identity: the spirit of 'servant' and the spirit of 'prophet'. China and the whole of Asia have a different cultural setting from the West. I believe that the first step for Christians in Asia is to play the role of 'servant', 'just as the Son of Man did not come to be served, but to serve (Matthew 20:28)'. This servant-role is also the necessary foundation for exercising a prophet-role. Indeed many opportunities of service are open to the Christian church in the contemporary Chinese society. In doing so, the church will play a positive role in the reconstruction of the wider society.

In the course of Chinese history, especially in the modern period, we have to recognise that there were many occasions of conflict between church and

---

1.   Phillip Jenkins, *The Next Christendom: The Coming of Global Christianity* (New York: Oxford UP, 2002).

state, and between Christianity and Chinese culture. Due to their close connection with missionaries, Chinese Christians were treated with suspicion and even hostility in the Chinese society. These confrontations are familiar to us all. We see such conflicts in the Rites Controversy in the past and in the disputation over 'canonisation' at the present.[2] With such historical burdens and remaining sensitive problems, it is not easy for Christians today to actively 'seek the welfare of the city' in China. But Christians should not give up. Biblical teaching can offer them the wisdom and orientation to avoid or overcome such difficulties, and find a new way to seek the welfare in and for China. It is unnecessary and futile to reiterate the disputes, conflicts, and clashes in the past. Rather, we should reconcile differences through dialogue and mutual understanding. To reach harmony or consensus, the main common ground is to 'seek the welfare of the city' together, rather than to demand exclusive uniformity in faith or in ideology. Here, 'the city' refers to the structural ordering of mankind, while 'the welfare' means harmonious coexistence between diverse cultures and religions. To realise this 'welfare' we need 'service', not 'occupation' (as missionaries in the first half of the twentieth century regarded their activities in China). We welcome cultural inclusivism, not exclusivism. Christianity as a universal religion with its ecumenical characteristics should in fact be congenial to 'inculturation'. If Chinese Christians would be confident and persevere in their service, it is not difficult for them to bring faith, hope and love to China, which means the real welfare for the Chinese.

In seeking the 'welfare' of our common 'city', Christians in Asia can play an active role in the establishing of a harmonious society. This would also contribute to the peace in the world. In so doing, they can avoid the 'disenchantment' with Christianity that is prevalent in the West today. Christians in Asia would then initiate a process of 'desecularisation of the world' in place of the secularisation processes that are taking place in the West.[3] People in Asia would then be able to meet together in a common pilgrimage towards holiness, a journey—for the Christians—towards the 'heavenly kingdom', the 'city of God'.

---

2. On 1 October 2000, Pope John Paul II canonised 'one hundred and twenty Chinese martyrs'. This provoked strong objection in China's mainland.
3. See Peter Berger, *The Desecularization of the World: Resurgent Religion and World Politics* (Grand Rapids: Eerdmans, 1999).

16

Christian Social Engagement in Asia

Daniel KS Koh

1. Introduction

Christian social engagement in the public arena is not an uncontroversial subject. Within the Christian community, controversies have centred, for instance, around whether Christian social engagement is a priority for the church. There are Christians who would insist, even in a post-Lausanne world,[1] that the priority of the church is to evangelise. If Christians were to be interested in social engagements, such engagements are considered of secondary importance. They merely function as tools to serve the church's evangelistic goal.

Increasingly, however, there are those who think that the focus of the church should be in protecting her peculiarity. Whatever the church does, it has to be done on terms set out by the church with little or no regard for ambiguities and the possibilities for finding common grounds and shared rationalities in a fragmented world of competing claims. Others have decided that social engagement, while welcome, should be done minus the faith content. But this often means that, unlike those who are assertive about Christian particularity, this group thinks that Christian identity should be downplayed. For them, doing what is good in the public arena is social engagement and there is no need to explain it as *Christian* social engagement. Theology takes a back seat. Faith is privatised and should not be mixed with public activities

Nevertheless, in spite the contentious views, by adopting the theme based on Jeremiah 29:7, the organisers of the conference decided very early that Christians should be socially responsible and publicly engaged in fostering the

---

1. See John Stott, *The Lausanne Covenant: An Exposition and Commentary* (Minneapols: Worldwide Publications, 1975), and *The New Face of Evangelicaiism,* edited by Rene Padilla and John Stott (London: Hodder and Stoughton, 1976).

common good. This perspective is adequately supported by the various papers presented at the conference. Without downplaying the importance of Christian peculiarity as people who follow, and are formed by, the teachings and tradition of the church founded by Jesus Christ, the organisers obviously recognised and affirmed the need for Christians to 'seek the welfare of the city' both as citizens of God's Kingdom and as citizens of the world created by God.

2. Perspectives: biblical, historical and contemporary

The range of papers presented at the conference is wide. Oliver O'Donovan's contribution is a model of what a nuanced essay that addresses complex issues should look like. He offers a theological understanding of political authority that also deals with the concomitant ideas of freedom, power and right.

In different ways, Tan Kim Huat, Bruce Winter and Paul Barnett draw lessons from the Bible and biblical times to explain how Jews and Christians had understood their identity and how, despite occasional and sometimes bloodied conflicts with the political authorities, in the main they had sought the welfare of the cities where they resided. Though Jews and Christians encountered persecutions and sufferings at various time in history, the teachings of the Bible, particularly Jeremiah and 1 Peter, issue clear advice for the people of God to take an active interest in the welfare of the city where they dwell.

Michael Nai-Chiu Poon looks to the early church for lessons. Hwa Yung discusses the contribution of the church to the emergence and development of civil society. Other papers offer examples of the significant Christian contributions to societal well-being (Kenson Koh, for example), specifically in Singapore (Richard Magnus and Robert Solomon) and also in China (Cao Shengjie and Zhuo Xinping).

The two opening addresses were given by Ye Xiaowen, the Director-General of the State Administration for Religious Affairs of the People's Republic of China, and Lim Siong Guan, a senior officer with the Singapore Civil Service. Both of them, with long experience in government services, offer overviews of their respective government's perception of what religious groups may contribute to the wider society and their assessments of the boundaries in which religions can operate in the public square, although Lim, who is a Christian, states at the outset that the views he offers are personal and 'do not necessarily reflect the views of the government'.

Since Christians have to live with and work within a given political context, with boundaries and policies governing public discourse and social engagements usually set out by the government of a given country, it is not unwise to pay attention to and pick out salient points on views expressed by those who are close to the government, Lim's caveat notwithstanding, if we want to be responsible and responsive participants in seeking the welfare of the city. This is particularly important for Christians living as the minority in countries where the Christian faith is regarded as a late-arrival and often associated with Euro-North American interest. Mainly for the reasons just stated, I shall give more space to interacting with some of the issues raised by Lim and Ye.

3. Views closer to the centre of political powers

The paper from Lim spells out the general hope for a multi-racial and multi-religious Singapore that is 'safe, stable and secure' which, Singaporeans have always been reminded, is vulnerable and can be easily undermined, if not governed firmly and fairly.

Broadly speaking, unlike a theocracy, in the context of the city of this world, the authority for, and arbiter in, the management of the state is the government and not the religious institutions.[2] It is the responsibility of the government to legislate laws and introduce policies that will ensure justice and social order for human flourishing. In such a democracy, even if the citizens have reservations about its usefulness, a law like the Maintenance of Religious Harmony Act, can be understood as having been put in place to regulate inter-religious relationship, in the hope of minimising the possibility of inter-religious conflict, which is an easily combustible possibility in a multi-racial and multi-religious society. Yet in acknowledging the complex challenge of governing well and fairly—ultimately in any country, not least in a plural society like Singapore—when it comes to matters of faith, no political leader should assume the role of a pope and no sensible parliament should think that it is the Vatican.

Laws can have a critical auxiliary role in regulating life and inter-religious relationship. But their effectiveness must be predicated on good governance that is transparent and just, and where the political leadership is provided by men and women who have been legitimately elected at regular intervals.

No matter what claims a government may make on its people, the citizens are more inclined to accept the authority of the government, not so much because of the threat of punishment under certain laws, but more so because

---

2. See also Oliver O'Donovan's paper, 'All Authority is from God' elsewhere in this book, for an excellent theological understanding of what this authority entails.

of the respect and goodwill which the political leaders have earned. Furthermore, any wise government should also know that religious people who are nurtured and nourished by their own faith community are more inclined to take final authority on what they believe and how they ought to behave, not from a president or from a parliament, but from the faith community and the teachings of that community. A political authority that is as much exposed to and tainted by sins, for example, in the self-serving claims and counter-claims of this good but imperfect world, cannot and should not assume for itself the religious authority which it does not have.

Ye's address is broad and diplomatic, though it includes some gentle chidings against those who distort religion 'to interfere in the internal affairs of other nations'. He also denounces the 'unilateralist' tendency in some Western culture. Against perpetrators of conflicts, Ye expresses his wish for a harmonious and peaceful world, something which, to use an American expression, is as desirable as 'motherhood and apple pie'. What might have raised some eyebrows is the claim of China having a 'tradition of peace and harmony'.

The claim may seem out of place. Yet there is nothing ostentatious about making such a claim. In the same way we would allow others to claim, for example, that Islam or Buddhism or Christianity is a religion of peace and harmony, if we understand such a claim more as a statement of aspiration rather than a reference to a faultless reality. But claims, we do know, must be tested by history and practice. And in this sense, religious groups in China and China's neighbours will be watching with interest how this claim is acted out in China's management of religious plurality and in the conduct of China's international affairs, particularly so when China is now regarded as a super-power in the making.

There is, in Ye's address, expression of appreciation for the positive contributions which religions can bring to foster peace and harmony in the city of the world. But discerning readers will also notice with concern the lingering suspicion that 'certain aggressive aspects of Western culture have led to a self-centred conviction in the superiority of Western culture'. It seems to me that this suspicion directed at the 'unilateralist' West, is clearly a reference to the United States of America and American 'unilateralism', for example, in the 'unilateralist' decision taken by the Americans to invade Iraq, which China did not support and, it should be added, that not every Christian supports. But those who are aware of the deep-rooted suspicion that the Christian faith is a Western religion, or a religion closely associated with the West, should be alerted to the possibility of being misunderstood as a willing voice of Western unilateralist agenda.

Without being misguided by blind nationalism, the challenge then is for sensible and sensitive Asian Christians to keep a critical distance from American, and for that matter, from any international political power play which may raise questions about Asian Christian commitment to the welfare of the city where God has placed us. If Christians in Asia are to be recognised as people who are truly interested in 'seeking the welfare of the city' and not as alleged purveyors of Western ideology, then a more critical and contextual approach to Christian social engagement in Asia is required for the sake of authentic Christian witness.[3] The upshot of taking such a critical and contextual approach is that it will also allow the church in Asia to speak with confidence and integrity against not only the pretensions of any foreign power but also the pretensions of national claims and cultures, without having to carry the burden of being branded as an apologist for Western interest, however that might be (mis)construed.

Both Lim and Ye emphasise the desirability of stability and peace. Lim is unequivocal in stating that 'social stability is an absolute must in Singapore'. On the other hand, Ye makes known that 'it is not only a political commitment of China to advocate and preserve peace, but also a natural extension of Chinese civilisation'.

Ordinarily, Christians who have the welfare of the city at heart would not disagree with the need to foster stability and peace in a given society. They would, in fact, pray for and work towards establishing peace and stability. A more important issue which Lim might not realise is that when one emphasises stability and peace, especially so when it is expressed in absolute term, one shows a lack of critical awareness that political authorities are capable of misusing if not abusing power. This might be an indication of a poverty in understanding structural sin which has often given rise to injustice when the coercive instruments of the state are used to control legitimate dissent or grievances in the name of protecting stability and peace.

Lest Christians become too conceited, I should add that the inadequate understanding of human sinful nature and structural sin is not a problem peculiar to people outside the church. This is in fact a problem for the church in Singapore, and I suspect for many churches in Asia as well. From my limited observation, there is a glaring lack of critical contextual theological rigour—both in touch with theological development elsewhere and at the

---

3. A point I have argued in 'Resident Aliens and Alienated Residents' elsewhere in this book.

same time interacting with the rich heritage and aspiration of Asia—needed for assessing and critiquing societal ills and issues.

4. Looking ahead

'Seeking the welfare of the city' should not be left at the level of providing social services and contributing to peace and social stability, important though that might be. The challenge ahead, which the conference did not address, is how to take the church in Asia to another level of critical contextual Christian theological reflection and Christian social engagement, a level that would enable it to take on the ideological and structural challenges, claims and counter-claims of our time, in our ongoing commitment to help enhance community well-being in the city of this world—blessed, informed and judged by the values of the city of God.

Author Index

Subject Index